Think
Before
You Speak

The Complete Guide
to Strategic Negotiation

Roy J. Lewicki

Alexander Hiam

Karen Wise Olander

JOHN WILEY & SONS, INC.

New York • Chichester • Brisbane • Toronto • Singapore

Preface

Many readers will use this book for self-study, and I trust will find it more than adequate. But I want to add a brief note for the many others who are engaged in training and development work in the field of negotiation. This book reflects both the academic work of its lead author and his practical experience leading seminars on negotiation. *Think Before You Speak* rises to such a high standard in large measure because of the expertise of the lead author, Roy Lewicki, who has devoted much of his academic career to researching and teaching negotiation. The other co-author, Karen Olander, has specialized for many years in making tough subjects clear through superior communication skills, and you will enjoy her touch throughout the book. If you are designing a training session, you will find its contents provide a natural structure for the event. Wiley can provide multiple copies of the book at discount if needed as a handout in training sessions (and if you have any trouble arranging this let me know and I can help).

In addition, I recommend the use of assessment instruments in conjunction with the presentation of negotiating strategies (in Chapter 5). Trainees can use an instrument to diagnose their own disposition toward a particular style or strategy. Negotiators can also use instruments to assess the other party's style and disposition, and to diagnose the situation in order to pick the most effective style in a particular negotiation. Some of the commercial instruments use the same two-dimensional model of negotiating situations and the same five negotiating strategies we present in this book.

Available: Assessment Instruments for Training and Planning. I have also developed a product line linked to this book for use in training and planning activities. It includes:

> **Descriptive Style Assessments,** which are designed to be cleaner, easier-to-use versions of industry-standard instruments.

Behavioral Style Assessments, which link negotiating style to social, emotional, and cognitive dispositions using an innovative new model.

Situational Strategy Selector, which students and negotiators can use to find the best strategy or style for a specific negotiation.

I am happy to answer any questions from readers about training and development activities or any other topics. We are eager to hear from people who use the book in academic courses or corporate training sessions and workshops, and are willing to provide support as needed to facilitate its use. You can reach me at Alexander Hiam & Associates, at 413-253-3658. We like to hear from our customers, and readers are the author's best customers!

ALEX HIAM

Amherst Massachusetts
1996

Contents

Contents

vi

Contents

Contents

Chapter 1

The Advantage of Strategy

Do you negotiate frequently? If you think not, you are like most readers and you are wrong! When dealing with other people, many of us negotiate *more than once in every waking hour,* but we do not recognize the majority of these "negotiations" as such. We may not take seriously even the fewer, more major negotiations of our day or week. But by overlooking opportunities to negotiate strategically, we settle for suboptimal results. We either get less than we could have, or we end up wasting time and energy on conflicts and problems we have created through poor negotiation.

Even those of us who have already studied negotiation may suffer from both problems—overlooking opportunities for negotiation, and negotiating poorly. Why? Because we are generally trained in only one of many negotiating styles and try to apply it in every situation. We lack the breadth of knowledge to negotiate strategically.

Think back on the events of a recent day. Did you negotiate? Did you win? Following a fictional character through her daily events may help you answer those questions. Helen, we will call her, awoke to the alarm clock at 6:45 A.M. She waited a moment, but Jim did not stir, so she climbed over him to turn the alarm off. Irritating, especially with her bad back. Jim's son Noel, from his prior marriage, was staying with them for the week while his mom traveled, so Helen went to his door and called to him, then headed for the kitchen to pack his lunch for school. Then she went upstairs to get ready for work. But the bathroom door was closed and the shower water was running—Noel? No, Jim was no longer in bed. It must be he. But that meant no time for her to shower before work, since it was her turn to drive the car pool to work and she had to leave home early to get everyone else. She wished she had remembered Noel was coming when they

1

discussed the car pool schedule at work—it would have been more convenient to drive next week!

Helen has not gotten very far in her day, and already she has ended up on the wrong side of four negotiations. Did you take note of them? She accommodated Jim's irritating habit of sleeping through the alarm. She generously packed a lunch for his son, and by so doing she lost her opportunity to take a shower before rushing to her car pool. To Helen, all three interactions with her family are probably losses and there's no point losing in any situation unless you gain something in the future from it. These sacrifices were not likely to be noticed and reciprocated. And her fourth loss—agreeing to drive in an inconvenient week—also accomplishes nothing in the long term. It is an example of suboptimal results due to incomplete information—a remarkably common problem for most negotiators. But let's not overly dwell on Helen's morning, as her working day is likely to hold many more negotiation situations for her.

Helen left the house a little late, and a little mad at Jim, who had driven off without offering an apology. Perhaps that is why she drove faster than usual on the freeway, and why she was pulled over by a state trooper. Even worse, she forgot how outspoken Fred, who was riding in the front seat, can be—or she certainly would have told him to keep his mouth shut! The police officer had clocked her at only five miles over the speed limit and seemed ready to let her off with a warning, when Fred started arguing with him.

Fred is a senior manager at her company, and he often loses his temper at subordinates. He was angry this morning since he had an early staff meeting, and he told the officer in no uncertain terms how inconvenient the situation was for him. Now Helen had a speeding ticket to pay and Fred was going to be even later for that meeting.

What mistake did Helen make this time? Another common one: She failed to plan and control communication in her negotiation with the police officer. Many negotiations turn sour when the wrong person gets involved or the wrong message is communicated. This point was brought home to Helen later that morning when her project team met. The team was charged with cutting costs out of the assembly of one of her company's products. They had begun to work with suppliers to reduce prices, and one of the suppliers was resisting the changes they proposed. Then Helen had called an old friend at the supplier company, who was able to get his firm to agree to a concession. Just as a solution was in sight, however, her friend took a new job and left the company. Now the supplier refused to sign the new contract. Her boss was impatient and wanted her to disband the current team and start all over again. But Helen knew this would hurt her relationships with the team members—all of them key personnel from the main functional areas of her firm. She suspected that these business relationships with team members were more important than the small price cut her boss wanted her to obtain from the supplier. But how could she get her boss to see it that way? She was not sure what to do, but she knew she had some difficult negotiations ahead of her.

Before even taking her lunch break, Helen has had to cope with many negotiations. Some seem trivial, some are minor but irritating, and others are vital to her career or personal success. These situations and similar ones we all face daily are important for four reasons.

First, we care about the results. We care because we have one or more *goals* that we hope to accomplish, and our goals often conflict with other people's goals. The traffic cop wants to meet his quota for tickets, but we want to minimize travel time and cost. Our boss wants a quick, forced solution to a problem, but we have to live with our associates afterward, so preserving our relationships is more important. If people shared all their goals, they would not have a problem or at least the problem would be one they could solve together easily. In fact, as we will soon see, aligning our goals is a useful negotiating strategy in contexts where collaboration is feasible and important, but it can be a wasteful, even damaging, strategy in other situations.

Second, we have *emotional* as well as rational issues and responses to negotiating situations. This is perfectly natural since negotiations involve other people. And when we blunder through negotiation situations without recognizing or planning them, then we operate more out of our emotions, almost by default. But emotional responses get in the way of good negotiating, and it takes a careful strategy to prevent passions or gut instincts from spoiling the outcome.

Third, we often care about the *outcome* of the negotiation. The outcome is how the parties resolve to behave and what that gives us as a result. It may be close to one of our goals, or may be very disappointing. And it may be critical for us, or may not have a big impact. The outcome is the traditional focus of negotiators, and it is, therefore, helpful to keep it in context, but only as *one* of the four main concerns of strategic negotiation.

The fourth is our *relationship* with the other people involved in the negotiation. All negotiations affect relationships, and the importance of a relationship must therefore be considered carefully in the development of any negotiating strategy. Often outcome and relationship issues conflict. Helen accepted a negative outcome in some of her negotiations because she wished to maintain a relationship; for example, she didn't shake Jim and tell *him* to turn off the alarm clock.

These four concerns are the cornerstones of a strategic approach to negotiation (see Figure 1.1). In the discipline of strategic planning, they

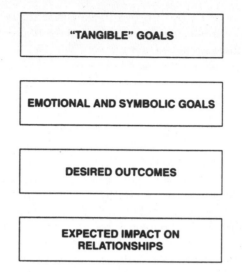

Figure 1.1 The Four Major Concerns of Negotiation

would be termed *strategic issues,* defined as the elements that have a major impact on your strategy and that do not have obvious answers.[1] It is important for any strategist to identify and think about strategic issues before planning or acting. But most negotiators omit this critical step, and as a result often adopt flawed strategies.

In this book, we will learn how to take a strategic approach to negotiations—both the occasional formal ones and the far more frequent informal negotiations that fill our days and affect the quality of our lives and work. This means, first, clarifying our goals and the goals of those with whom we must negotiate. Second, it means substituting a careful, rational plan for the impulsive, emotion-based approach we naturally tend to take to such situations. And third, it means optimizing outcomes or relationships, or—if you are really good—both.

In the initial chapters of this book, we will examine the elements you must analyze to develop a sound strategy including your position, the other party's position, and the context of the negotiation. You will discover information in each of these areas that you must take into account in your strategies and plans.

How much information you have makes a big difference and is a difficult issue for negotiators. Usually you can get good information on your *own* side, but it is often harder to get information on other parties. We will see that the negotiation process itself can be used as a vehicle for obtaining information about the other side, its goals, constraints, strategies, and perceptions.

Planning and preparation require that you:

- Know your goals.
- Anticipate the other party's goals.
- Do your homework.
- Understand the negotiation process.
- Design a strategy to *manage* the negotiation process and reach resolution.

As you analyze the various negotiating situations that arise in your own work week and personal life, you will discover that the strategic issues are *answered differently* in each case. This implies the need for a different strategy in each case. Applying the one approach you are already comfortable with is a guarantee that your strategy will be wrong in the majority of situations. In Chapter 5, we will discuss multiple strategies for negotiation. Once you select a strategy, you can move on to Chapters 6, 7, and 8, which explain *each* of the strategies in depth. It is important that you master *all* negotiating strategies and become proficient at using them in context. This is the secret of strategic negotiators: They vary their approach as required by the circumstances so as to optimize personal performance in all the formal and informal negotiation events of life and work. Their flexibility gives new meaning to the dictum that you should think before you speak.

Adaptability is important. You must plan your actions and move toward a goal. But negotiation is a process. If you stay focused only on your goal and ignore other cues, you may miss opportunities to improve your strategy or learn more about the other parties in the negotiation.

As you work through Chapters 2, 3, and 4, you will be accumulating and analyzing information to help you in the strategic negotiation process. In this chapter, we will outline the basic steps of analysis. In Chapter 2, you will analyze your own strengths and weaknesses so that you can make convincing arguments for yourself or against the other side. In Chapter 3, you will research the other side's position and incorporate that information into your plan. Chapter 4 looks at situational concerns such as rules and regulations, timing, constituencies, and power.

As you move through the chapters, you will be able to fill in the information pertinent to each factor in the negotiation—you, the other party,

Figure 1.2 The First Rule of Strategic Negotiation

and the situation or context. By the time you come to Chapter 5, you will understand the strategic issues and be ready to select a strategy based on the information you have collected. Then in the following chapters, you will implement the strategy you have chosen, selecting and perfecting the most appropriate and sophisticated negotiating tactics for each strategy. Executing the strategy well makes a big difference—almost as big a difference as choosing the right strategy in the first place.

When you are doing your analysis and strategizing, be sure to allow yourself plenty of time. It is tempting to plunge into the negotiations, but this will be harmful to your case. It will keep you from selecting and implementing the best strategy for the situation. The best single piece of advice about negotiation you will ever hear is: Wait! Take it slow! Some strategic negotiators like to post a warning like the one shown in Figure 1.2 near their desks or on their refrigerators at home to remind them of the importance of this rule. Note that it applies to the analysis phase, ensuring you listen and think before jumping to conclusions; and it also applies to the selection of a strategy. Don't start negotiating until you have taken the time and care needed to select the best strategy. Otherwise, you will accidentally start implementing some strategy, most likely the wrong one.

STEPS IN THE ANALYSIS PROCESS

The following steps have been identified by researchers as the best approach to the planning process.[2] To a strategic negotiator, they are particularly applicable to analysis of the four key strategic issues identified in

Figure 1.1. A truly strategic approach required us to front-load the process with analysis. These planning steps are therefore most appropriate for the first stage of strategic negotiation, the analysis of strategic issues. Strategic negotiators are superior to conventional negotiators because they follow specific rules—the first one being that they take time to think about the negotiation before most negotiators do. Analysis is needed no matter what strategy you are going to use for negotiating. It will indicate which strategy to employ. Here are the steps for analysis; each will be examined in depth in the following chapters:

1. Define the issues.
2. Assemble the issues and define the agenda.
3. Analyze the other party.
4. Define underlying interests.
5. Consult with others.
6. Set goals for the process and the outcome.
7. Identify your own limits.
8. Develop supporting arguments.

Let's look at these steps in more detail.

1. *Define the issues*. In this step, you analyze the conflict situation. You look at it closely and decide which are the major and minor issues. You consider past experience and information about your party, as well as the opposing party.

2. *Assemble the issues and define the agenda*. In this step, you list all the issues in order of importance. In Chapter 2, you will look at your goals and prioritize them.

3. *Analyze the other party*. You will likely find it more difficult to obtain information on the other party than on your own side. Nevertheless, this is vital to planning a good strategy. Chapter 3 deals with researching the other party.

4. *Define underlying interests*. At this point, you define the interests and needs that underlie the issues you defined in Step 1. To do this, you assess each issue and ask the question, "Why? Why is this issue important to me or to the other party?" For example, *why* do you want this item or goal? Why is it important to you? When you assess other parties in Chapter 3, you will look at the underlying reasons for their preferences.

5. *Consult with others.* In this step, you look to others for further information. You may have "constituencies"—people that you are negotiating for, or to whom you must explain and interpret the outcomes you achieve. These people are often called "stakeholders." You will also consult with the other side. Any parties to the negotiation should be brought into the situation as early in your planning as possible.

6. *Set goals for the process and the outcome.* Management of goal-setting depends on successful completion of previous steps, so if you have done your homework well, you will know which items to fight for and which to be flexible about. You will also need to take into account the other parties' preferences in these areas. The management aspects of planning include setting up the schedule, the site (location), the time frame, the principal players, and the procedure to use if negotiation fails.

7. *Identify your own limits.* Knowing your limits is extremely important. Your limits will be dictated to a large extent by your goals, priorities, and more detailed information such as bargaining range points and alternatives. We will take a detailed look at these issues in Chapter 2.

8. *Develop supporting arguments.* Once you have defined your goals and preferences, you need to develop arguments to support them. Facts and information found during the research phase will help you in this effort. You will also decide on the methods for presenting the information.

Even the simplest of negotiations may contain a mixture of needs, powers, interests, and skills among the "players," which means that the outcome is never totally predictable. But planning helps you to gain some control over the variability of the outcome. As negotiations progress, the variables may change, but if you have planned well, you will be better prepared to adjust. The more information you have ahead of time, the better able you will be to minimize the surprises.

The book's outline follows the negotiating process described in this chapter and can be used as a process guide or manual, helping you work through each step to a successful conclusion. The first few times you use it, you will want to work through each chapter carefully. Once you are familiar with strategic negotiation, however, you will find you can turn to Chapter 5 to select the best strategy, and then use the chapter describing that strategy as a guide to implementation. On occasion, you may also need to dip into later chapters, which describe special problems and resources, such as how to use third-party help (Chapter 11) or how to negotiate with many different people and positions (Chapter 14). But, in general, the strategic negotiation process becomes quite simple to use with experience.

We recommend that you take advantage of the many negotiation situations arising in your work and life to apply strategic negotiation as you read this book. Learning by doing is the most effective way, and since you are negotiating anyway, there are many opportunities to apply what you read directly to negotiations you face on the job or in your personal life. We can't guarantee the results, but we can guarantee that study and practice are beneficial in the long term. Many lawsuits have been avoided, careers made, and marriages saved through good negotiation!

Chapter 2

Assessing Your Position

Let's look at a negotiation situation in the real world. The members of a Boeing aircraft design team, working on the passenger oxygen system for a new plane, found themselves in conflict with another Boeing design team. The first team had found a nice spot for the passengers' oxygen masks, in the back of each passenger seat. But the second team had chosen this same spot for the "gasper," the little nozzle that provides a stream of fresh air to passengers. You can't put two pieces of equipment in the same space. What to do next?[1]

If you were on the oxygen system team, you would first need to assess your team's position. Is this the only location for the mask that is likely to work, or is there room for flexibility? Will you suffer personal costs, such as a bad work review, if your team's design is scrapped? Does your team have the backing of senior managers who outrank the other team's backers? Even if there are alternative approaches, do you have enough time and other resources to redo your design? And what are the costs of a change in your design to the project's overall time and budget targets, and to the ultimate quality of the plane? Answers to questions like these would help you and your team decide what the important issues are and how flexible you could afford to be in resolving the conflict. You would also want to know the options for dealing with the conflict. For example, are there resources within Boeing to handle this problem and minimize the costs of solving it?

In the past, this sort of problem would have been discovered on the production floor at Boeing, long after the design teams had finished their work. It probably would have led to extended bickering, escalating up the ranks of management. The team that had to move its piece of equipment would have absorbed a lot of trouble and extra expense, and the production schedule and budget might have been compromised. Therefore, each team's positions would have been staked out aggressively. Future careers

10

could have been at stake for the team held responsible for the mistake. But, because Boeing is improving its methods for finding and resolving such conflicts *early* in the design cycle, a computer program quickly spotted the problem making it less costly and embarrassing for either team to change positions. And Boeing now offers third-party help in the form of an "integration team," which rushes in to help the two design teams come up with a win-win solution. The early identification of this problem, coupled with the immediate use of a third party to help resolve the conflict, allowed the two teams to avoid a major conflict. And no doubt, their initial assessments of the situation showed that the costs of arguing and delaying the project were far higher to both teams than the costs of collaboration and compromise.[2] What both teams wanted was a quick, easy solution, and the company offered the resources to achieve such a solution. (What was the solution? Our sources did not say, so you'll have to buy an airplane ticket to find out.)

Whenever you are in a negotiation situation, your first move, before you say or do anything, is to take stock of your own position and decide exactly what you want. Assessing your "position"—your arguments or "your side of the story"—is the first step in negotiation. In this chapter, we will investigate your position and insert it into the analytic framework suggested in Chapter 1. Once you have thoroughly planned *your* position, you can move on to looking at the problem from the *other party's* point of view (Chapter 3). Then in Chapter 4, you will add the *context* of the negotiations to this analytical framework. Only then will you be ready to pick a negotiation strategy from among those presented in Chapter 5.

Does it sound like a lot of work? Yes! Absolutely! Planning and analysis are work. It takes time. But if you want to negotiate successfully, analysis and planning are the keys. You need to plan not only for your position but also for that of the other party, and for the situation. And after you have done it formally a few times, it becomes instinctive and easy to use informally as well.

As part of our framework for complete negotiation analysis, we will examine your position—your side of the story.

THE KEY QUESTIONS

The major questions that underlie this chapter are "*What* do I want out of this negotiation?" and "*Why* is it important to me?" To find the answers to these questions, you need to conduct a careful investigation. We cannot emphasize enough how important it is to plan so that you know where you are going, no matter what negotiation strategy you ultimately select.

In the first section of this chapter, we will use the analytical framework introduced in Chapter 1 to discuss the many issues you need to consider as you take stock of your position and resources. Then, we will go through the specific steps for planning your side's position in the bargaining. It is important to be diligent in collecting information so that you are thoroughly prepared and are not taken by surprise.

Some of the information you collect here may help you make decisions in other areas. Even though this chapter concentrates on you and your position, there is always overlap with the other party and with the situational factors. All three factors—you, the other party, and the situation—are interrelated. For example, your behavior affects how the other side behaves, and that behavior tends to dictate the moves you make. Likewise, the location of the negotiations (their turf, your turf, or a neutral place) can affect your behavior and theirs. The extent of their power, and yours, will affect the outcome, too.

Goals

Goal-setting is a critical aspect of analyzing and planning your position. Think about what you want to attain in this negotiation. List your goals in concrete, measurable terms such as dollar amounts and percentages. It is not very helpful to say that your goal is to buy a car for less than a half-year's salary. It is more meaningful and easier to evaluate a specific goal such as "I will spend no more than $5,000." Then, if a counteroffer puts a car's price at $6,000, it will be clear that you have not yet achieved your goal.

A dollar amount is a *tangible* goal. So is a benefit in salary negotiations, or a particular interest rate when you are negotiating a loan. But many negotiation situations also contain *intangible* goals, such as "making a successful transaction" or "keeping everyone in the family happy" or "looking like a good negotiator to my friends" or "being viewed as a fair and honorable person." Intangibles will be more difficult if not impossible, for you to quantify. Further, you may not be able to tell whether you have accomplished them. You may only realize them after the negotiation has been completed. Nevertheless, it is important to be aware of intangible goals and to name them whenever possible.

Many, if not most, bargaining situations contain *multiple* goals. Be sure to list all your objectives for this negotiation. Likewise, eliminate any goals that do not apply to the case at hand. Loading too many objectives into the negotiation may make it impossible to achieve settlement.

Priorities

One way to sort out goals is to prioritize them. Ordering them in terms of their importance, assigning each one a dollar value, or using some other procedure to define value will assist you in comparing goals and deciding which are most crucial. This process may also help you eliminate the goals that are unrelated to the present situation. If you calibrate priorities precisely, it will make it easier to decide which ones to pursue.

Later in the negotiations, when you want to make tradeoffs or concessions with the other party, you will see the value of setting priorities. At that point, you will usually be ready to give up a less important goal to gain a more important one. If you know the relative value of each of your goals, you will be able to evaluate the various tradeoffs. For example, you might not insist on having four new tires put on a used car if the seller is willing to come down in price by $500.

Assessing priorities allows you to establish *packages* of goals for various alternative offerings during negotiation. For example, a car stereo and automatic transmission may be more important to you than air conditioning and automatic windows. If you evaluate these packages of goals with the same rating system you used for individual goals, you will be able to compare their relative worth. When you have anticipated a package that is offered to you during negotiation, you will be able to evaluate it quickly and not lose valuable time figuring out its worth.

Bargaining Range

The second rule of negotiation is that as part of goal-setting, you will need to define your bargaining range including a starting point, a target point, and a resistance, or "walkaway," point (Figure 2.1). Each of these points may be defined in monetary terms, or in other ways that allow you to define their relative value. The points may also be associated with *intangibles*—psychic outcomes that are harder to define, such as esteem or success—but that are nevertheless important. We will concentrate here on the *tangibles*, which are the more substantive (and usually economic) outcomes.

The *starting point* is your first offer to the other party. Where you set this point may depend on the market rate, how badly you want the outcome, the time frame for the negotiation, the other party's anticipated starting point, concessions you may be willing to make, or how negotiations have gone in the past. Some of these factors depend on the context of the negotiation, which will be discussed in Chapter 4. For now, consider

**DEFINE
YOUR
BARGAINING
RANGE**

Figure 2.1 The Second Rule of Strategic Negotiation

a simple example. You make an offer on a house that has a price tag of $175,000; therefore, the seller's starting point is $175,000. In most circumstances, buyers will not pay the seller's price, but will offer less—your starting point or opening offer might be $140,000.

The *target* is the point where you want to settle. It is your intended outcome. In the case of the house, say your target is $150,000.

The *walkaway point* is the figure at which you will break off negotiations. The walkaway point is usually beyond your target; it is the "point of no return." In the case of the house offer, it is the highest amount you will pay (or, from the seller's point of view, the lowest amount the seller will accept.) Your walkaway point for the house in our example might be $155,000. Although you would prefer to pay the lower target amount of $150,000, you are willing to go as high as $155,000—but no higher.

Whether you will be able to negotiate with the other party at all will depend on the seller's bargaining range. If your range and the seller's range overlap—that is, the most you will pay is above the least that the seller will accept—then bargaining can occur. Otherwise, there can be no negotiation. If the seller's walkaway point for the house is $160,000, then there can be no negotiation.

Bargaining range is primarily associated with competitive situations, where each side takes a stance and there is give-and-take adjustment until the two parties reach a compromise point between the two extremes. In Chapter 6, we will discuss the methods for setting your bargaining range if you are negotiating in a competitive situation.

Alternatives

Your negotiation analysis and planning should also include establishing an Alternative. (Well-known authors Roger Fisher and William Ury have called this a BATNA,[3] or Best Alternative to a Negotiated Agreement.) An

Alternative is an acceptable alternative outcome or settlement to the issues under negotiation, such as a second but acceptable house in a nearby neighborhood, or a different car with the same equipment. An Alternative can provide you with power during bargaining because, if the deal under consideration does not work out, you can switch to your BATNA and still be satisfied.

Think of Alternatives to the present situation that would be acceptable to you, and prioritize them if you have more than one. If you can assign each one a rating on a scale comparable to the one you used in prioritizing your goals, this will also be helpful. Then you can see exactly where your Alternative fits in terms of tradeoffs and limits. We discuss Alternatives further in Chapters 3, 5, and 6.

Underlying Needs and Interests

Beneath your defined goals and objectives, you may have deeper, underlying needs, interests, concerns, or fears.[4] Interests can be *concrete* (tangible), such as money or interest rates; or they can be more *abstract* (intangible), such as a friendly interchange with the other, or preservation of your image. A major concern may be protection of the relationship between the two parties, about which we will say more later. You may also be concerned about principles,[5] such as what is fair or right. You may be attentive to the *ethics* of the situation or what has happened in the past. (We will discuss legal and ethical issues in Chapter 13.)

You will usually have a mix of underlying needs and interests. As you will see in the next chapter, the other party will also have needs and interests, some similar to yours, some different, depending on each party's values and belief systems. As negotiations proceed, there may be a shift in concerns on either side or both. Thus you may find it challenging to define your underlying interests and concerns. Nevertheless, the need to be aware of them is the basis for the third rule of negotiation (Figure 2.2).

One way to get at underlying interests is to ask yourself the *"why"* question that we mentioned at the beginning of this chapter: *Why* do you want a particular goal? For example, do you need a car to get to work, or do you want a particular model to show people that you are successful? Are you looking for a house in a particular section of town because it is a better neighborhood, or do you need a larger house because your family is expanding?

Another way to look at underlying needs is to ask what will happen if you accomplish the goal. Then ask yourself what will happen if you *do not* achieve your goal.

Figure 2.2 The Third Rule of Strategic Negotiation

Frequently, we are not aware of underlying motivators, but it is important to look for them and define them if possible. You may assign a low priority to a goal and trade it for something else during negotiation, only to regret your action afterward because the underlying interests were important to you.

Researching your underlying interests will enable you to share them with the other party and thus find common interests. Although the two parties in a negotiation may appear to have conflicting goals, the underlying needs of each party may be similar. The result could be a collaborative solution that will meet both parties' goals and needs.

For example, two coworkers who are arguing over whether a window should be open or closed are unable to find a solution.[6] A third person asks each one to explain the problem. The one person wants the window open to get fresh air. The other person wants the window closed to avoid a draft. The third person suggests opening a window in the next room, which will provide fresh air and at the same time avoid a draft. This solution meets both parties' goals and needs and is a good example of following the fourth rule of negotiation (Figure 2.3).

Figure 2.3 The Fourth Rule of Strategic Negotiation

Resources

Assess your resources. These can be concrete assets, such as other people, files, and data to support your side. Resources also include personal traits, characteristics, and skills that are assets to you in this situation.

In many negotiations, information is your most important resource. It may be used to construct a set of arguments to persuade the other side, or to provide counterarguments to the other's persuasive efforts. For example, if you are buying a house and you happen to be a builder, you are less likely to be "taken" than if you know nothing about houses. However, if you know nothing about houses but your best friend is a builder, then you have access to an excellent resource you can use to your advantage.

Your negotiation experience can also be a resource, particularly if you have had past success in the same area as the issues presently under consideration. If you are not experienced, think of experts you can call on to assist you.

Another resource is your creative ability in problem-solving. This is particularly helpful in collaborative negotiations, where the two sides attempt to find common ground and solutions that will enhance both sides. And if you are not particularly creative, do not despair. You may be able to consult with someone else who can offer the problem-solving ability or the creativity that you need; you will also find that creativity is a muscle you can strengthen with exercise.

When you inventory your resources, identify your strengths and weaknesses. Because weaknesses represent areas of vulnerability, the other side will try to identify them and take advantage of them in a negotiation. You need to protect such weaknesses or offset them with other strengths, particularly if the other party is competitive. Stay alert—weaknesses will surely take you by surprise later if you do not account for them now.

Recurrence of Negotiation

A factor that dramatically affects negotiations is whether the parties regularly relate to each other. In organizations, many negotiations are recurrent; the parties have regularly dealt with each other in the past and will continue to do so in the future. A purchasing agent regularly negotiates with a supplier over prices and delivery; a manager regularly negotiates with her boss about budget and personnel. Other negotiations may occur only once, as when the company buys a real estate parcel to build a new manufacturing plant.

You need to decide whether your own negotiation is a one-time event or will continue over time or fold over into additional negotiations with the same party, with multiple meetings. For a one-time negotiation, your approach may be different than for a series of meetings. The stakes may seem higher in a one-meeting bargaining session, and this may affect your strategy and tactics. What you expect and what actually happens may differ, but you should factor your expectation into your planning, and then change it if necessary.

If you expect the negotiation to continue over time, you need to consider your relationship with the other party and how you can structure it to avoid antagonistic behaviors. When we discuss researching the other party in Chapter 3, we will look at relationship issues in more detail.

History

Another area to examine is your history of negotiation. In this chapter, history refers to *your* experience in two areas: general negotiating experience with other parties, and specific negotiating experience with this party. Your experience will, to some extent, affect how this negotiation will go. Your past experience can bias your approach to this negotiation, either favorably or unfavorably. If you had success in the past, for example, you might expect a positive outcome again.

It is also wise to research previous cases in which similar issues were under negotiation. The outcome of such cases may be instructive to you as you prepare your negotiation plan.

In Chapter 3, we will discuss the need to look at the history of the other party's negotiations with others and with you.

Beliefs about How to Negotiate

Do you hold basic beliefs about what negotiation is and how to go about doing it? We hope that you are gaining new ideas and points of view to take into the negotiating arena, but you may still cling to a picture of "the typical negotiation," where two warring parties battle each other verbally until one gives up and gives in, and the other gets all the goodies.

A typical assumption about negotiation is that a fixed amount is available (the fixed pie) and that you have to get as much of it as you can. While this may sometimes be true, holding such a point of view can cause you to miss opportunities to negotiate solutions that can make both parties happy.

Trust

An important aspect of negotiating is trust. Since the topic of this chapter is you, the question here is "How trustworthy are you?" If you value trust, then you will likely expect to be trustworthy yourself and to trust the other party as well.

Expectations can influence situations of all kinds. For example, if a teacher expects poor behavior from a student, it often occurs. If the teacher looks for good behavior, the student frequently lives up to the teacher's expectations. A bit simplistic, perhaps, but human behavior is an amazing blend of simple and complex.

So if you have experienced situations in the past where you were trusting and the trust was returned, then you would expect to be trusting in this situation. However, you will probably adjust this view as you research the other party in the next chapter. Your expectations of their trustworthiness will be based on *their* history of negotiation and other historical information. You will adjust your assessment as negotiations progress and you can observe their trustworthiness at close hand. They will also adjust *their* view of *your* trustworthiness as they see you in action.

What should you expect? Well, if you do your research carefully, you will have a good sense of the situation. Whatever you expect will direct your moves. If you are distrustful (even for good reason), your behavior will probably be less than open. But trust can be built, based on observed behavior. And if you expect the relationship between you and the other party to continue into the future, then you will have to establish a degree of trust. We say more about this in Chapter 4.

We cannot stress enough the importance of assessing yourself as accurately and honestly as possible. The objective of this personal assessment is to plan an action for each possible action that can occur during negotiations. With a firm plan formulated before the negotiations begin, you will be prepared for most eventualities.

Authority and Constituencies

Another variable in negotiation is the authority or power you have as a party to decide on the actual outcome of the negotiation. Are there policies in place that will govern your actions, either protecting you or restricting you? Are there rules or regulations by which you must abide? In a corporation, are you negotiating at the request of someone higher up? Will you be able to resolve the disagreement yourself, or will others have the final say in the outcome?

"Higher-ups" and "others" who may affect negotiations are called "constituencies." These individuals or groups may be physically present at the negotiations or not, but they maintain accountability over you and hold you responsible for the outcome you achieve. Whether a constituency is large, such as all the members of a labor union, or small, such as the members of your family, it exerts some kind of positive or negative influence on you as a bargainer.

In some cases, negotiators simply have to take into account the position and concerns of the constituency. In others, the constituency has the final say in the negotiations. For example, in union-labor negotiations, the agreement has to be voted on by the union membership (the union negotiator's constituency) and okayed by the board of directors of the corporation.

For planning purposes, it is necessary to know how much bargaining authority you will have and how supportive your constituency is likely to be. In some cases, everything you negotiate will have to be cleared and approved by some higher authority; in others, you may have carte blanche to find a resolution.

We will discuss constituencies further in terms of the *power* they can exert in negotiations in Chapter 4.

Strategy—Firm or Flexible?

If you want to remain flexible during negotiation, you might think that having a plan would be restrictive. You might be tempted, therefore, to go into a negotiation without a plan and just "wing it." The problem is, you could be caught short by an unanticipated proposal or countermove by the other party. If you have not set goals and prioritized them for your side, it will be difficult to evaluate whether or not a new offer moves you closer to your intended outcome. If you have done your homework, you will have a good idea of what to fight for and what to let go.

The best approach is to build some flexibility into your plan by establishing goal packages and alternative scenarios.

Your flexibility will also be influenced by your constituencies, and by your own style. Although some people are comfortable just letting nature take its course, that might not work if you have a strong, directive constituency. A relaxed style may send signals to the other party that you are either poorly organized or a pushover. You could open yourself to aggressive tactics by the other party.

Flexibility implies a willingness to be open to the other party and to invest time in the proceedings. If you cannot spend time on analysis and planning, then the negotiations will proceed differently than they would with time and effort. If you display flexibility and openness during negotiation, your willingness to share information may encourage the other side to do likewise. Both your appearance and degree of flexibility can influence the situation.

Personal Traits

Some of your personal qualities and attitudes will be called into play during negotiations, so it is important to assess these traits ahead of time also. For example, how do you feel about *rules* and *fair play?* How concerned are you about your *reputation* and *image?*

Your standards, principles, and values will affect the proceedings. If your position is to take care of yourself first and foremost, then that will dictate the negotiation strategy you select and how you carry it out. If you value fairness, you may make a concession to be fair but not be happy about it. How you behave will also affect how the other party behaves.

You should also beware of displaying any stereotypes or biases. Prejudices of any sort can work against you if the other party sees these weaknesses and decides to take advantage of them.

Good communication skills are essential. If you need to brush up on your skills, take a look at Chapter 12.

Characteristics such as persuasiveness and tenacity can affect the outcome of negotiations. Integrity and character may be hard for you to evaluate in yourself, but you probably have a good idea of your reputation. Rest assured that the other party will be checking on these aspects of your personality. The other party will be reticent to negotiate with you if you appear to be a deceitful person.

THE ANALYSIS PROCESS

Now that you have all this information, it is time to put it into your analytical framework. Allow plenty of time for this process. Although it is tempting to just go ahead with negotiations, beware! An early start could be harmful to your case. Likewise, now that you have a better picture of your position, you might want to skip researching the other party (see Chapter 3). That, too, could be a serious mistake.

As you go through the analysis steps, be sure you thoroughly understand your strengths and weaknesses at each stage. This will help you make convincing arguments for yourself or against the other party. Remember

**FOLLOW THE
EIGHT
STEPS OF
NEGOTIATION
PLANNING**

Figure 2.4 The Fifth Rule of Strategic Negotiation

that this process is applicable no matter what strategy you are going to use for negotiating. The specific tactics you will use for a particular strategy may differ, but the basic planning will not. (Tactics are discussed in Chapters 6, 7, and 8.)

The fifth rule of strategic negotiation is to follow the eight steps of negotiation planning (Figure 2.4). Consider again the analytical process introduced in Chapter 1:

1. Define the issues.
2. Assemble the issues and define the agenda.
3. Analyze the other party.
4. Define underlying interests.
5. Consult with others.
6. Set goals for the process and outcome.
7. Identify your own limits.
8. Develop supporting arguments.

Look at these steps in light of the material you have collected during the course of this chapter:

1. *Define the issues.* Analyze the conflict situation from your own point of view. Look at the issues, and decide which are major issues for you and which are minor. Past experience can be helpful. Take into consideration the research you have done, including your past history in negotiation. Based on the issues, make a list of experts in the field who may be able to contribute advice, information, or expertise.

2. *Assemble the issues and define the agenda.* List all the issues in the order of their importance. This should be relatively easy because of the

work you did earlier on prioritizing goals. You may find that some of the issues are interconnected and therefore have to be kept together.

3. *Analyze the other party.* Although it may be difficult to obtain information on the other party, researching the other side is vital to planning a good strategy. At this stage in your analysis, you should start to think about your relationship with the other party, for this will affect all your ensuing moves as you design your negotiating plan. In particular, your history with the other party and the degree of interdependence between the parties will affect your interactions. All the research you have done thus far will influence how you work with (or against) the other party.

4. *Define underlying interests.* To define the interests and needs that underlie the issues you specified, remember the question "Why." *Why* do you want this item or goal? Why is it important to you? When you investigate the other party's goals in the next chapter, you will again use the *why* questions to get at the underlying reasons for the other party's preferences. This will help you understand "where they are coming from" and will enable you to find common interests and differences.

5. *Consult with others.* Unless this is a very simple negotiation, other people will probably be involved. For example, if you are negotiating a bank loan, the loan officer probably has to clear it with higher-ups. Or perhaps you are buying a car to use primarily to drive to work. If your spouse will be driving it occasionally, you will probably need input on the choice of car.

Constituencies, as we stated, can affect negotiation to a greater or lesser degree, depending on the situation. A constituency that is even superficially involved may need to be consulted.

You will also consult with the other party, perhaps on issues, or even on how you will negotiate. Talks with other parties can be amicable or hostile, depending on the situation. Nevertheless, any parties to the negotiation should be brought into the proceedings as early in your analysis and planning as possible so you can begin to see the whole picture. We will return to this step again in Chapter 3.

6. *Set goals for the process and outcome.* Be sure you have a clear picture of your preferred schedule, site (location), time frame, who will be involved, and what will happen if negotiations fail. You will need to take into account the other parties' preferences that surface in your consulting with them. Be sure you know which items are important enough to fight for and which to be flexible about. Such prenegotiation talks will tend to

set the tone for the bargaining session itself. (You may want to save this step until Chapter 3.)

7. *Identify your own limits.* It is very important to know your own limits. These will arise from having a clear picture of your goals and their priorities, your bargaining range points, and your alternatives or BATNAs. If you know your limits you will be able to adjust your plan as necessary. For example, if an item is rejected by the other side during bargaining, you will more readily be able to reevaluate it and decide what your next move should be.

Be sure your limits are realistic. It is fine to have an absolute minimum or maximum acceptable point, but consider having a range for flexibility. The priority ratings you gave to your issues when you were defining them will also help you set limits. You want to do better with the more important issues and be more flexible on the less important issues. You will be in an even better position for negotiating if you have anticipated possible packages that might be offered by the other party, and assigned them values on a scale similar to the rating scale you used for your own packages. They will help you make comparisons.

8. *Develop supporting arguments.* Once you know your goals and preferences, think about how best to provide supporting arguments for those goals. You need facts to validate your arguments. You will have accumulated many of these during your research. Methods for presenting facts include visuals, such as charts, graphs, and other visual aids; people, such as experts; and records or files, especially from respected sources. Other similar negotiations can provide clues for how to proceed.

Use them regularly to help your negotiation planning. In the next chapter, when you look into the other party's views and interests, you may be able to find a common basis for negotiation as a result of understanding their position.

The process and outcome of the negotiation will be affected by the other party's qualities, and by the interplay of behaviors and moves of both parties. In Chapter 4, we will talk about the situational factors (such as power) that can affect negotiations.

Chapter 3

Assessing the Other Party

While it can be difficult to diagnose your own needs and position, under-standing someone else's position is far harder. Some negotiators assume it is too difficult, and do not even bother. Their strategy is simply to take care of their own needs, and let the other parties take care of theirs. This is a mistake; while it may be appealing at first glance, in practice it is likely to produce undesirable results ranging from suboptimal outcomes to failure to agree and even to conflict escalation. A look at a real-world ne-gotiation situation helps clarify the importance of understanding the needs and positions of other parties to the negotiation.

Tom Stoner started Highland Energy Group in 1989 to help organiza-tions convert to energy-efficient technology. But the work required large investments in technology and staff, and Stoner had to raise venture capital to get the business off the ground. That meant negotiating with any poten-tial investors who would give him an audience.

Negotiations generally fall into two categories: planning for an upcom-ing negotiation and dispute resolution. The cases and stories we have met so far in this book have largely been examples of dispute resolution nego-tiations: how Boeing design teams should deal with conflict, how an employee should cope with the conflicting requirements of her team rela-tionship and her boss's demand to fire the team and obtain a better out-come. Disputes arise often, but opportunities for planning also arise and can be used to avoid future disputes or create future opportunities. You can engage your team, boss, or spouse in a planning negotiation rather than wait for a problem to grow so large as to require a dispute negotiation. And, when you engage in creative exercises such as business planning, you create opportunities for others to become involved in the creation process, presuming that a successful planning negotiation takes place.

In any negotiation, and especially in planning negotiations, the other party's position can offer the key to a successful strategy. Tom Stoner's experience reflects this principle. He recognized that the systems he wanted the firm to bring to market were untested. Large-scale conversions from old to newer, more energy-efficient technologies were not in the mainstream. Most investors knew little about the technology, and his firm had no track record to convince investors that the technology would work. He knew his own position and needs; that was the easy part. But the fundraising task required him to understand the motivations of investors. Stoner recalls the result of his analysis of potential investors: "I needed to create the belief [in the investor] that these systems would work." But how? Most investors were too busy and skeptical to take the time needed to learn about the technologies. So Stoner targeted HFG Expansion Fund, a venture capital firm founded by Tim Joukowsky, an old friend from college who was willing to learn about the idea. Stoner recalls, "Tim and I went for nice long walks. You can learn a lot about another party's position by going for a long walk with him—and he can learn a lot about your company's technology and plans." (Recall the famous "walk in the woods" that President Jimmy Carter took with President Anwar Sadat of Egypt and Menachem Begin of Israel, resulting in the Camp David accords.)[1] The plans made sense to Joukowsky, but he still had reservations about Stoner's ability to carry them out because of their highly technical nature. Knowing this, Stoner agreed to bring in a technically oriented business partner, and finally HFG was ready to invest. After more than a million dollars in venture capital, followed by private offering for second-round financing, the company finally won its first major bid in 1993 and is now one of the major contractors to utilities in its industry.[2] This success story would not have been possible without Stoner's commitment to understanding the needs of the other party in his early planning negotiations, because—the sixth fundamental rule of strategic negotiation—the *other party is the key* to your success (Figure 3.1).

During negotiations, you will have many opportunities to learn about the other party. If you can manage to "take a long walk" with them, so much the better. But you do not have to be friends to learn what you need to know about the other party's position. Knowledge of the other party's concerns and issues will come both from what is said and what is *not* said. If you are a good reader of body language, you may learn a lot by just watching the undertakings.

Warning! It is not enough to find out as you go along. You need to create an effective plan for this negotiation, and the more you know ahead of time the better. That doesn't mean you can learn everything the first time

**The
OTHER
PARTY
holds the
key to your
success**

Figure 3.1 The Sixth Rule of Strategic Negotiation

through—planning is an ongoing activity, and as you learn things about the other party—their interests, preferences, primary concerns, areas where they are committed or flexible, and so on—you will want to revise your plans accordingly. However, many negotiators avoid making ANY assumptions or inferences about the other side, and delay any consideration of the other's probable concerns and issues until negotiations begin. This is a mistake. If you already know some things about the other party or can make reasonable assumptions about what they *probably* will do, you can factor this information into your own personal planning.

In this chapter, we will discuss the information you need to gather about the *other* party—personality, values, social environment, and preferred outcomes—and ways to uncover that information. What you do with the information will differ somewhat depending on which negotiation strategy you ultimately choose. But no matter what the type of negotiation, you still need to learn all you can about the other party.

Remember that while you are researching the other party, they may be checking up on you. Giving and obtaining information can be a somewhat delicate matter, especially if you feel that you need to guard some details, such as weaknesses, for fear that they might use them against you. This behavior is typical in the competitive negotiation process, which we discuss in depth in Chapter 6. In contrast, in the more open communications that characterize collaborative negotiations, both parties share information openly and extensively: The objective is to find a common ground and a solution that will satisfy both parties. The Collaborative Strategy is the subject of Chapter 7.

Your research on the other party somewhat parallels your research on your own position (see Chapter 2). There are some differences, however, which we will note as we go along. At the end of this chapter, you will take the new information you have collected and incorporate it into your negotiation planning structure, as we did in Chapter 2.

Before you begin your detailed research on the other party, think once again about your relationship with them. How important is it? Your relationship (or lack of one) will direct the process of data collection and influence your choice of negotiating strategy. (We will discuss strategy choice in Chapter 5).

We need to repeat again the importance of planning before you enter a negotiation. Do not skip this step! While it may seem much harder to get information on the other party than it was to figure out your own position, it is equally important. The better idea you have of what to expect, the better prepared you will be, and the more successful you can be in your bargaining session. As stressed earlier, you need to know not just the information but the "why" behind it.

One final word. Gathering information on the other party ahead of time will help you in your analysis and planning. However, if you are unable to obtain material beforehand, do not worry. First, decide whether you can make any reasonable inferences or assumptions about the other side. For example, if you are buying a used computer, you can assume that the seller will start with the price that was advertised or posted on the computer. Second, you can pick up details as you go along. And even if you have "perfect" information on the other party to begin with, you will probably see changes and adjustments as negotiations progress. This is the result of interaction between two parties and the growth of a relationship, whether positive or negative.

RESEARCHING THE OTHER PARTY

You will need to conduct research about the opponent in the following areas:

- Their objectives.
- Their interests and needs.
- Their alternatives.
- Their resources.
- Their reputation, negotiation style, and behavior.
- Their authority to make an agreement.
- Their likely strategy and tactics.

We will consider each of these separately.

Their Objectives

It is easy to make assumptions about the other party's objectives. Although they may be true, be careful not to jump to conclusions. For example, if you are considering buying a used guitar, you may believe that the seller is trying to get as high a price as possible. That may be true, but aim to learn specific information rather than relying on guesswork. Perhaps the seller has to sell it, but would rather do business with someone who will take good care of the guitar. Perhaps the seller is in a hurry and just wants to sell it fast.

If you discuss the negotiation with the other party, you may discover their objectives in what they say, or emphasize, or do not say. Or, perhaps, at this early stage, the other party may not have carefully formulated objectives. And if they reveal several objectives, you may not know which ones are more important. Once negotiations begin and progress, you will be able to formulate a general idea of the other party's objectives, and you may be able to infer by the type and size of their concessions what appears to be more (or less) important to them.

Likewise, you may not be able to ascertain the other party's bargaining range before you begin negotiations, but once you get underway, their starting point will become clear. If you hit their walkaway point, you will know it from their words and actions.

Some commodities are so widely exchanged that you will be able to find informative books and articles about them. For example, numerous books on purchasing an automobile present negotiation advice as well as a great deal of information about dealer costs, the price of options, and so on. Similar information is available about houses, antiques, and artwork. If you want a basic idea of what to expect before starting your negotiations, read about commonly accepted ranges in similar transactions. You can consult with experts in this area, or ask other negotiators about their experiences. Bear in mind that each negotiation is different because of the different people involved and the different array of goals and concerns.

Indirect methods of obtaining information include observing the other party, looking through documents and publications, and asking sources who know the other party. The direct method is to ask the other party, but you may not receive an accurate response because they may wish to "keep you in the dark." They may limit what they say, so you will not know whether you have a full picture of the situation. In Chapter 6, we will discuss tactics for screening information in competitive situations.

Their Interests and Needs

Underlying interests and needs for your party were introduced in Chapter 2. The other party's interests and needs are no less important. In fact, if you expect to find a common ground with the other party and to create a collaborative solution, then you *must* know the underlying factors of the other party's position. Without knowing their needs, you might assess the situation as competitive when in fact there may be some common ground that can serve as a basis for finding a good collaborative solution.

If you can, ask the other party the *why* question: Why are these objectives important to you? And related questions: How did you come to this position? What if you cannot accomplish your goals? Have your needs changed since our previous discussion?

How you word these questions will help or hinder you in obtaining responses. For example, if you say, "How did you ever think you could get *that* objective?" you will probably put the other party on the defensive, possibly even set up a combative relationship. Consider carefully how you phrase your questions, based on your own objectives. We discuss communication skills in Chapter 12.

After you ask a question, listen carefully to the answer. For one thing, you will be gaining information. For another, you will be indicating to the other party that you are truly interested in hearing what they have to say. This may encourage them to listen to your needs. Your purpose is to figure out the other party's thinking and logic which you can learn most easily by asking direct questions.

Try to find out the other party's walkaway point. This is usually difficult, but it can give you a sharper sense of the other party's bargaining range and how well it meshes with yours.

Their Alternatives

You need to know whether the other party has any alternatives and if so, how strong or weak they are. A strong Alternative can be used as a sort of "prod" to push the negotiations on. If the other party has a strong Alternative, they do not have to continue bargaining with you. If they have a weak Alternative, then you may be in a better bargaining position. If the other party is unwilling to share information, it may be difficult to find out such details before you begin negotiations. However, you will learn more during the bargaining.

Their Resources

Knowing about the other party's business and background will assist you in gauging what to expect in negotiation. Therefore, you need to research the other party's business history, previous negotiations, and financial data, as appropriate. You can make phone calls or site visits, assuming that it is not a hostile relationship. If it is, then you may prefer to use less direct methods of fact-finding. Public companies will be listed in stock reports, reported on in the media, and described in legal documents.

You may want to investigate any past negotiations by the other party.[3] Historical information about negotiation successes and failures with this party will help you assess your own chances of success.

You will want to learn as much as you can about the bargaining skills and experience of the other party's team members. The more experience they have, the stronger their position.

Their Reputation, Negotiation Style, and Behavior

Although historical information about the other party's successes and failures in negotiation may be informative, you cannot be sure people will behave as they have in the past. However, this information, in combination with the preferred type of negotiation, may give you a good picture of what may occur. For example, if they have a reputation as hard bargainers, then you may expect difficult competitive negotiation.

As previously mentioned, beliefs and expectations affect how we go into negotiation. Thus, if you believe that there can be only one winner, you will behave accordingly during negotiation. Likewise, if the other party holds a particular belief about how negotiation should work, then this will affect both their behavior and the outcome. What makes the situation hard to assess is how the two parties will interact when put together under possibly stressful circumstances.

Another important element in negotiation—trust—was discussed in Chapter 2. As you add the information on the other party to your planning framework, you will see that trust can become a complex issue. If I trust you to be open and honest, and you are, we have one sort of communication. If I trust you and you are *not* open and honest, then I will adjust how I respond to you, and our communication will change. Both lack of trust and unrewarded sense of trust can affect negotiations.

Their Authority to Make an Agreement

You need to know whether the other party will be working alone, or with others, and whether a constituency will influence their agreement-making capability. Further, do they have the authority to make agreements or are they limited by other parties, or by company rules and regulations? Limited decision-making authority can be an advantage or a disadvantage, depending on the situation. For example, a negotiator may use limited authority to advantage by saying, "It is out of my hands" (when it may or may not be). On the other hand, the same negotiator may become stuck on a concession point if he or she cannot concede a point without some sort of permission from a constituency.

We will be discussing constituencies and their inherent power at greater length in Chapter 4.

Their Likely Strategy and Tactics

A variety of strategies and tactics can be used in negotiation; we treat these in detail in Chapter 5 and thereafter. You will want to anticipate the other party's likely stance. We will formally name the strategies in Chapter 5, but for the moment, try to estimate and characterize in general how the negotiations will go. On the one hand, the other party may be conciliatory and open to accommodations and flexible solutions. On the other hand, the other party may be hard-nosed and appear ready to fight you tooth and nail. And there are a number of other possibilities between these two extremes. As you do your research, you will develop a good picture of how the other party is likely to operate.

In Chapter 9, we will take up the issue of how to go about changing the other party's stance to one that is more aligned with yours.

CONCESSIONS

It can be useful to know what points the other party might be willing to concede during negotiations, but this is fairly difficult to find out beforehand. You probably will not know until the concessions actually occur. However, once there is a concession, you can make some educated guesses about whether there may be others and their probable magnitude. You will be able to base your expectations on the behavior and interplay you have seen demonstrated thus far in the negotiations.

A few words on concessions: Each side will most likely make at least one concession. Once one party makes a concession, it is more or less expected—negotiation protocol, if you will—that the other side will follow suit. If they don't, you can usually count on one of two explanations: They want to achieve 100 percent of what they are asking for (their opening bid and walkaway point are identical), or they are very competitive and are trying to force you to make more concessions before they give in anything. We discuss concessions for the Competitive Strategy in depth in Chapter 6.

Understanding the Other Party

At this point, if the relationship between the parties is important (and even if it is not), you may want to try to "get into the other person's shoes" by using role reversal. This can help you understand the other person's motivations and needs. We discuss role reversal at length in Chapter 12.

THE PLANNING PROCESS

Now we turn back to the planning grid again. You should have assembled enough information to understand and evaluate the other party's strengths and weaknesses. Adding the detail you have discovered about the other party to your basic plan will help you expand and improve it.

Look again at the planning steps we considered in Chapters 1 and 2:

1. Define the issues.
2. Assemble the issues and define the agenda.
3. Analyze the other party.
4. Define underlying interests.
5. Consult with others.
6. Set goals for the process and outcome.
7. Identify your own limits.
8. Develop supporting arguments.

See what needs to be added to your plan, based on the information that you have collected in this chapter:

1. *Define the issues.* This time, try to look at the conflict from the other party's point of view. See if you can determine their major and

minor issues. Does past experience with the other party add any information? Remember that you may be able to further expand on this section once negotiations begin and the communication between the two parties reveals more information. So make notes about anything you can't identify in their perspective—this will serve as an outline for questions you will need to ask later on.

2. *Assemble the issues and define the agenda.* Are there agenda issues for the other side that need to be added, based on your understanding of the other party's position? During negotiations, more issues may need to be included in the agenda and you will have to come back to this step. You may also have to reevaluate your own issues in light of the new information from the other party.

3. *Analyze the other party.* This step is the crux of your work in this chapter. You may find it helpful to summarize the other party as you see them now. This evaluation will most likely have to be adjusted as the negotiations proceed, and you gain further knowledge and information about the other side.

4. *Define underlying interests.* What are the interests and needs underlying the other party's issues? Just as you asked "Why?" to discover your own underlying goals and interests, now use this method to find out why the other party wants a particular item or goal, and why it is important to them. If you cannot have discussions with the other party before the negotiations begin, you may find it harder to fill in this section of your plan now, but it is of great importance to understand their position as soon as possible. Once again, make notes; this will help you to define the questions you want to ask when you meet the other side.

The reason for looking at the underlying issues for both parties is to invent solutions that speak to those interests rather than the overt objectives.[4]

5. *Consult with others.* Add to your plan any information that you find on others involved in the negotiation, including the other party's constituencies. Even though you will probably not be in a position to consult with the other party's constituencies, it is important to know about them and the ways they might exert influence over the situation.

You may consult with the other party, perhaps on issues, or even on how you will negotiate. Talks with other parties can be positive or negative, depending on the situation, but it is important to include any parties to the negotiation as early in the process as possible. For your discussions with others, you will need to decide how much information to tell, and likewise, how much you can believe of what you are told.[5]

Bearing in mind the type of negotiation strategy that the other party might use, evaluate the responses. For example, if you expect the other party to be forthcoming with information and offering an open relationship, then you can trust the answers. On the other hand, the other party may try to protect their information, or even alter it to protect their self-interests. Good planning in advance often helps you know when they might not be telling you the truth.

6. *Set goals for the process and outcome.* Take into account the other party's preferences for schedule, location, time frame, participants, and procedure for failed negotiations. Remember that any discussions you have before the actual negotiations will tend to set the tone for the bargaining session itself. See if there are commonalities or strong differences in your preferences and theirs.

7. *Identify your own limits.* Look at this section of your planning to see whether anything you have learned in this chapter affects the limits you set in Chapter 2.

8. *Develop supporting arguments.* Given the information you now have on the other party, do your supporting arguments make sense? Is your presentation appropriate? Be sure you bear in mind the other party's views and interests. As a result of understanding the other party's position, you may now have information that will enable you to appeal to them on a common basis of concern.

SUMMARY

Understanding the other party is vital to planning a good strategy. Now we move on to the third and last aspect of good analysis and planning, the negotiating context or situation. The context presents a number of factors not related directly to either you or the other side, which nevertheless must be accounted for in your analysis. We will take these up in Chapter 4.

Chapter 4

Context and Power

Effective negotiation planning requires attention to three critical elements: what you want, what the other side wants, and the context (or situation) in which the negotiation occurs. Each of these elements is important, and further, they interact to make negotiation a rather complex and dynamic set of events. In this chapter, we examine the context of the negotiation, to see what factors affect the negotiation process. We will examine two major context sets: situational elements and the relationship between the parties (see Figure 4.1). Situational elements, such as deadlines, constituencies, options, and rules and regulations are important to understand because they frequently affect which side has more power in the strategic negotiation process. As you look at these various factors, try to assess whether they are positive or negative for your party. Following the discussion of situational elements, we will examine the relationship between the parties and show how that affects the way the parties negotiate.

SITUATIONAL FACTORS IN NEGOTIATION: DEFINING THE POWER[1]

Much of what we have said in the two previous chapters suggests that negotiation is largely a two-party event, and that the critical elements of planning are in understanding one's own goals, interests, target points, and so on. While these are important aspects of negotiation, situational factors also tend to have subtle but important impact on the process. These are often called "power factors," because using them in a particular way can contribute a distinct advantage to a party's negotiating position.

36

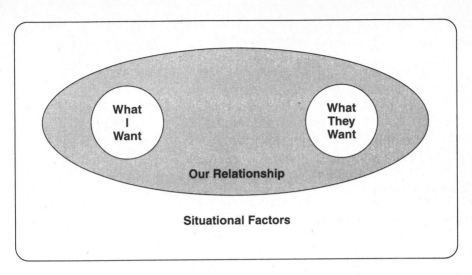

Figure 4.1 The Social Context of Negotiation

In contrast, if situational factors are effectively "balanced," both parties can employ their negotiation power to assure a mutually effective agreement (see Figure 4.2).

Nature and Type of Information and Resources Available

The key source of power in negotiation is information. Your planning is based on the information that you have, or can obtain from various sources. Once you know your own objectives, you need information to

> **POWER gives you leverage over BOTH the outcome and the relationship**

Figure 4.2 The Seventh Rule of Strategic Negotiation

support and buttress them. Once you know the other party's objectives and the underlying factors for their point of view, you will need information to refute their position or to support it. Much of negotiation is simply an exchange of information, and using information to convince the other party that you have a better, stronger, or more valid case.

When negotiation begins, you will make an opening offer, with a limit in mind. You will have set the opening, target, and walkaway points based on such information as the going market rate, the time frame, the other party's range, possible concessions, and generally accepted standards for a particular negotiation, all of which you will have assembled and determined beforehand.

To be prepared with a good plan, you need good information. Having a good plan will move you toward a positive outcome.

Since we have discussed at length the information you need to collect for your side and for your assessment of the other party, we now turn to some of the more general aspects of information and how they can provide power in negotiation.

Accuracy. You will base your negotiation requests on the information you gather, so it must be correct. The more accurate the information, the greater the power it gives you. If it is not accurate, you can lose face with the other party. There is nothing more embarrassing than to try to build a strong and compelling case, only to have the other side correct you and tell you that your facts are wrong. Unfortunately, you may not be able to get accurate information from the other party, especially if they are trying to maintain power by withholding or altering data. As a negotiator, you also have to decide whether you want to do the same thing—we discuss this more extensively in Chapter 13.

Expertise. Being able to assemble the facts into a coherent, coordinated presentation can help your image of being skilled in the area. One way to emphasize your pertinent skills and abilities is to offer information that only an expert would know. Likewise, you can refer to people who can vouch for your expertise. If the negotiation takes place in your office, the presence of diplomas, certificates, and other validating materials and credentials can add to your image of being an expert. As mentioned earlier, you can balance lack of knowledge to some extent by engaging the services of an expert to assist you.

In addition, expertise in negotiation itself is extremely helpful. The more experienced you are in negotiation, the more power you wield.

Communication Skills. In addition to the quality and accuracy of information, how that information is communicated can also contribute to your power. For example, how you structure the message to the other party affects their response. It can put you at an advantage or disadvantage. It can support your position, or it can undermine the other party's position. It can make them feel more or less confident in the information they have already assembled. Similarly, your style of presentation can affect the other party's response. Personal characteristics, which we treat later in this chapter, can assist you in getting your message across. Even your body language may help you appear credible and trustworthy. We discuss communication skills more extensively in Chapter 12.

Resources.   You can obtain power through a variety of nonhuman resources, especially if these are scarce. (If I have all the oil, or own all the real estate in a key neighborhood, then I am in a powerful position.) Supplies and equipment can provide power. Money, in all its varieties (insurance, stocks and bonds, benefits, to name a few) is a powerful tool. Time, which we treat separately later in this chapter, can also be a powerful tool in negotiation.

In summary, a negotiator can gain power if he/she has more information than the other, has more accurate or unique information, has greater expertise, or has better and more persuasive communication skills to present this information. In contrast, if both parties possess this information or have these skills, then the power of information will be balanced between the parties.

Constituencies and Their Support and Authority

In a simple two-party negotiation, perhaps where you and a friend are deciding which movie to see, there are no other parties to influence your decision. The two of you discuss your preferences, come to an agreement, and go to the movies. But in most negotiations, there are multiple parties. Behind you as a negotiator, there may be a department or a management group, a spouse or family members, or some other group who has goals and objectives in this negotiation. The existence of such a constituency can become a powerful influence in your negotiation and its success.

Constituencies serve two major roles. First, a constituency helps to define the objectives of the group. Even if you are the sole negotiator for the group, if you have a constituency, then the chances are that the constituency has had some input into shaping your objectives. Second, a constituency evaluates your work. How influential or powerful the constituency is can affect how well you are able to negotiate. The evaluation by the constituency will affect your reputation as a negotiator, both now and in the future. As a result, negotiators with a strong constituency must negotiate in a way to please that group of people and keep them happy; if they are not happy, then they can either embarrass you in negotiations, or may even "dismiss" you from your negotiating responsibilities.

If the constituency is powerful, yet removed from the negotiation process, they may expect extravagant results from you as the negotiator without fully understanding the situation. In fact, that is frequently the experience of negotiators with powerful constituencies. Because these groups are "out of touch" with what can actually be accomplished, they tend to form unrealistic expectations. The challenge then becomes educating the constituency to the difficulties of negotiation and exactly what the possible outcomes are. Unfortunately, they may not fully hear you.

The extent of control or power of the constituency can be positive or negative. It can be limiting to the negotiator always to have to go back to the constituency for "permission" to make an agreement or a concession. On the other hand, having to adhere to a review process can provide the negotiator with some control over the situation. In this case, the negotiator can always say to the opponent, "I'd like to give you that, but I can't make a decision right now. I have to talk to my superiors."

In an ideal relationship, a constituency is supportive of the negotiator's work and worth, and will back the negotiator on whatever needs to happen. Yet it is often useful to convey to the opponent that you do not completely have this control; in this way, you can use the constituency as an excuse to not give in to their concerns. For example, you and your spouse may have talked about the car you want to buy and the price you are willing to pay before you went into the dealership. But if the dealer presses you to complete a deal you are unhappy about, you can always say, "I have to talk to my spouse first before I can make an agreement."

Time Pressures and Deadlines

There is a "Murphy's Law" of negotiations: they tend to take as long as the time period that is allotted for them. This means that concessions usually do not occur until close to the end of the allotted time, or just before the negotiations are due to end.[2] There are a variety of reasons for this. One is that the parties tend to stall, hoping that the other will make concessions first. A second is that a deadline gives a party a "reason" to offer a concession, whereas they would not have wanted to do so earlier in the negotiations, for fear of appearing weak. Thus, I am willing to concede that you have an important point, but only because we have to complete this negotiation today. Finally, a deadline can serve as an excuse with one's constituency: "We held out as long as we could, but time was running out and we had to come to an agreement." Deadlines therefore also serve as a way for a party to explain to a constituency why a concession was made, without looking weak and admitting that one simply caved in.

As long as both parties are operating under the same deadline, then neither side has a power advantage. However, if one party does not have a deadline, and the other one does, then the more flexible party (the one without the deadline) gains some power. The party with the deadline will be moved by the urgency of the situation to make concessions. A classic example of the power of deadlines is negotiation between labor and management, where each side has a lot to lose if negotiation is not completed on time. The union will go out on strike and management will have to find ways to cope with the loss of labor. In 1994, the strikes by both professional baseball and hockey players were affected by deadlines—the point at which the parties could salvage or lose an entire season.

If you have a deadline and the other party does not (or says they do not), one way to try to balance the power is to set some kind of deadline for the other party, such as by offering a very attractive negotiating package, but then requiring that they have to decide in 24 hours. Thus, even if time was not important to them before, now you have made it so. For example, an automobile dealer will often attempt to close a sale with a hesitant buyer by offering a price reduction that is available "only today!" Similarly, companies often make job offers to graduates that are only effective for several weeks, so that students cannot accumulate several good job offers and "play the companies off" against each other.

Legitimacy Factors—The Power of Rules and Regulations

In our everyday lives, we are governed by formal rules, laws, and regulations that set certain limits for our behavior. We are also constrained by societal norms and cultural expectations. Parents set "rules of the house" for their children; teachers set "rules" for classroom behavior.

Likewise, in organizations, policies, regulations, and rules give the organization power and authority, and shape the behavior of employees, customers, suppliers, and so on. If we want to remain a part of that organization (or society) and do business with that organization, we are obliged to follow its rules. These rules are clearly made for the benefit of the organization and often limit what is negotiable, how it can be negotiated, and what procedures must be used if one does not simply want to "follow the rules." The objective is to protect the interests of the organization. We call this use of rules and regulations to control and maintain power "legitimacy."

We cannot challenge something that is "policy." Or, if we try, it takes time, money, and persistence, often ending in frustration. Thus, bureaucracies often have a lot of power, simply because they make it difficult for anyone to do anything outside the established rules, regulations, and procedures. For example, in accepting a new job, you might ask for a higher salary than is being offered. The manager might say to you, "If it were up to me, I would gladly give you a higher salary. But it is our company's policy to offer this amount. It cannot be adjusted." (A savvy negotiator might then request other benefits that are not part of the policy, or ask how the policy can be modified, or who has the authority to do so. Or a savvy manager who is doing the hiring might look for other benefits to offer you that are within the manager's authority to grant.) Other types of legitimacy include formal authority—usually granted from the institution, and past performance. If you have the authority to make an agreement, for example, you have more power than someone who has to keep returning to a constituency for authorization to proceed.

Position in a company or organization can also provide legitimacy and therefore, power. Organizational charts, and the job descriptions that accompany all the boxes in the chart, grant the occupants of various positions more or less authority. The higher your box is in a chart, the more likely it will be that you have more "position" authority. However, as organizations have undergone tremendous transformations in the past 10 to 20 years, the power that goes with "position" has changed dramatically. Whereas once we might have looked at an organizational chart to see where the power lies, nowadays responsibility, authority, and position look more like an interconnected network[3] or spiderweb of relationships than like the traditional chart with boxes. On the traditional organizational chart, authority (and power) usually lies at the top. In the network design, to see where the power lies, look for the parts of the network where critical information or resources are assembled, exchanged, or disseminated. These will tend to dictate which segments of the network are most central or have the most crossing paths. Other ways of ascertaining the division of power are by looking at how critical the position is, seeing whether it carries a lot of flexibility and discretion in making key decisions, or finding out whether it is a highly visible position. All would be indicators of more contemporary views of "position power."

In summary, if you have legitimacy on your side, you have a great deal of power in negotiation. If you are negotiating against an institution or someone representing an organization that has a lot of legitimacy, it will be very hard for you to achieve your objectives. The way to balance legitimacy power is to have other power factors on your side, and to invent clever ways to challenge the institution's authority and legitimacy in this situation.

Alternatives or Options to the Agreement

In Chapters 2 and 3, we discussed the key role of Alternatives, or options to completing this deal. Such options to the issues under negotiation can be powerful tools for a number of reasons. First, they allow us to avoid feeling compelled to complete the current negotiation. If we have good Alternatives, we are not obliged to pursue this negotiation at all costs. Once we start negotiating, many of us tend to believe we have to see it through, even if we end up with a poor deal, because a poor deal is better than no deal. (Not necessarily true!) Once we make a public commitment and invest time, money, and energy in the task, we may think we have to see it through to completion.[4]

However, when you have a good Alternative (or several), you gain power. You can pursue the current negotiation only so long as it is better than your Alternative. If it is not, then you can simply walk away and accept your Alternative. Hence, having Alternatives—even ones that aren't very good—gives you more power than having no Alternative at all! The threat that you will exercise other options can help you persuade the other party to make a deal that meets your needs.

Your Own Personal Qualities

There are a number of personal qualities that can give a negotiator power. These include three P's: persuasiveness, persistence, and personal integrity. There are also a number of related qualities, which we will discuss here.

Remember that your behavior affects other people's behavior, and their actions affect what you do. Thus, as events progress in negotiation, behaviors may change. The interplay may not be easy to predict.

Your personal reputation can provide power if it is positive. Someone with a reputation of being honest, or always successful at negotiation, has power over someone who does not have an established reputation or has a poor one. Your past performance can add to or detract from your reputation.

Persuasiveness. Earlier in this chapter, we talked about persuasiveness in relation to good information. But it is also a personal quality, because people differ in their ability to be persuasive. Success in negotiation will depend to a large extent on your ability to persuade the other party. You may persuade them to see things your way. You may convince them that their approach is all wrong. Or you may persuade them to try a collaborative approach. No matter what your intent, if you have persuasive skills, it will help your case immeasurably. Persuasiveness is power.

Persistence.　A second personal quality necessary for successful negotiation is persistence. A negotiator must be able to persevere through ups and downs to accomplish the objectives. Stay with it. Don't give up. As any child knows when trying to coax a parent into doing something, "no" doesn't necessarily mean "no." "No" can mean maybe, try again later, keep asking, and so on. Persistence will often yield something! This may mean sticking it out through emotional exchanges, or patiently waiting while the other party consults with their constituency. Tenacity can be a source of power if used gently but firmly.

Personal Integrity.　Character has a lot to do with power. Your reputation for personal integrity and being trustworthy can go a long way toward giving you a powerful position in bargaining. If the other party knows that you will stick by an agreement that you make, and you share information honestly, then they need not fear underhanded tactics. They may be more willing to negotiate. If you are known for your integrity, the other party will generally trust you.

Usually high trusters believe the other party will be trustworthy and that they need to be so themselves. Low trusters expect untrustworthiness so they are less inclined to be trustworthy themselves. As we said earlier, what you expect tends to be self-fulfilling. This can be a powerful tool in negotiation. However, if your actions and behaviors during a negotiation change, for example, if you give incorrect information or use underhanded tactics, the other party will likely become less trusting.

If a party has been in a situation with you or with someone else where their trust was broken, then they will be less willing to trust you in the current situation. This, of course, is a disadvantage.

Environmental Factors

The environment of the negotiation can provide a source of power. Aspects of the environment include the nature of the problem, previous outcomes or precedents, location and configuration of the site, schedule or agenda, negotiating process, record keeping, social and cultural context, and gender.

Nature of the Problem. The nature of the problem will govern some of the decisions made about other environmental factors. If it is a "simple" one-issue, one-event negotiation, there may not be a need for finding a location or setting up an agenda. If it is a new car bargaining session, for example, you probably will not need to find a location—it is usually at the car dealership. On the other hand, in a salary negotiation you might be able to select the location, say your boss's office or yours. You will have to decide where it would be better to meet and have a voice in the selection of the site if it is important to you. Perhaps you will want to use a neutral location, given the nature of the negotiation.

Previous Outcomes or Precedents. Another seemingly powerful tool is previous outcomes, especially in a similar situation. But details are different in each situation, so while knowing about previous outcomes can be helpful, it may not be predictive of the present outcome. If this issue has been negotiated by other people in similar circumstances, the results of those negotiations can set a precedent for the current dealings. The more frequently an issue has been negotiated before, the more those negotiations will limit the range of possible outcomes in the present situation. When precedents exist, they will define the most likely outcome. For the current negotiation to produce a different result, it would have to be demonstrated that this situation was different, unique, or in some way exceptional, and hence not subject to the previous precedents. Depending on whether precedents are going for you or against you, they will strengthen or weaken your negotiating position.

Location and Configuration of the Site. Sometimes it is helpful to hold negotiation on your own "turf," where all your resources are readily available. At other times, you may want to select a neutral site. And, on occasion, you will have to meet at the other party's site. Each of these situations has advantages and disadvantages. In general, negotiators tend to do better on their home turf; so you need to decide whether you want to take the advantage for yourself, give it to the other party, or call for a neutral site where neither has an advantage. For example, Geneva, Switzerland, is often used for international disarmament talks; the United Nations is often used for debating international treaties; and championship sporting events are usually held in "neutral" stadiums.

The arrangement of the room can also be a power factor. Frequently in diplomatic negotiations, there is lengthy discussion of site and configuration factors, such as the shape of the table and the seating arrangement. Certain positions tend to hold more power in terms of the process, while other positions are important for highly symbolic reasons. For example, the person who is running the meeting will usually select a location at the head or the center of the table. The person sitting straight across from the leader usually holds some power, which can be used positively or negatively. A person to the right of the leader has more power than the person to the left.[5]

Schedule or Agenda.   The agenda for a bargaining session or series of sessions can be used as a power tool also. The structure of the undertaking and the process can favor one party or the other. For example, the scheduling of breaks and the length of them can be used manipulatively, if both parties are not involved in deciding. (And they may not be, if such decisions are not important to one of the parties.) Intervals between sessions can be a controlling factor as well.

Power is also contained in the process of developing the agenda. If one party would like to have issues talked about in a particular order, sequence, or time frame, then it is to their advantage to dictate and control the agenda. Anyone who has seen a meeting manipulated by parliamentary procedure—what items get discussed, in what order, and whether they get discussed at all—knows how much power can be contained in dictating and controlling the agenda. In contrast, if one wishes to share this power, then both parties ought to collaboratively structure the agenda.

Negotiating Processes.   The process of negotiation is related somewhat to scheduling and agenda, but is more about how things will proceed than the actual content. For example, is negotiation formal or informal? Are there rules that need to be followed, in terms of what gets discussed, who must be present, and so on? Labor-management negotiation may follow fairly strict rules, whereas car bargaining may follow a sort of pattern but not be bound by formal rules. Person-to-person bargaining usually has no rules at all.

Record Keeping.   Another factor that may contribute to the power of one party or the other is how negotiation processes and decisions are recorded. Normally, most people don't like to be appointed "secretary" and have the responsibility for taking notes or minutes. Most would prefer that others do this task. Yet the position of writing and keeping the records of negotiation progress and decisions can be a very powerful one. The recorder is the person who writes down what is actually decided, and those notes/minutes are the "memory" of the negotiation. Therefore, the recorder can write things down in a way that creates advantages or minimizes disadvantages for his or her side. Particularly when the negotiations are over complex issues, or multiple issues, or multiple time periods, the wording of an agreement may be very important. The more important the exact words and language will be to the future of the agreement, the more critical it may be to assume the responsibilities for record keeping.

Social and Cultural Context

The social and cultural context will have an effect on the negotiation. When there are ethnic, cultural, racial, or gender differences these need to be taken into account. Because situations are increasingly diverse, it is important to develop tolerance for differences instead of taking advantage of them.

We will not discuss social and cultural issues here, except to note that there are programs to increase awareness of differences. Many feel that there is power in recruiting participants with diverse backgrounds to contribute the components of solutions.[6] We discuss the impact of intercultural differences further in Chapter 15.

Gender. It is easy to generalize that men and women negotiate differently, forgetting that within the population of women there are individual differences and likewise for men. Not all males are alike, nor are all females; nevertheless, differences have still been observed in the way men and women approach negotiation.[7] There are four basic areas of difference:

1. *Relationships among the parties negotiating.* Women are more apt to be concerned about the broader situation, and feelings and perceptions of the participants, than men, who usually want to resolve the matter at hand without considering the larger view.

2. *View of the negotiation.* Men tend to see a bargaining session as a finite, separate event, whereas women see it as part of a larger relationship with the other party.

3. *View of power.* Women tend to want to see everyone in the bargaining situation be equally empowered, whereas men tend to use power as a way to achieve their own goals.

4. *Dialogue.* Women use interaction and dialogue to achieve understanding, whereas men tend to use it for their own ends—to persuade the other party of their point of view.

The point about men's and women's approaches to negotiation is not that one approach is better than the other, but simply that they are different. Women perceive negotiation differently.[8] And this may explain, in part, why they have been found to be treated differently in negotiations. In fact, both women and blacks were found to be treated differently in the bargaining situations of buying a car and negotiating salary.[9] Opening offers made to women were worse than those made to men, and the outcomes were worse for the women buyers, too. When women used the same tactics as males, they appeared to be penalized for doing so. This seems to indicate that individuals should implement negotiating strategies in a manner most comfortable to them. The secret to success in negotiation is to improve upon your own technique rather than to copy another's. If you start with relatively less power, then you need to build your position and drag out the negotiation if needed to do so. But don't try to emulate someone with more power unless you can get the other party to go along.

SUMMARY: APPROACHES TO POWER

So what can you do when you know there are one or more power factors at work in the negotiation? It depends to some extent on how you view power or the lack of it. If your objective is to find a solution that will keep everyone happy, then you probably want to equalize the power. However, if you want the best outcome for yourself and you do not care about the other party, you will probably want to do everything you can to increase your power advantage. (Note that we do not advocate this position, we are just looking at various points of view. Power is a factor of negotiation that you need to be prepared for, especially if the other party seeks to take advantage of it.)

Power also has a lot to do with perception. The other party may see you as having more power than you do. Further, they may believe you have the ability to use it. So, just the image of power can be effective in accomplishing your goals. Many will argue, in fact, that the *image* of power is more important than real power. In addition, use of power is to some extent based on experience. As you learn what works in a particular situation, you will adjust your behaviors accordingly.

Some people use power more successfully than others. It can be used positively or negatively, as noted previously. Remember also that negotiation is usually a changing situation, with the parties making moves and countermoves, so that the behaviors and actions provide a moving target that is sometimes hard to zero in on.

RELATIONSHIPS

Power factors are also elements of individual personalities (e.g., persuasiveness, integrity) and key elements of the relationship between the parties. In addition, many of the elements we have mentioned will definitely have an impact on the relationship between the parties. For example, the relationship of superior and subordinate in a negotiation over salary will have a great effect in the bargaining,[10] and the bargaining process will have an impact on future relationships.

Much of the interpersonal behavior in a negotiation will depend on what the two parties view as most important: the outcome or the relationship. If the outcome is more important, and relationship issues do not count for much, then most personal qualities will not really provide you with much power. If the relationship is important, power may figure more, but it will not be used in a strategy of one-upmanship. In Chapter 5, we will discuss the importance of concern for outcomes and concern for the relationship, and how they affect the choice of strategy.

Remarkably, negotiation research reveals much less about how to define what the key relationships factors are, and how they affect (or are affected by) the ongoing negotiation process. Yet much of the negotiation that actually takes place—between coworkers, spouses, parents and children, suppliers and customers—occurs in the context of an ongoing relationship. Our paucity of understanding is because it is much more difficult to study these relationship factors in a research laboratory; as a result, much of negotiation research has studied negotiation processes between "strangers" who do not know each other and will not have a relationship in the future, rather than people who do know each other and will continue to work with each other.

Several researchers[11] have begun to study relationships and their impact on negotiation. These studies have identified a number of key factors that will either directly affect the negotiation process between parties, or will be affected by those negotiations as the parties sustain their relationship after the negotiation is over. We will mention only a few of the major ones:

1. *Trust.* We talked about trust in Chapters 2 and 3 when we talked about your own trustworthiness and the trustworthiness of the other party, and again in the previous section when we discussed personal integrity. While trustworthiness is a key quality of individuals, the level of trust between parties is a key factor in a relationship. The more people trust each other, the easier it will be to take risks with them, know what they will do and understand how they will react, and be able to coordinate with them to achieve a good outcome.[12] However, if the parties are competitive with each other, then the trust level is likely to decline.

2. *Commonality.* The more the parties have in common, the more likely they will be able to build a relationship and sustain it. Commonality also leads to predictability and understanding the other.

3. *Respect.* Parties who have respect for each other are likely to treat each other better. Respect contributes to a desire to treat the other fairly and honorably, and attend to their needs and concerns.

4. *Cooperation/Competition.* The parties differ in their level of cooperation/competition with each other. This may be a function of different goals, personalities, or many of the other situation factors described earlier. This factor may also directly affect the strategic choice process we describe in Chapter 5.

5. *"Exchange" or Transactions.* This element reflects the basic outcomes or resources that the parties want or expect from each other. This may be information, products, goods and services, contracts, budgets, assistance, and so on.

6. *Scope.* This element describes how many different "facets" there are to the relationship. A husband and wife have a relationship with a broad scope—they work and relate to each other in a variety of different ways. In contrast, a supplier and customer may relate to each other in only one or two ways, based on the simple exchange of products or services.

7. *Affect.* This element reflects how the parties feel about each other—their emotional reactions and feelings. Strong relationships are likely to have a great deal of affect, which may also lead to a high level of intimacy and romantic attachments. Using affect—being emotional—can also be an effective tool in negotiation.

8. *Acceptance.* This element reflects how much the parties accept each other. It can also relate to the amount of conflict in the relationship, such as the frequency of fights, disagreements, or inability to get along with each other.

9. *Empathy.* Being sensitive to the other party's needs involves the ability to look at their perspective.[13]

10. *Power.* This is a key element of a relationship. Is one party more "powerful" than the other, in that this party almost always gets what they want while the other seldom achieves their preferred outcome? In contrast, are the parties relatively equal in power, so that, on balance, both parties win a number of their transactions?

PERSONALITY CHARACTERISTICS

The personality characteristics of the individual negotiators are often difficult to separate from "relationship characteristics." A number of personal qualities such as the following ones can affect the relationship dynamics in negotiation:

- Attitude toward conflict (their personally preferred style of managing conflict, which parallels the strategy options outlined in Chapters 5, 6, and 7).
- Degree of assertiveness and cooperativeness.[14]
- Level of cognitive complexity (ability to think about issues in more or less complex terms).
- Level of self-esteem.[15]
- Belief in their ability to negotiate effectively.
- Belief that events are controllable (or not).
- Personal need to be in charge or in control of situations.

For example, if the person's style tends to be competitive, then the person is less of a risk taker, will demonstrate more internal control, will show a high need for power and control, and is less concerned about the other person's possible reactions of dislike or anger. On the other hand, a person who tends to operate collaboratively will be more cooperative, more trusting, more creative, and more capable of dealing with complexity.

Although many researchers have studied the potential impact of personality factors on negotiation, the true impact of these factors remains elusive.[16] In general, and over the long term of the negotiation process, the situation and relationship factors will have far more impact than individual personality elements.

THE ANALYTICAL PLANNING PROCESS

Now that you have analyzed the situation of the negotiation, consider once again the eight analytical planning steps outlined in Chapter 1 and see if you need to add anything in light of what we discussed in this chapter. Note that while the process initially requires an emphasis on information gathering and analysis, it shifts naturally toward a planning approach as more information becomes available. Information has implications, many of them immediately obvious and therefore leading to ideas for plans and strategies. As you stop now to assess the information and insights you have gained, you are on the verge of generating an effective plan for your negotiation. In fact, you may already have formed some plans in your mind. But remember the strategist's planning sequence: First, strategies, then plans, and finally, tactical implementation. The point is, you need to resist the temptation to make specific planning decisions, such as what opening position to take. Hold back for one more chapter, and you will discover that more fundamental strategic decisions will shape all these planning decisions. With that warning, we will now review what you have learned about the negotiation through your analysis, based on the eight steps of the analytical process.

1. *Define the issues.* In this chapter, we looked at situational issues such as deadlines, constituencies, options, rules, regulations, and power. How do these affect your definition of the issues for you and the other party? Are there any changes? Did you overlook any issues that have now become clearer and which should be added to the list? Does your study of the situation change anything about the issues you have planned already? Will you need any other experts to help with any of these issues?

2. *Assemble the issues and define the agenda.* Look at your prioritized list of the issues. Has anything changed? Should any of the issues be changed from major to minor or vice versa?

3. *Analyze the other party.* Take another look at the other side, given the context and power factors that you learned about in this chapter. Perhaps the balance of power looks different now. Decide what you want the balance of power to be (even in your favor) and take steps to adjust as suggested in this chapter.

4. *Define underlying interests.* In addition to the interests and needs you defined for your party and for the other party, are there others attributable to the constituencies that we discussed in this chapter? If so, use the question "Why" to look for the reason behind the issues. If you have a supportive constituency, then it may not be crucial to understand their interests. But if they are likely to apply pressure, you need to be sure that you understand them and that they understand you.

5. *Consult with others.* Even the simplest negotiations include other parties, who frequently need to be consulted. If any new party has surfaced in your awareness, add them to the plan now and ask for their input.

6. *Set goals for the process and the outcome.* Look at the schedule, site, time frame, parties, and contingency plans. Given the discussion of power factors in this chapter, does any new information need to be included in your planning?

7. *Identify your own limits.* Does any of the new situation information affect the limits you have set? Will you still be able to avoid going beyond

your limits? For example, what if you do not want to spend any more than a week on this negotiation, and you have discovered that regulations require that after the first meeting there has to be a two-week hiatus? Be sure that you have set realistic limits that you are comfortable with.

8. *Develop supporting arguments.* Will your planned presentation be possible and even appropriate, in light of these new situation factors? For example, if you have decided to use visual aids, will the meeting room allow you to do this? Or, are the experts you want to have testify available for the dates of the bargaining session? Can the resource files be obtained and available for the time period you need? Although these issues may seem unimportant, as negotiations progress you will be glad you have planned carefully to encompass them.

You may want to study other negotiation situations in which there were similar deadlines, rules, and so on. Bear in mind, however, that each negotiation is unique and unlike any other.

Congratulations! You have done your homework well by analyzing the negotiation in full. With the knowledge you have gained about your position and that of the other party, as well as the situation posed by your relationship, you can answer the strategic issues we first met in Chapter 1. What are your rational goals, what you can plan and hope to get out of the negotiation? And what are the other party's goals? Next, are there emotional or other irrational issues to consider; for example, does the other party have a history of taking a tough, conflict-oriented approach in negotiations? What about the outcome of the negotiation: How important is it to you and the other party and how do you each see it? And, finally, how do you and the other party view your relationship: Are there, for example, power issues to consider? Or will the other party be unable to accomplish long-term goals if the relationship is damaged? The answers to such questions vary with each negotiating situation, but there are good answers to all the important questions you can think to ask—if, that is, you have stopped to gather and analyze information about your own position, the other party's position, and the situation.

Now you are ready to consider various strategies to use for negotiation. Chapter 5 will give you an overview of the strategies, then Chapters 6, 7, and 8 will provide detailed descriptions of how to implement the various strategies.

Chapter 5

Selecting a Strategy

After you have analyzed your own position (Chapter 2), that of the other party (Chapter 3), and looked at the contextual issues of the negotiation (Chapter 4), you are ready to select a strategy to use in negotiating with the other party. This lengthy preparation allows you to negotiate strategically, adopting a style and plan that is best suited to the situation. As we have noted before, most people skip this preparation; as a result, they negotiate blind. The right strategy greatly improves your odds of a successful outcome.

In this chapter, we will look at five basic strategies that can be used for negotiation. Each strategy applies to a particular set of circumstances and has its own advantages and disadvantages. If you have done your homework in Chapters 2 through 4, you will be well prepared for selecting the appropriate strategy or combination of strategies for a particular negotiation situation. Note that we say *combination* of strategies. Most negotiations involve a mixture of issues, and each may be best handled with a different strategy. There is usually no single "best" strategy. Variations in the positions of the parties and the context of the negotiation will affect each negotiation differently. And as negotiations continue over time, each side will make adjustments that may call for shifts or changes of strategy by the other side (see Figure 5.1).

KEY FACTORS THAT DETERMINE THE TYPES OF STRATEGIES

The five basic types of negotiating strategies depend on your combination of preferences for two basic concerns: the *relationship with the other negotiator* and the *outcome of the negotiation itself*. The strength or importance of each of these two concerns, and its relative priority, should

---

The WRONG
strategy
guarantees

FAILURE!

Figure 5.1 The Eighth Rule of Strategic Negotiation

direct the selection of the optimal negotiation strategy. The other party may select a strategy in a similar manner. If they do not, you will want to give serious consideration as to whether you should share this strategic negotiating model with them. Your chances of a good outcome are often better if both parties agree to play by the same rules. The interaction of the two parties' choices will further influence the negotiation process that actually occurs, and this will have dramatic impact on the outcomes. We will now describe each of these concerns.

Relationship Concerns

First, how important is your past and future *relationship* with the other party? How have the two of you gotten along in the past, and how important is it for the two of you to get along, work together, and like each other in the future? Perhaps it is very important. Perhaps it does not matter at all. Perhaps it is somewhere between these extremes. If maintaining a good relationship with the other party is important to you, then you should negotiate differently than if the relationship is unimportant, or if it is unlikely that you can repair the relationship.

The importance of the relationship between the two parties will be affected by a number of factors: (1) whether there is a relationship at all; (2) whether that relationship is generally positive or negative (whether the two of you have gotten along well or poorly in the past); (3) whether a future relationship is desirable; (4) the length of the relationship and its history, if one exists; (5) the level of and commitment to the relationship; (6) the degree of interdependence in the relationship; and (7) the amount and extent of free, open communication between the parties.

For example, if you are negotiating the purchase of a new car, you may never have met the salesperson before and may not expect to have a continuing relationship. Therefore, your relationship concerns are low.

However, if your business uses a fleet of cars and you expect to work with this person on deals in the future, your relationship concerns are high, and this will affect negotiations. Or if you are buying the car from your neighbor, and want to continue to have a good relationship with that person, you may negotiate differently than if you are buying it from a stranger.

In the case of a party with whom you have an ongoing relationship, it may be congenial, or it may be antagonistic if earlier negotiations have been hostile. If it is a congenial relationship, you may wish to keep it that way, and avoid escalating emotions. If the relationship has a history of hostility, you may prefer not to negotiate, or you may want to lower the emotional level in the negotiations. This is important if you expect the relationship to continue in the future.

You should have a good sense of what to expect from the other party, based on your assessment in Chapter 3.

Outcome Concerns

The second factor affecting negotiating strategy is the importance of the *outcome* of the negotiation. How important is it for you to achieve a good outcome in this negotiation? Do you need to win on all points to gain the advantage? Or is the outcome of only moderate importance? Or does the outcome not really matter in this negotiation? For example, let us return to the car-buying example. If you are buying a car from a dealer, price may be the most important factor, and you may have absolutely no interest at all in the relationship. If you are buying the car from your neighbor, and you want to keep a good relationship with your neighbor, then you might not press as hard to get a good price. Finally, if you are buying the car from your mother simply so that she doesn't have to worry about it any more, you probably are most concerned about the relationship and care very little about the outcome.

Most of the planning and preparation described in the earlier chapters has focused on the outcome. Hence, we will not say much more about outcome concerns here. The important message in this chapter, however, is that the priority of each of the two negotiating concerns, relationship and outcome, will direct the strategy you choose to use for a particular negotiation. The relationship may be your top priority, especially if there is a relationship history and you want to maintain the relationship. In contrast, in many other negotiations, the outcome is the most important factor, as in the example of buying a car. Or, relationship and outcome may *both* be important. This will require working together with the other party in some fashion to effect a result. If the relationship concerns have a strong influence on the matter at hand, and you decide to emphasize them over the outcome, then you will select a different strategy than you would select where the outcome is more important.

If we show the relationship and outcome concerns on a graph, with high and low priorities for each represented, it looks like Figure 5.2. The vertical axis represents your degree of concern for the relationship, and the horizontal axis represents your degree of concern for the outcome. When we look at the various quadrants created by different levels of concern for relationship and outcome, five distinctly different strategies emerge:

1. *Avoiding (lose-lose).* This strategy is shown in the lower left of the diagram. In this strategy, the priorities for both the relationship and the outcome are low. Neither aspect of the negotiation is important enough for you to pursue the conflict further. You implement this strategy by withdrawing from active negotiation, or by avoiding negotiation entirely.

2. *Accommodating (lose to win).* This strategy is represented in the upper left of the diagram, where the importance of the relationship is high and the importance of the outcome is low. In this situation, you "back off" your concern for the outcome to preserve the relationship; you intentionally "lose" on the outcome dimension in order to "win" on the relationship dimension.

3. *Competitive (win-lose).* The lower right of the diagram represents high concern for the outcome and low concern for the relationship. You

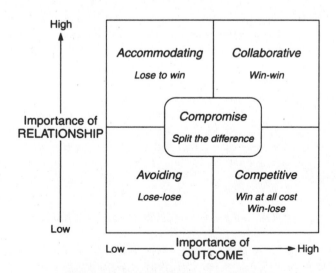

Figure 5.2 Negotiation Strategies

use this strategy if you want to win at all cost, and have no concern about the future state of the relationship.

4. *Collaborative (win-win).*[1] The upper right part of the diagram defines a strategy where there is a high priority for both the relationship and the outcome. In this strategy, the parties attempt to maximize their outcomes while preserving or enhancing the relationship. This result is most likely when both parties can find a resolution that meets the needs of each.

5. *Compromising (split the difference).* In the middle is an area we will call a Compromising, or "satisficing," strategy. It represents a combination approach that is used in a variety of situations. For example, it is often used when the parties cannot achieve good collaboration, but still want to achieve some outcomes and/or preserve the relationship. Thus, for example, if the parties cannot achieve good collaboration, but do not want to pursue the outcome and abandon the concern for the relationship (or vice versa), then a Compromising Strategy can be effective. It is also often used when the parties are under time pressure, and need to come to a resolution quickly. Each party will give in somewhat to find a common ground.

These brief descriptions are ideal or "pure" negotiating situations where there may be only one issue at stake. In contrast, most real-life negotiation situations are frequently complex, and thus are often best addressed by using a mix of strategies. Remember, too, that the other party will be formulating a negotiating strategy. You will find your analysis of the other party (from Chapter 3) helpful when you are selecting the appropriate strategy for a particular situation, because you may want to adjust your strategy choice based on what you expect the other to do. If the parties are able to agree on one strategy, negotiations will be easier. In real-life situations, however, each party may start with a different strategy. How to handle this situation is discussed further in Chapters 9 and 10.

We now look at the five basic negotiating strategies in detail. Although you may be inclined to use one particular strategy, it is a good idea to study the components of each strategy carefully. In this way, you can be prepared for the other party's moves, if they use a different strategy than you anticipated.

AVOIDING STRATEGY (LOSE-LOSE)

The Avoiding Strategy is used infrequently, but has merit in certain situations. Our nickname of this strategy is actually a misnomer, since an active choice of an Avoiding Strategy is not necessarily a "loss" on either the relationship or the outcome. However, since we tend to refer to the more active pursuits of relationship and outcomes as "winning," we will call the Avoiding Strategy a "loss" in terms of the outcome and the relationship.

Why would one choose an Avoiding Strategy? Because negotiations can be costly (in time, money, and relationships) and there are many cases where negotiators would have been better off to drop the matter entirely! The person employing an Avoiding Strategy basically sees negotiation as a waste of time—or not worth pursuing. This person may feel that his or her needs can be met without negotiating. In addition, this person may decide that the outcome has very low value and that the relationship is not important enough to develop through the negotiation. As a result, the party reasons that neither the relationship nor the outcome is sufficiently important (at least compared with the costs) and so takes no action or simply refuses to negotiate.

If the "avoider" refuses to negotiate when the other party wants to, this may have a negative effect on the relationship. Even when the outcome is unimportant, many people will prefer to avoid angering the other party. A more moderate method of avoidance may be to not raise any objections to the proceedings, or simply to not show up. If the other party insists on negotiations, and it is important to preserve the relationship, then you might switch to an Accommodating Strategy.

The Avoiding Strategy also is a possibility when a party can pursue a very strong Alternative outcome. If a strong Alternative is available, the person may choose not to negotiate. For example, if you are looking at two different houses to buy, and both meet your needs, you may choose not to negotiate with one seller because you feel the price is too high and the person is inflexible. So you simply select your Alternative and pursue an Avoiding Strategy in the first negotiation.

Alternatives can provide you with bargaining power in other situations, as we will see. If you have no Alternatives, or only weak ones, you may also choose not to negotiate. We will discuss Alternatives in more depth later in this chapter.

ACCOMMODATING STRATEGY (LOSE TO WIN)

An Accommodating Strategy is used when the relationship is more important than the outcome of the negotiation. The person using this strategy may prefer to primarily concentrate on building or strengthening a relationship. Since other people are usually happy when we give them what they want, we may simply choose to avoid focusing on the outcome and give it to the other side, thus making them happy. A second reason is that we may want something else in the future. Since many social relationships are built on rather informal expectations and rules of exchange,[2] giving something away now may create the expectation that they need to give us what we want later on. So we give them their preferences now, to obtain a better future outcome. A short-term loss is exchanged for a long-term gain.

For example, in a manager-employee relationship, the employee may want to establish a good relationship with the boss now to have a good evaluation, a raise, or a better position in the future. The employee may choose an Accommodating Strategy and not push for a salary increase now, at her 3-month review, if it is expected that this will put her in a better position for a raise at the 6-month review.

The Accommodating Strategy may be used to encourage a more interdependent relationship, to increase support and assistance from the other, or even to cool off hostile feelings if there is tension in the relationship. If the relationship is ongoing, then it may be particularly appropriate to "back down" now, to keep communication lines open and not pressure the opponent to give in on something that they do not want to discuss. In most cases, this strategy is *short term*—it is expected that accommodation now will create a better opportunity to achieve outcome goals in the future. For example, a manager might not urge an employee to take on an extra task right now if the employee is overloaded with projects and the manager can find another person to complete the task, especially if the manager knows that a big project is coming next week, and everyone is going to have to put in overtime.

In a long-term negotiation or over a series of negotiations, it may happen that one side constantly gives in. This precedent may be noted by the other side and seen as accommodating behavior (which it is). It should not be construed as an invitation to the other party to be competitive. But sometimes it is. If this happens to you, the other party will begin to compete and take advantage of your guard being down. You will need to learn how to use the damage control and reconnection strategies in Chapter 10 to overcome these problems.

The Accommodating Strategy is not usually considered a formal strategy in negotiation. Many negotiation books do not even mention Accommodation as a viable strategy; however, most of these books also are based on "high outcome concern" strategies (Competing or Collaborating) and spend less time on specific strategies to improve or strengthen

the relationship. There are two important times to consider an Accommodating Strategy: first, if the outcome is not very important to you, or pursuing the outcome is likely to create too much tension and animosity, and
second, if your primary objective is to improve the relationship. In addition, you might decide to switch to an Accommodating Strategy during negotiations, particularly when they reach a point where you no longer wish
to press for a resolution.

COMPETITIVE STRATEGY (WIN TO LOSE)

When many people think of negotiation and bargaining, this is the
strategy they think of. The Competitive Strategy is used frequently, so it is
important to understand how it works, even if you do not plan to use it
yourself.

In a Competitive Strategy, the outcome of the negotiation is more important than the relationship. Because the outcomes (resources, gains,
profits, etc.) are seen as finite and limited in amount or size, the person
engaging in a Competitive Strategy wants to get as much of those outcomes as possible. (We will use the term "competitor" to denote the person using the Competitive Strategy.) We call this strategy "win to lose"
because it is likely that while competitors may gain on the outcome, they
strain and endanger the relationship between the parties. The thinking and
goals in this strategy are short term: to maximize the magnitude of the
outcome right now, and to not care about either the long-term consequences of this strategy or the relationship. The relationship with the other
party does not matter, for one of several reasons: (1) this may be a one-
time negotiation with no future relationship, (2) the future relationship
may not be important, (3) the relationship exists, but was poor to begin
with, or (4) the other party may have a reputation for hard bargaining or
dishonesty, and this strategy is adopted for defensive reasons. At any rate,
this strategy is undertaken with the assumption that the future relationship
with the other party is unimportant, but the specific outcome *is* important.

The Competitive Strategy tends to emphasize the differences between
the parties, promoting a "we/they" attitude. Thus, the relationship during
negotiation in a competitive situation will be characterized by lack of trust
and even by conflict. This contrasts with the Collaborative Strategy in
which differences are minimized and similarities emphasized.

The goal in the Competitive Strategy is to get the other party to give
in, and thus to satisfy the competitor's needs now. It is based on the "I
win, you lose" concept. The competitor will do anything to accomplish

the objectives and obtain as much of the pie as possible. This can include a variety of behaviors, including hardball tactics, which we discuss in Chapter 6.

Critical Factors in a Competitive Strategy

A Well-Defined Bargaining Range. In a Competitive Strategy, each side has a bargaining range, which consists of a *starting point,* a *target,* and an *ending point* or walkaway. Bargaining occurs because the bargaining range for each party is different. During bargaining, you attempt to bring the two ranges into overlap so that each party is satisfied.

The *starting point* is announced or inferred as the negotiations begin. Starting points will be different for the two parties. In new-car negotiations, for example, the buyer will have a lower starting point, the seller, a higher one. Usually, the buyer makes gradual concessions upward, while the seller will make gradual concessions downward, with the expectation that the two will be able to meet somewhere in the middle. In labor negotiations, labor is usually expected to ask "high" and management to offer "low," again with the expectation that concessions on each side will result in finding a meeting ground.

Both parties will have a walkaway point, which is the cutoff point, beyond which they will not go. The walkaway point of the other party is usually not known, and is not stated. In fact, they will actively try to keep you from learning their walkaway point, because if you knew it, you would offer them something slightly above it and expect that they would agree! If talks break off because this point has been reached, then you may surmise that the walkaway point of the other party was probably close to, or at, the last offer that the other side made. If this point is not reached, and the parties agree to a resolution, this point may never be known. In future chapters, we will explore ways of discovering competitors' walkaway points and learn how to turn this knowledge into better outcomes.

As long as the bargaining range for one party in some way overlaps with that of the other party, then there is room for bargaining. (By "overlap," we mean that the most the buyer is willing to offer is above the least the seller is willing to accept.) If the ranges do not overlap (and this may not be known at the beginning of the negotiations), then there may be no successful negotiation. The parties will need to decide whether to adjust their bargaining ranges, or to end negotiations.

A Good Alternative. An Alternative or BATNA[3] (Best Alternative to a Negotiated Agreement) is an option that can be pursued if the current negotiation fails. It is an outcome outside the scope of the negotiation with this other party, and can be pursued if it appears more attractive than any potential outcome from this negotiation. Alternatives are good to have because they can be weighed against the value of any particular outcome from this negotiation, to decide which is most advantageous. Not only is an Alternative an evaluative tool, it is also a power tool that can be introduced into negotiations in the manner of "I have this Alternative that is equally good and costs less. Can you improve on what I will get if I pursue my Alternative?"

Alternatives interact with walkaway points to influence the choices you make. For example, say you currently make $25,000 in your job and you are job hunting. You decide that you want to find a job making at least $30,000. What do you do if you find a job you like, but it only pays $28,000? Do you take it or not? If there are no other such jobs available (no Alternatives) because the economy is sluggish, then you might take the $28,000 job. However, if many Alternative jobs are available for the taking, then you may hold out for a higher salary. On the other hand, suppose you lose your $25,000 job and you are offered $24,000 for another similar job. Will you take it? Perhaps under these circumstances, you will be more likely to do so. In any negotiation, it is wise to be well-informed of your Alternatives and, wherever possible, to use them to your advantage.

Tactics. The Competitive Strategy is also characterized by a number of tactics calculated to enhance the competitor's position and place the other party at a disadvantage. These include behavioral tactics such as bluffing, being aggressive, and threatening, which can give the competitor power over the other party. We take up the subject of competitive tactics in Chapter 6. While these tactics work sometimes, they also have the problem that they can potentially backfire on the person using them, so they must be employed carefully.

Results and Drawbacks of Using a Competitive Strategy

The Competitive Strategy can be successful, in spite of being one-sided. People using this strategy usually come away from a negotiation with the belief that they obtained the best that they could.

Negotiations that rely on a Competitive Strategy can be costly and time-consuming, especially if each party holds out for all its demands. Much time is spent researching, pressuring, and "psyching out" the other party. Further time is consumed making moves and countermoves, trying

63

to figure out what the other party will do. Competitive Strategies are often compared with strategies used in chess, military warfare, and other tactical, competitive battles. The time spent in these activities is very different from alternative uses of that time; for example, in the Collaborative model, this same time could be spent on mutual exploration of issues, sharing of information, and an attempt to find mutually acceptable solutions.

Time and goodwill may also be lost if the competitor anticipates that the other party will be competitive and prepares a Competitive Strategy. If the other party had not intended to be competitive, they may switch strategies when they discover that you have decided to be competitive, thus escalating emotions and increasing conflict. Not only do you lose time, but you may have alienated the other, hurt the relationship, and toughened them so that they are now willing to give you far less than they might have on the outcome dimension.

A major problem with the Competitive Strategy is that it is frequently used by inexperienced or untrained negotiators who believe that competition is the only viable strategy. They may be missing opportunities by automatically selecting the Competitive Strategy. It is important to select a strategy only after thorough investigation of the issues, an understanding of what strategy the other is likely to pursue, and some clear decisions about the relative importance of the outcomes and the relationship with the other party.

Likewise, it is possible to underestimate the other parties in a competitive situation. Remember that they, too, have adopted the mission to win at all costs. When using a Competitive Strategy, we tend to underestimate the strength, wisdom, planning, and effectiveness of the other party and assume that even though they are preparing to be competitive too, we can beat them at their game! If you do not pay close attention to their behavioral and verbal clues, you may set yourself up for manipulation by the other party.

Finally, we need to beware of something called the "self-fulfilling prophecy." A self-fulfilling prophecy is something we believe so strongly that we actually make it come true. It often happens in negotiation when one party expects the other to behave in a particular way, and as a result, actually makes the party behave that way. This tends to come true if the other party is using the Competitive Strategy because they think you are. Anticipating that the other is going to be competitive, we prepare to be competitive ourselves. The cues we give off in this preparation—our language, tone of voice, gestures, and behaviors—let the other believe that we intend to be competitive. So they behave competitively, which only assures us that our initial assumptions were right.

THE COLLABORATIVE STRATEGY (WIN-WIN)

A Collaborative Strategy is one in which both parties consider the relationship and the outcome to be equally important. This strategy is also referred to as cooperative or "win-win."[4] In a Collaborative Strategy, the parties to the negotiation either begin with compatible goals or are willing to search for ways to pursue their goals so that both can gain. This is in sharp contrast to the Competitive Strategy, in which the parties believe their goals are mutually exclusive, and only one side can win. The relationship between the parties is very likely an ongoing one, with some established history of give-and-take, so that the parties trust each other and know that they can work together. In addition, collaborative strategies are often initiated when the parties know that they want to establish long-term goals for particular outcomes and for the relationship. For example, many local governments are finding that they simply cannot sustain the operating costs of the past, especially in view of the voters' unwillingness to accept higher taxes. Knowing that city budgets have to be cut, departments need to work collaboratively, with *each* department taking a cut, and try to find creative ways to help each other stay in the black or at least minimize the red.

To make this strategy work, *both* parties to the negotiation must be willing to use the Collaborative Strategy; if only one side employs it, and the other uses a different one, the chances are that both parties cannot achieve both an optimal outcome and preserve or enhance their working relationship. A Collaborative Strategy is particularly appropriate within an organization, when two parties have common ground, or in situations where two parties have the same customers, same clients, same suppliers, or same service personnel. In any of these cases, the parties have or want to establish a working relationship, and to keep it working smoothly.

For a Collaborative Strategy to work, there must be a high degree of trust, openness, and cooperation. The parties look for common needs and goals and engage in mutually supportive behavior to obtain them. Both parties realize that they are interdependent and that their cooperative effort can solve the problems and meet the needs of both sides.

In collaboration, communication between parties is open and accurate. This contrasts greatly with the Competitive Strategy, in which the negotiators have a high level of distrust and guard information carefully to prevent the other side from obtaining the advantage.

The parties in a Collaborative endeavor have support from their constituencies. The constituencies trust the parties to find common ground and support them in doing so. Doing so may mean not achieving absolutely everything the constituency wanted on the substantive issues, and the constituency has to accept this as valid. In contrast, in the Competitive Strategy, the constituencies usually push the negotiator to get everything he or she can, regardless of the future of the relationship.

Collaborating parties respect deadlines and are willing to renegotiate the time frame if necessary to achieve their goals. Contrast this with the Competitive Strategy, where time is used as an obstacle or as a power ploy to accomplish one's own ends.

The Collaborative Strategy is hard work, but the results can be rewarding. It takes extra time and creativity to build trust and to find win-win solutions. But the outcome and relationship results are usually better for both parties.

Keys to Successful Collaboration

The Collaborative Strategy has traditionally been underutilized, because most people do not understand the fine points of the strategy and because it is less familiar than the Competitive Strategy. Many negotiations are based on the competitive model, which is the way most people view negotiation—as a competitive situation where one is better off being suspicious of the other, and the fundamental object is to get all the goodies.

Of key importance in a Collaborative Strategy is commitment. Both parties need to be committed to (1) understanding the *other* party's needs and objectives; (2) providing a free flow of information, both ways; and (3) finding the best solution(s) to meet the needs of both sides.[5]

Understanding the other party's goals and needs is critical to the Collaborative Strategy. We suggested that this is important in a Competitive Strategy as well, but for very different reasons. In a Competitive Strategy, you may know or think you know what the other party wants; but your objective in learning this is to facilitate your own strategy development, and also to strategize how to beat the other side by doing better than them or denying them what they want to achieve. In a Collaborative Strategy, your objective is to understand their goals and needs so that you can work with them to achieve their goals as well as your own. Good collaboration frequently requires not only understanding their stated objectives, but their underlying needs—*why* they want what they want. In the Collaborative Strategy, both parties must be willing to ask questions and *listen carefully to the answers,* to learn about the other's needs.

Second, to provide a free flow of information, both parties must be willing to *volunteer* information. The information has to be as accurate and as comprehensive as possible. Both sides need to understand the issues, the problems, the priorities, and the goals of the other. They need to fully understand the important context factors in the negotiation (see Chapter 4). Compare this with the Competitive Strategy, in which information is closely guarded, or, if shared, often distorted.

Finally, having listened closely to each other, the parties can then work toward *achieving mutual goals* that will satisfy both parties. To do this, the parties will need to minimize their differences and emphasize their similarities. They will need to focus on the issues and work at keeping personalities out of the discussions. Collaborative goals differ from Competitive goals. In competition, the goal is obtaining the largest share of the pie, at any cost, without giving away any information or conceding on any issue. In collaboration, each party must be willing to redefine their perspective in light of the collaboration, knowing that the whole can be greater than the sum of the parts. In this light, having a strong knowledge of the problem area is a definite advantage. While a lack of information can be overcome, starting out with the knowledge is definitely an asset.

In Chapter 7, we will discuss how to implement a Collaborative Strategy. To achieve success, each party *from the beginning* must send signals to the other that will help build trust between and among those negotiating.

Obstacles to the Collaborative Strategy

Both parties to a negotiation must be willing to collaborate if this strategy is to be successful. It will be difficult, if not impossible, to employ a Collaborative Strategy under the following circumstances:

- One party does not see the situation as having the potential for collaboration.
- One party is motivated only to accomplish its own ends.
- One party has historically been competitive; this behavior may be hard to change.
- One party expects the other to be competitive and prepares for negotiation based on this expectation.
- One party wants to be competitive and rationalizes this behavior.
- One party may be accountable to a constituency that prefers the Competitive Strategy.
- One party is not willing to take the time to search for collaborative items.
- The negotiation or bargaining mix may include both competitive and collaborative issues. (Sometimes, the two parties can collaborate on

collaborative issues and compete on competitive issues. Our experience however, is that competitive processes tend to drive out collaborative processes, making collaboration harder to achieve.)

Most of the foregoing obstacles reflect a conflict between the parties' preferences for strategy. It may be possible to get the other party to take a different stance if it appears to be desirable in light of the information. (See the discussion of how to build collaboration in Chapter 9.) Communication is of major importance when you are trying to establish a collaborative relationship. We take up specifics of communication in Chapter 12.

COMPROMISING STRATEGY

Ultimately, most negotiating situations are mixed; some bargaining elements are competitive in nature, and others can be approached collaboratively. There are times when the relationship is only somewhat important, and the outcomes are only somewhat important. This is where the fifth strategy comes in.

The Compromising Strategy may be thought of as an "adequate for most occasions" approach to negotiation. In this strategy, each side will have to modify their priorities for the relationship and for the preferred outcome(s). In both cases, the parties are making a decision that Compromising is preferred because, on the one hand, *both* parties gain something (an advantage over Accommodation or Competition), both parties gain *something* (as opposed to nothing—an advantage over Avoiding), and yet Compromising does not require all the intentional effort required for Collaboration. For example, if a manufacturing facility has a mandate to contain costs, the union and the factory representatives (whose relationship is usually competitive) will want to find an acceptable way to achieve this. The union will want to avoid layoffs. The company may propose a wage freeze. So the two parties may agree on a small wage increase offset by a decrease of the labor pool by attrition rather than layoffs; this is a Compromise.

While negotiators usually don't start off planning a compromise (particularly if a Competitive or Collaborative Strategy is possible), Compromising is often seen as an acceptable "second choice." There are three major reasons to choose a Compromising Strategy (particularly as a "default" alternative to other Strategies):

1. A true Collaborative Strategy does not seem to be possible. One or both parties don't believe that true win-win can be achieved

because it is simply too complex or too difficult. Or, the relationship may already be too strained for the parties to work together in a manner that fosters and supports good collaboration.

2. The parties are short of time or other critical resources necessary to get to Collaboration. Compromising is usually quick and efficient. While it may be suboptimal on the quality of the outcomes achieved, the tradeoff between achieving a great outcome and the time required to do it may force one to pick time over quality.

3. Both parties gain something (or don't lose anything) on both dimensions. As opposed to pursuing a Competitive Strategy (and maximizing outcomes at the expense of the relationship) or an Accommodating Strategy (and sacrificing outcomes for the relationship), Compromising assures some gain on *both* the outcome and relationship dimensions.

WHEN TO CHOOSE WHICH STRATEGY

Now that we have reviewed the five basic strategies, we come to an important part of this chapter: how to decide which strategy you should use for a negotiation. There are two key factors to consider:

1. How important is the outcome to be gained from this negotiation?
2. How important is the past, present, and future relationship with the opponent? The following paragraphs describe ways to decide about these two questions and other factors to consider in answering them.

Situation

Look at the *situation* and try to figure out which strategy might be best in those circumstances. Do I care a lot about the outcomes in this situation? If I do, am I willing to sacrifice my relationship with the other person? Or, conversely, is the relationship so important that I am unwilling to endanger it by pursuing the outcome? Alternatively, consider the conditions under which each strategy is most effective (see Figure 5.2). Which of these conditions apply to the present situation?

Remember that each strategy has both advantages and disadvantages. One strategy is more or less appropriate depending on the type of conflict and the situation.

Preferences

Analyze your personal *preferences* for the various strategies. You will probably be more successful using a strategy that feels comfortable. Research has shown that people in conflict have distinct *preferences* for employing certain strategies in conflict situations.[6] These preferences lead individuals to develop distinct *styles* with which they approach many situations. Based on past experience and history, some people have strong biases toward being competitive, collaborative, compromising, accommodating, or avoiding in conflict situations. The stronger your preference for a particular conflict management strategy (style), the more often you will choose it, the more "biased" you become in seeing it as an advantageous strategy, and the more likely you will be to see that strategy (style) as appropriate in a variety of situations. Thus, if you normally respond to conflict (and negotiation) situations in a competitive manner, then you are more likely to see the Competitive Strategy as widely appropriate—even when it may not be. Similarly, the less likely you are to avoid conflict, the more likely it is that you will not choose the Avoiding Strategy—even when it may be the most appropriate thing to do. Therefore, understanding your preferences and "biases" is critical, because they will affect your tendency to overselect or underselect strategies in particular situations.

Your preferences for a particular strategy are also influenced by subtle issues such as your *values and principles*. These may be harder, in some ways, to define than your goals, priorities, or limits. But, how you evaluate the following will have a great impact on your willingness to use (or not use) certain strategies:

- How much do you value truth, integrity, manners, courtesy?
- Is respect an important issue for you?
- How important is fair play? (And, for that matter, how do you define "fair"?)
- How much of your ego is involved in this—your reputation, your image? How concerned are you about how you will see yourself—or others will see you—if you get what you want, or don't get what you want?

Experience

Next, consider your *experience* using the various strategies. The more experience you have, the better you become at using that strategy—and, probably, the more likely you are to use it. Experience is one of the key factors that works to shape your *preferences.*

Style

Think about your own style as it interacts with the *other party's style,* and consider the possible consequences. What will be the effect of such a combination? For example, two competitive parties might have more conflict in their negotiation than a competitive party negotiating with a party that usually yields. While it would be too complex to explore all the possible interactions between each of your five possible styles and the styles of the other in detail, we have summarized the possible combinations in Table 5.1. (Some of the cells in the left side are blank because the information is contained in the "matching cell" on the right side.)

Perceptions and Past Experience

Consider your *perceptions and past experience* with the other party. How you feel about the other party, and what you want to have happen in that relationship in the future, will drive your strategy. How well do you like each other? How much do you communicate? How much do you need to work with the other in the future because you are dependent on what they can do for you? How much do you trust them? Your level of trust with the other party will be based on your past experience with them, and on the history and results of other negotiations they have conducted with you or with other parties in the past.

Other Factors

Finally, there are other factors that may affect the selection of strategy but that might be less in your control. Nevertheless they should be part of the planning process. These reflect the following situational or context issues (discussed in Chapter 4):

- Is this negotiation voluntary or imposed? Are both parties going into it willingly, or has it been assigned by a manager, or some other constituency whose voice and support are influential?
- Is the situation highly structured? Are there rules, laws, and management mandates that will direct the negotiation?

71

Table 5.1 Likely Interactions between Negotiators of Different Styles

	Avoiding	Accommodating	Competing	Collaborating	Compromising
Avoiding	Both parties avoid pursuing their goals on the issues, and do not take any action to endanger the relationship.	Accommodator shows strong concern for the Avoider, particularly the relationship; Avoider attempts to minimize interaction.	Competitor will dominate or Avoider will escape. Avoider attempts to minimize interaction, while Competitor tries to "engage."	Collaborator shows strong concern for both issues and the relationship while Avoider tries to escape. Collaborator may give up.	Compromiser shows some concern for both issues and relationship; Avoider tries to escape. Compromiser may give up or Avoider may engage.
Accommodating		Both parties avoid pursuing their goals on the issues, give in to the others' goals and try to smooth over relationship concerns.	Competitor pursues own goals on the issues, while the Accommodator tries to make the Competitor happy. Competitor usually wins big.	Collaborator shows strong concern for both issues and relationship; Accommodator tries to make the Collaborator happy. Relationship should be very strong, but the Collaborator may achieve better outcomes.	Compromiser shows some concern for both issues and relationship; Accommodator tries to make the Compromiser happy. Relationship will improve, Compromiser may entice the Accommodator to pursue some issue focus.
Competing			Both parties pursue their goals on the issues and ignore any concern for the relationship; create conflict, mistrust, hostility.	Collaborator shows strong concern for both issues and relationship, while Competitor only pursues issues. Competitor usually "wins" and both parties become competitive.	Compromiser shows some concern for both issues and relationship, while Competitor only pursues issues. Competitor usually "wins" and both parties become competitive.

Collaborating

Both parties pursue their goals on the issues, show strong concern for the others' goals *and* sustaining trust, openness, and a good relationship.

Compromiser shows some concern. Collaborator shows strong concern for both issues and the relationship. Minimally, good compromise or better.

Compromising

Both parties pursue their goals on the issues in a limited way and attempt to "do no harm" to the relationship.

73

- Is the agenda already established? (Can it be changed if necessary?)
- Finally, realize that the setting plays an important part in the proceedings and in the results. Consider not only the physical environment but elements of the psychological setting, including the players, both individuals and groups; their cultures and behavior; and established norms, standards, and processes.

CAN YOU MAKE A "NO STRATEGY" CHOICE?

Some people whom we have taught in negotiation have argued that it is possible to adopt *no strategy*. You refuse to make an explicit strategic choice, and "let the chips fall" to determine what you will do next. This allows you "maximum flexibility" to adjust your approach based on what your opponent does first, or as the proceedings change.

This approach has some distinct advantages. You get a chance to find out how your opponent wants to negotiate first, which may tell you a lot about your opponent. It also keeps you from making a commitment to a strategy that may not work or get completed; for example, to be Accommodative while the other is being Competitive. However, a "No Strategy" choice is often the lazy negotiator's way of avoiding a key part of the planning and preparation process. We do not think this is a good choice! While a "No Strategy" choice may give you some negotiating leeway, it could also put you in a precarious position if you have not planned well. The result will be that the opposition gains an advantage over you before you realize what is going on!

If you know that you care about the relationship, or the outcome, or both (or neither), select a strategy and begin to plan around it. If you are proactive about strategy choice, you are much more likely to get what you want than if you wait for the other to initiate action. As we have pointed out, you can always adapt your strategy later as necessary.

MOVING FORWARD

Once you decide which strategy is best for you, it is time to take all the information you have gathered and to proceed to implement that strategy. In the next two chapters, we discuss implementation of the two most popular strategies: Competitive and Collaborative. In Chapter 6, we discuss implementing a Competitive Strategy. In Chapter 7, we review the steps in implementing a Collaborative Strategy. Compromising, Accommodating, and

Avoiding are discussed in Chapter 8. We suggest that you read each of these chapters to familiarize yourself with the characteristics of the strategies.

As with planning a trip, it is wise to know *where* you want to go and *how* to get there. It is important to have a well-developed plan that includes specific moves and countermoves. Your game plan can be modified as needed. Modifications will be based on what the other party says and does. Plans start with a strategy. If you are negotiating, select a strategy now and then refine your plan as you read the following chapters.

Chapter 6

Implementing a Competitive Strategy

As we noted in the previous chapter, the Competitive approach is most effective in the right circumstances—when the outcome is important to you and the relationship with the other party is less important, and/or when you expect that the other party is likely to be Competitive. Similarly, the other strategies work best in specific circumstances. Thus, the strategic negotiator can beat the odds by consciously planning to employ the right strategy for the right situation, rather than betting on any single strategy for all negotiations (or, even more problematical, by not intentionally planning a strategy and letting one's opponent make the choice).

Before we explore the competitive strategy, we want to introduce you to two fictional characters[1] to help illustrate the different strategies and train people in their use. Once we describe these people, we will tell their story in five different ways, to illustrate the five different paths that result from the five strategies. Their names are Sara and Felice, and you will be following their negotiations in future chapters as well.

Sara and Felice have been friends for many years, ever since they took a high school art class together. After graduation, Sara attended an art school then went on to land a job in a respected interior decorating firm. Felice inherited enough money from a wealthy great aunt to avoid serious work and has spent much of her time traveling and dabbling in the arts. She sits on the boards of her city's art museum and opera company, and has decorated her house and summer cottage with the works of well-known artists and furniture designers. Felice admires Sara's work and is very interested when Sara suggests they start their own interior decorating business. Sara has the talent and a growing reputation among clients, but lacks the funding needed to open the new business on her own. We will visit Sara and Felice periodically as they approach the discussion of this partnership, using each of the five negotiating strategies. In this chapter, Sara and Felice will use a competitive strategy.

SITUATIONS WHERE A COMPETITIVE STRATEGY MIGHT BE USED

Before we discuss in depth how to implement a Competitive Strategy, we will recap the appropriate circumstances for a competitive strategy:

1. First, the goals of the parties are *short term*. There is no desire to establish or nurture a long-term relationship.
2. Second, the parties assume that their goals are *incompatible*. The issue(s) under discussion are seen as a "fixed pie"; what one gains, the other loses, and there are a limited number of ways in which it can be divided. Your objective is to maximize your piece of the pie. If there is more for you, there is less for the other party. And vice versa. So the aim is to get as much as you can.
3. Third, the *tangible* or more quantifiable, objective benefits are the most important to you—factors such as price, interest rate, number of items, delivery terms, and wording of a contract. The price is the most common tangible benefit in competitive negotiations. *Intangibles,* or psychological factors such as esteem, principles, precedents, or the overall well-being of both parties (now and in the future) are less important in competitive negotiations, though they need to be taken into account as well.
4. Finally, you are likely to use a Competitive Strategy when you *expect the other party to take a competitive stance.* From your research on the other party in Chapter 3, you probably have a good idea of what strategy they will employ. If you know that the other party is going to be Competitive, then a Competitive Strategy may be appropriate (see Table 5.1). However, if you are only guessing, and the other party uses a different strategy, whatever you have planned may not work. And even if the other party is likely to employ a Competitive Strategy, you may find it desirable to try to shift to a Collaborative negotiation to increase the outcome possibilities for both sides. We discuss this at length in Chapters 9 and 10.

Sara and Felice are sitting at the kitchen table in Felice's luxurious apartment, discussing how to split ownership of the proposed business as they drink coffee. You might wonder as you read this why Sara has allowed the negotiation to take place at all without careful analysis and planning; for example, why allow Felice to gain the twin advantages of time pressure and location? This is exactly our point—competitive negotiations often occur as a result of just such a lack of planning and forethought!

"What it comes down to," Sara said, "is that I have the experience and you have the money. People in the decorating industry know my name and my work; we'll get our first jobs because of my reputation. Nobody knows your work unless they've been in your living room, but I believe you have some talent. With my knowledge and your financial backing, I think we could go far . . . I think we ought to split the profits 50/50."

Felice poured them both another cup of coffee and then said, "What do I get out of this deal?"

"Well, you'll have an opportunity to learn from me," Sara answered, "and of course you'll control one quarter of the shares." She gulped some coffee and grimaced as she burned her tongue.

"If I'm going to put up all the money, I need to get most of the profit, or you need to repay half of the investment to me," Felice demanded.

Sara was furious. "What kind of a friend are you? You know that I can't possibly pay back that much money, and I can't make a living from a tiny part of the profits. Besides, if you have more shares than I do, you'll be in control of the business, and that's not fair to me."

Felice took her time, adding cream and sugar to her coffee, stirring and sipping before she answered. "The way I see it," replied Felice, "you don't have much of a choice. No one else will give you the money, and I know how much you want to do this. We'll split it 80/20, or you'll repay your half with interest, or there's no deal. I'll give you until next Friday to decide."

"But Felice, you know I can't wait that long to get started! If I had more time, I could line up a dozen backers, but we're supposed to start on our first job the day after tomorrow. You've really got my back against the wall! Here's my final offer: we split it 60/40 and sign the papers right now!"

"Make it 70/30 and I'll accept," countered Felice.

Sara thought a long time. "Fine," she said, "but *only* because I have no other choice."

Usually, given the opportunity, most people will engage in a Competitive Strategy because that is the most familiar. Felice and Sara fell into their competitive negotiation without much thought. For Felice, it produced a very positive outcome. However, whether the relationship between them will survive in the long run is far more questionable. The attitude with which Sara accepted Felice's offer makes it likely that she will view the agreement as one-sided and unfair. She also probably regrets not having started with a proposal of 80 percent for herself and 20 percent for Felice, given where the negotiation wound up! It is highly unlikely that Felice was thinking about that aspect of the negotiation since her whole focus was on the economic side of the partnership.

So even if you think you know how the Competitive Strategy works, you need to be thoroughly prepared, if for no other reason than it is easy to fall into a Competitive process, and it is much more likely that this will happen when the parties have not intentionally planned their strategy! Effective planning returns us to some of the elements of the "checklist" we have discussed earlier—knowing *all* the issues, not only from your point of view, but from the other side's perspective as well. We will now review the elements you need to plan for.

BARGAINING RANGE

In a competitive situation, the focal point is the bargaining range, which consists of four points: a starting point, a target point, a walkaway point, and an Alternative. Each party's bargaining range is different from the other's. An important part of planning your moves for competitive negotiation is to define these points for your side and to do the best you can to deduce those for the other side (see Figure 6.1 for a diagram representing these points).

The *starting point* is where you commence bargaining. It is your initial offer to the other party. You will need to do a lot of research to define your starting point. It will depend on the market rate; the urgency of the situation, both for you and the other party; the anticipated range (starting and walkaway points) of the other party; the number and value of concessions you are willing to make; and the time frame for the negotiations. For

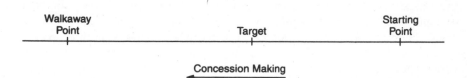

Figure 6.1 Key Points in Competitive Negotiation—(One Party)

example, on a car with a price tag of $15,000, you might offer $12,000 as a starting point. Or, in labor negotiations, a firm might start out by offering labor a 3 percent wage increase, when they expect the union to ask for 8 percent. In house buying, it might be customary in negotiations to offer 80 percent of the asking price.

You may or may not know the other party's starting point. Cars usually have sticker prices; houses have advertised prices. In labor negotiation, labor usually has stated goals, and often the parties are familiar with each other's tactics. In many cases, these "price tags" have anticipated that bargaining will take place, and thus the price may have even been inflated by some percentage, expecting that the other will make an offer that is less than 100 percent of the price. But often, starting points for the other side are not so clear. For example, you may not know or be able to find out how much your boss has been authorized to increase your salary.

Even if you do not know the starting point of the other side, you will know it after you make your opening offer or bid; when the opposing party comes back with a counteroffer, it represents their starting point. The two parties' starting points are rarely the same—if they were, there would be no need for negotiation.

The *target* is the settlement point you want to attain. It is your hoped-for outcome. The target may be defined in monetary terms, or in other tangibles such as benefits, shorter working hours, and the like. There may be "intangibles"—psychological factors such as esteem—associated with the target as well. As we mentioned earlier, intangibles are harder to define and may seem less important because they are less concrete. Nevertheless, you should define them during your planning.

The *walkaway point* is the point at which you will break off negotiations, either temporarily or permanently. The walkaway point may be somewhat beyond your target, but it will be the absolute maximum you will agree to pay if you are the buyer (or minimum you will agree to if you are the seller). In the case of a car deal, it is the highest amount the buyer will pay, or the lowest amount the seller will accept.

Sometimes you can figure out the target point for the other party. For example, if the other side does not expect to negotiate, their target point is the stated price on the car or the advertised house price; if they *do* expect to negotiate, the target is probably some percentage less than the stated price. However, you may never know the other party's walkaway point. It is not usually the same as the target. If the negotiations are broken off, you can suspect that you were in the neighborhood of the other party's walkaway point, but you cannot know for sure (see Figure 6.2).

Even though each party has a starting point, target, and resistance point, the two bargaining ranges may not overlap at all. If this is the case,

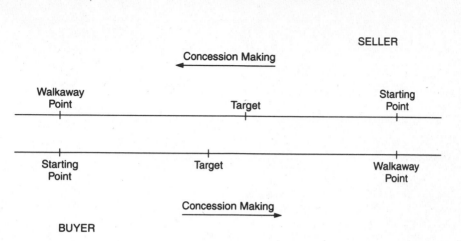

Figure 6.2 Key Points in Competitive Negotiation—(Two Parties)

no negotiating can occur unless at least one party adjusts the points of its bargaining range. To illustrate overlap, if the maximum I will pay for a used car is $13,000 and the dealer will not take less than $14,000, then our bargaining ranges do not overlap. In this case, we need to reevaluate our bargaining ranges, especially our resistance points, and either adjust them or end the negotiations (see Figure 6.3).

Based on this format, we can also analyze the negotiation between Sara and Felice (see Figure 6.4). Sara believed that both parties brought an

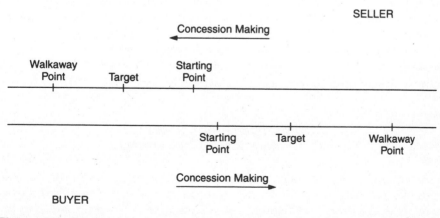

Figure 6.3 Competitive Negotiation—No Overlap in Bargaining Range—(Two Parties)

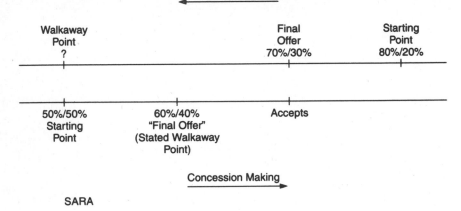

Figure 6.4 Competitive Negotiation—Felice and Sara

equally valuable commodity to the partnership—knowledge/experience and revenue—and, as a result, each should get an equal part of the profit. Felice, on the other hand, believed that the risk of her money was far more serious—particularly if the business failed—and that she should get a much bigger percentage of the profits. So the negotiation began with each party putting their "opening offers" on the table. Sara moved to 60/40, and stated that this was her "final offer"—an effort to make Felice believe that she had to make a concession to this point. But Felice called her bluff and counteroffered with 70/30. Sara, having no Alternative—no one else with whom she could do a business deal—then had to choose between moving off her "final offer" to accept Felice's offer, counteroffer again, or terminate the negotiation. Sara accepted the offer, but probably feels both angry about the way Felice behaved and unhappy with the settlement she will have to live with until she can renegotiate their financial arrangement.

Alternatives—An Important Consideration in Bargaining

Your planning should include establishing an Alternative or BATNA,[2] if possible. The role of a BATNA, the Best Alternative to a Negotiated Agreement, was discussed in Chapter 3. An Alternative is a viable option to the current settlement or agreement to the item(s) under negotiation, and can provide you with power in the bargaining process. Without an Alternative, your position in bargaining is much weaker. As we just pointed out, because Sara had no Alternative, her only choice was to either accept Felice's undesirable offer, or not go into a business with anyone. As a result, she was forced to make a very unhappy but necessary choice. Or, returning to our used car illustration, there might be a second car, with a price tag of $12,000 that you believe to be of equal value. If you cannot come to an agreement on price for Car 1, then you could cease negotiation and switch to your Alternative, Car 2.

Suggestions for Defining Your Bargaining Range

Define Your Walkaway Point in Advance.   Know ahead of time the point at which you want to stop bargaining. If you do not, you may have to drop out of the negotiation when the price gets "too high," or else you may end up spending more than you intended.

Have a Good Alternative.   An Alternative provides you with a bargaining chip in negotiations. Without an Alternative you will be in a weaker bargaining position. If there is no good Alternative, be sure you know this during your planning (but also be careful not to tell your opponent this!). It will help the process of setting points on your bargaining range.

Focus Only on This Deal.   To maximize the results of this deal, you need to ignore your relationship with the other person, and other peripheral or low-priority issues. Staying focused on the matter at hand allows you to keep control and therefore gives you power in the negotiation. Note again that this may not be a good approach if you are bargaining with a party with whom you will have future negotiations or relationships. A prime example is if both parties work for the same company, and will need to work together at some time in the future. And it also means accepting that this deal is not worth it unless you achieve or exceed your Alternative.

Get as Much Information as You Can without Giving Much (if any) Away.   The more information you have, the better. This is also true of the other party. Research the other party carefully; talk with them if possible; ask questions. Try not to share much information about your own position. Knowing all you can about the other party's position and bargaining range will help you set your own position. We will say more about researching the other party in a moment.

Set the Opening as High or as Low as Possible.   If you are a seller, set your price as high as possible; if you are the buyer, set your offer as low as possible. How you set your opening will be based to some extent on how urgent this deal is for the other party. For example, if the other party needs to sell in a hurry, you start with a much lower price than if the negotiation is of little importance to the seller or if there are many other potential buyers.

Setting the opening offer is often a tricky process. First, as we said, you want to set your opening as high or low "as possible." What we mean here is high or low enough to get a good agreement without being so high or low that the other party simply laughs, walks away, or declares that you are insincere and have no credibility! (Warning: they may do this even if your opening offer is reasonable, just to make *you* think they will never give in to your opening demands.)

A second reason this is a tricky process is that opening offers tend to set the range for negotiation. Once both sides have declared opening offers, psychological principles dictate that both parties begin to look to the middle of the range as the place where settlement is likely to occur. So if your price is $15,000 and I offer $12,000, both of us begin to look at $13,500 as a reasonable place to settle. If we want to settle lower than that, we need to make a lower opening offer (e.g., $11,000) and still have the other side accept this as a credible opening. This is why opening offers should be as high (or low) as you can go, without completely losing credibility with the other side.

OTHER ELEMENTS IN PLANNING

Multiple Issues

We have been describing a simple negotiation, where there is one issue and two parties are trying to resolve it. Planning becomes more complex when you must resolve "collection" of issues. In planning for a multiple-issue negotiation, you will need to list all the issues that need to be discussed in the negotiation, and then prioritize them. You may need to focus on only the major issues and save the items of lesser importance for another negotiation session. The lesser issues can often be used as "throw-ins" during the closing stages of the negotiation.

Costs

Sometimes, in negotiation planning, we only estimate the gains that we may achieve if negotiations are successful. But costs play an important part

Don't
compete
unless you
are
prepared to
LOSE!

Figure 6.5 The Ninth Rule of Strategic Negotiation

in negotiations, especially if there are delays. Likewise, costs are incurred if the negotiations are broken off. Both time and money are lost. In fact, as our ninth rule of strategic negotiation points out, you shouldn't attempt to use a competing strategy unless you are also prepared to lose and incur the estimated costs (see Figure 6.5)! Many people think that when they try to compete, they are automatically going to win. This is not true! In any case, it is important to know the costs not only for your side but for the other party as well. If the other party's costs of delay are high, you can use a foot-dragging tactic to create pressure for a resolution. This sort of manipulation is discussed further in the "Tactics" section later in this chapter.

Researching the Other Party

When you are planning a Competitive Strategy, it is very important to research the other party. Although you may pick up a lot of information as the negotiations proceed, it is important to obtain as much information as possible *before negotiating*. In Chapters 2 through 4, especially Chapter 3, you have looked closely at the other party and gathered information. As we have said, this information will help you set your bargaining points and other aspects of your strategy. You need to know what *value* the other party places on the outcome, something about the limits of their *bargaining range,* and their *level of confidence and motivation.* Based on this information, you can plan your position and strategy for bargaining.

It is not always easy to obtain information on the other party in a competitive situation. Although a car might display a sticker price so you will know the seller's opening, in other competitive bargaining situations such information might not be openly advertised. One method of research is to ask direct questions of the other party. This may not be productive if the other party is reluctant to share information. You can work indirectly by looking up records, checking public information sources, asking people who might know the party and their negotiating history, or talking with experts who have experience in the area under negotiation. For example, in buying a car, bookstores and libraries have books that advertise the wholesale price or dealer's cost for most automobiles, so you can learn a lot about the seller's profit from this information.

Sometimes, competitors use such questionable methods as bugs, special codes, or searches of wastebaskets or computer files to gain information. These methods can be tricky, as they can result in stalled or ended negotiations if the other party becomes upset by them. We specifically discuss these issues in Chapter 12.

Remember that gathering information "indirectly" is open to interpretation. It is not fact; it may seem to indicate one thing when in fact it means another. Once the negotiations begin, you should be prepared to confirm the validity of the information you have already collected.

Finally, while you are doing your homework, remember that the other party is unearthing information about you. It is important not to divulge to the other party any information about your side, such as a weak position or other vulnerability that could potentially be used against you in negotiations. This will be difficult to do if you are up against a skilled opponent, because they are used to prying information from you, sometimes in subtle ways.

The Role of Constituencies

In simple negotiations, there are usually two people: you and the other party. However, even in the simplest bargaining situation, there may be constituencies that influence the two bargaining parties. On a simple level of negotiation, such as buying a house or car, there may be family members whose input is part of the bargaining process, if only behind the scenes. These people represent a constituency. In a car dealership, though you may think you are bargaining only with the salesperson, just wait until you make an offer. It has to be taken "to the boss," behind closed doors, for discussion. A perfect example of a constituency—and often a manipulative tactic!

When a corporation bargains with a labor union, the constituencies are considerably larger. The corporate negotiator is backed by a host of people (various levels of management, stockholders, and others) who have goals and outcome preferences. Some have higher stakes in the negotiations than others. Likewise, the labor union negotiator is not alone. He or she represents not only the members of the labor union, but also the union's management. In complex negotiations, there may be a group of negotiators, each with one or more constituencies.

So, assuming that there are constituencies (either visible or behind the scenes), what is their role? In Chapter 5, we noted that the power of constituencies depends on the type of strategy being used. Constituencies are probably most influential in the Competitive Strategy, where they may exert undue influence and pressure on the negotiator. If the constituency has a lot of power, then the negotiator's own power and authority may be limited. This can be an advantage or disadvantage. On your own side, if the constituency is powerful, then this limits what you can accomplish on your own in the negotiation; every move or concession will have to be approved by the constituency. This can be an advantage if you do not want to be pressured by the other's competitive tactics, but it can be a disadvantage if you want to wrap up a deal quickly, or if you disagree with your constituency and want to come to an agreement quicker than they do. The same principles hold true when we are talking about your opponent's constituency. If they are tough and give your opponent very little power, then it will be very difficult to get a quick agreement, or put pressure on the opponent; if they are flexible and give your opponent a lot of power, then agreement may be easier when an agreement emerges that is within the bargaining range.

THE SEQUENCE OF EVENTS IN COMPETITIVE NEGOTIATION

The opening offer may be the hardest point to set, because you are basing it on information about the other party, which may or may not be accurate. Once you start negotiations, and the opening cards are on the table, you will have a better idea of what to do next. Whether to take an *extreme* position at the outset is a difficult question, as this stance has both advantages and disadvantages.

First, an extreme position sets a tone for the negotiations. It suggests that you are a tough, no-nonsense negotiator and that the other party will probably have to make many concessions (see the "Concessions" section later in this chapter).[3] An extreme offer leaves a lot of room for adjustments, which may give you more time to figure out the other party, but can also mean more lengthy negotiations. In contrast, a major disadvantage of an extreme offer is that the offer may be rejected out of hand, thus bringing negotiations to a halt. In many situations, the opponent will simply refuse any further negotiations and will walk away—particularly if they have a good Alternative. Therefore, while you may wish to convey toughness, this can be a drawback if there is ever to be a future relationship with the other party. The premise in the Competitive Strategy is that the relationship concerns are, at best, low and short term. Since the extreme offer can be problematic, you should use it only if you (also) have a good Alternative.

Your opening offer sets the tone for the negotiations. The other party's behavior will frequently mirror yours, so if you set up an adversarial situation at the outset, then the other party may expect to fight on each point of the negotiation. Both sides' behavior may become belligerent. A less strong opening stance can result in the other party having more reasonable expectations, which may lead to reasonable concessions and compromises. The other party will be confused if you start out with a reasonable offer and then take a tough stance, or make an outrageous offer at first, and then appear to be compromising and reasonable.

It is difficult to know what is more important here—toughness or consistency. If you have the choice, you are better off being consistently tough (or flexible) than being erratic in your messages. Toughness can produce better outcomes, but consistency in strategy helps your credibility with the other. If you start off being tough, you probably need to stay tough unless that behavior produced such a negative response in the other that you decide to be more flexible—but also sacrifice consistency, and some credibility.

CONCESSIONS

A series of concessions will follow each side's opening. Concessions are tradeoffs that a party is willing to make, usually with the expectation that the other side will respond in kind and in the same magnitude. For example, if you go up by $100 in your offer for a used car, the dealer may be willing to come down from the asking price by that amount. But if you only go up by $10, it is unlikely that the seller is going to come down by $100.

Concessions are usually built into the bargaining situation by the distance between your starting and ending points and those of the other party. There is enough space between your offer and the other's that each side can make some adjustments to their offer.

Concessions affect not only the tangible outcomes but also the intangibles such as esteem or reputation. When you make a concession, you are acknowledging that the other party is a worthy opponent. If you make a concession, however, and the other party either does not make one or else makes a very small concession, you may lose face and thus appear to be the weaker party—particularly to your constituency. The intangible—your reputation and image—thus figures in the negotiations prominently, particularly when constituencies are present.

If you find that the other side's concessions do not match the ones you offer, you may want to negotiate about how concessions are made. For example, you may say, "I need you to give me some indication that you are willing to negotiate in good faith, by indicating where concessions may be possible." Or, you can link concessions together: "If you agree to throw in that roof rack for the car, I'd be willing to offer you another $200." Another approach is to package concessions: "I will do A and B if you do C and D."

Pattern of Concession

The competitive strategist can learn a lot about the progress of the negotiations by looking at the pattern of concessions. When we talked about consistency, we implied that the pattern of concessions was important. It is! In general, negotiators begin by making large concessions, and then making smaller ones as they get closer to their target point, and even smaller as they get closer to their walkaway point. In addition, the tougher the negotiator, the fewer concessions they will make, and the smaller these will be in all stages of the negotiation.

Thus, if the other party's concessions are becoming smaller during each round, it is probably because they are close to their walkaway point and have less space for movement toward a resolution. This can also happen if the negotiations started at a point very close to their target or walkaway point, thus leaving little space for concessions. To avoid this situation when you are making concessions, you may find it helpful to save one small concession for the last round, if possible.

If the size of the other party's concessions vary, first large, then small, then large again, it may be hard to discern what is happening. Watch for behavioral clues from the other party. Or ask them what they are doing, if their behavior confuses you. (There may be times when you want to confuse your opponent, and this is certainly one way to do it!)

One caution about concessions: You may be able to push for concessions from the other party early in the negotiations, but be careful how much and how long you push. There may be a point of no return, where the other party has nothing left to concede, so you risk ending the negotiation if you push them past that point. This is another dilemma in Competitive negotiation. The other party may try to convince you that they can't make any more concessions, when they really can. You have to decide whether this message is really true, or just an effort to have you make the concessions, not them.

GENERAL GUIDELINES FOR EFFECTIVE COMPETITIVE NEGOTIATION

Once you get past the opening offers (or demands) of each side, and into a pattern of concessions, a number of things can happen. So from this point, it is a bit more difficult to state exactly what will happen next. We will thus offer some general advice on how to pursue a Competitive Strategy, and then discuss a number of the tactics that usually accompany it.

1. *Stick to your planned target and walkaway points.* Try not to be manipulated by the other party. Watch out for the tendency to find a midpoint between the other party's asking price and your first offer, and to settle there too quickly. Once both sides have stated their opening, there is a tendency to jump to the middle of those two points and offer a settlement. This is often called the "1-2-3 and it's over" process. They say $15,000, you say $12,000, and they say, "why don't we just settle for $13,500?" Don't say yes unless $13,500 is really your target (or better). Stick to your planned goals. Remember that you may be able to make a better deal if you make smaller moves.

2. *Do not reveal your target point too early.* Provide minimal information to the other party. If you let your target point be known, you will be open to manipulation, particularly if you think you can do better than your target point. So only let them know your target point if you can't possibly do better.

3. *Never reveal your walkaway point.* *Never* let them know your limits. If you let them know this, they will try to settle as close to your walkaway point as possible. Say as little as possible—even if they keep asking you questions about how far you are willing to go.

4. *Get the other party to make big concessions.* If you believe that the "pie" is limited in size, then you want to get as much of it as you can, while allowing the other side to get as little of it as possible. Keep trying to persuade them that it is up to them to make big moves in their position. This is the tenth rule of strategic negotiation (Figure 6.6).

RECIPROCATE
"UNFAIRLY"!

Figure 6.6 The Tenth Rule of Strategic Negotiation

5. *Keep your concessions few and small.* If you have to give in, do it in small increments, one item at a time. Be patient. Remember that time is on your side.

6. *Know the other party's level of concern for the outcome and the costs of ending negotiation.* You may learn this through direct information—for example, if a company claims it cannot withstand a strike, or if there is a push to settle quickly. To learn about their concerns while masking your own, ask them questions, but avert their questions to you. This information can be useful in planning your tactics.

TACTICS

In the Competitive Strategy, there is a lot of jockeying for position and "psyching out" the other party. Once negotiations actually get underway, there are likely to be changes in positions on each side. It may be easier, once the dust settles, to form a clearer picture of where the negotiations are going. As the other side makes a move, you will have a chance to reevaluate your position accordingly.

Sometimes tactics are used in the Competitive Strategy to better one's position while diminishing the other party's position. Since the objective in competitive negotiation is to maximize a single deal and to get the largest piece of the pie, the competitor wants to get as close as possible to the other party's walkaway point, or else get the other party to change their walkaway point so as to increase the bargaining range.

The purpose of such tactics is to manipulate the other party into thinking that this settlement is the best possible. Tactics can easily backfire, with the result that emotions may escalate and negotiations may be abruptly halted. We do not recommend these behaviors, but rather explore

91

them here for the purpose of preparing you in case these tactics are used on you.

Commitments

How can you show the other party that you are committed to this negotiation and to accomplishing your goals? There are a number of ways to show commitment. These include assertions, threats, and using public and political means to underline your commitment. However, whenever you take a strong stand on something, and especially if you make a threat, you have to follow through on it. The more public the threat is—even if it is only made directly to your opponent—the greater the pressure to "put your money where your mouth is."

There are two kinds of commitments: conditional statements of what you will do (threats and promises), and "final offers." Let's talk about threats and promises first.

Threats and Promises.   A commitment statement or threat might go something like this: "If you _____ , then I will _____ ." There are two kinds of commitment statements—threats and promises. A threat specifically states what happens if the other does *not* do what you want. Thus, a threat is, "If you do not _____ , I will _____ ." This sort of statement puts the other party on the defensive, while clearly establishing your commitment. Your own esteem and need to maintain credibility (that you do what you say you will do), coupled with public pressure, can be strong motivators to "make good" on such a statement. In contrast, a promise is, "If you do _____ , I will _____ ." Since you are usually offering to do something good for the other, these are more likely to help the other party open up and make them less defensive.

Like threats, however, promises can cause problems for you, particularly with your credibility. Just as with a threat, you may get stuck with a "promise" and actually have to deliver on the terms. It may put you in a difficult position. If you promise your son that you will buy him a new computer game if he cuts the lawn, you will have to follow through on your promise when he does it!

Both types of commitments—promises and threats—decrease your flexibility but enhance the likelihood that the other party will give you what you want. If you decide that a commitment statement would help your position, make it. To have it carry more weight, make it public. State it in front of several people, or a group. To make it even more public, go to the newspaper or radio, or take out an ad in the newspaper. To add support to your statement, find allies who will back you on it. Be sure that you can carry it out.

The other party may retaliate with a commitment of their own, which is preferable to avoid. In these situations, both sides are usually declaring that they are locked into their statements and unwilling to change their intentions. However, if both sides become entrenched in their commitments, the negotiations may end prematurely, because neither one is willing to back down.

"Final Offers." A final offer is a second form of commitment. Final offers are declarations that one party has made all the concessions they are going to make, and it is up to the other side to make the rest of the movement to close the gap between them. Once the parties have made several concessions, they decide they have gone far enough. This can happen when they are getting close to their target point (or have passed it), or when they think that you have a lot more to give and can be pressured into it.

It is usually pretty obvious when the other party has made their final offer. Often they state it explicitly: "This is our final offer." They may include with the final offer a concession of fair size, as it is a common practice to save one concession until the end. Your decision now is whether to give in and move to that point, or make a final offer of your own and hope that they will decide to make more concessions. It is not uncommon for two negotiators to make concessions that cover 95 percent of the distance between their opening moves, only to deadlock with final offers that leave the remaining 5 percent on the table.

Getting out of Commitments. Since commitments decrease your flexibility, you may need some sort of escape hatch or alternate plan to get out of such a commitment. Having committed yourself, what do you do if you need to get out of it? One way to "uncommit" is to say that the situation has changed or you have new information. Another is to let it die quietly. Or, to change the statement to more general terms. Negotiators often do this by choosing the language of their commitments carefully, so that there are "escape clauses" in their words. "I never said I would buy you a video game *this week*" (you can try this on your son but it probably won't work).

If the *other party* makes a commitment that it then needs to abandon, it is usually an astute move on your part to help them save face. This is where you will need to be less competitive than the strategy might dictate. If you keep the pressure on them, they are likely to either lock in to their unreasonable position and refuse to budge, or they will feel so embarrassed that they may plot to get even with you later. Instead, we recommend that you help them save face. You might allow them to change their offer, find a way for them to be flexible without looking foolish, say that this is being done "for the greater good," or make some other generous and supportive statement. Again, if constituencies are involved, you might actively compliment them so that their constituency can overhear.

Hardball. Playing the tough guy, starting out with an extreme offer, refusing to make concessions, making tough demands, and making final offers are examples of hardball tactics. They are calculated to put pressure on the other party, and may in fact work against one who is poorly prepared. But other parties can be moved to revenge. Then the negotiations become a series of moves and countermoves, all of which may be unproductive or time-consuming. The problems in using hardball tactics include loss of reputation, negative publicity, loss of the deal, and becoming the brunt of the other party's anger about what has happened.

Good Guy/Bad Guy. We have all seen this tactic in cop movies, where two investigators are questioning a suspect. First the bad guy leans heavily on the suspect, pushing him or her to the limits. Then the bad guy gets exasperated, storms out of the room, and the good guy takes over, trying to persuade the suspect to confess before the bad guy comes back. In negotiation, the job of the good guy is to try to cut a deal before the bad guy returns. A variation on this theme is for the bad guy to talk only when the negotiations are faltering—to "soften the other up"—and the good guy to take over when things are progressing smoothly. The disadvantages of this tactic are (1) it is usually obvious to everyone, (2) it alienates the other party, and (3) energy is spent on the tactic rather than on the negotiations.

Highball/Lowball. This tactic is to make a ridiculous first offer, either very low or very high, depending on the situation. The intent is to force the other party to reassess its position. If someone is selling a used computer and the buyer offers half of what the seller has asked, the seller who hasn't done his or her homework may very well think this is a fair offer and accept it. On the other hand, the seller may simply end the negotiations, thinking that there is no possible overlap. A skilled competitor may be able to turn the situation around and get the negotiations moving again, but there can be residual bad feelings that will be hard to counteract.

Bogey. In this tactic, you pretend that an issue is important when it really is not, then trade it off later in the negotiations for something that really is important. To do this, you need to know the priorities of the other party. In addition, you have to pretend that something is very important when it is not, and this can be difficult and confusing. If the other side is employing the same tactic, it may be impossible to sort out what is being negotiated. For example, if price is the most important element in a sale, while a good warranty is a second concern, you may make some outrageous demands on the warranty (which you know they will not give you), and then offer big concessions on the price instead.

Nibble. In this ploy, you wait until the end of the proceedings, when everything is almost decided and then ask for something that was never even brought up before as an issue. Just before the deal is ready to be signed, you try to press for one more concession: "Oh, gosh, I forgot to mention, can you have this ready for me to pick up in three hours?" This often works, unless the other side knows they are being "nibbled."

Chicken. This is another familiar "game." The classic example is of two teenager drivers racing directly at each other, each driver waiting for the other to "chicken out" and turn away. Chicken is used in competitive negotiation to bluff and threaten to get what you want. The objective is to hold your ground and intimidate the other party into giving way so you can win. The problems with this strategy are that (1) it has very high stakes, and (2) you must be willing to follow through on your threat. Escalation of war between countries, particularly with nuclear weapons, is often a game of chicken.

Intimidation and Aggressiveness. Many ploys are used to force an agreement in competitive negotiation. One is anger, real or feigned. Another is the use of formal documents such as contracts that force certain responses or postures. Yet another is to press someone to do something by appealing to their sense of guilt. Aggressive behaviors such as being pushy, attacking the other person's view, asking for explanations of positions—all can be used to coerce the other party.

Deadlines, Scheduling, and Delays. Scheduling can affect the outcome of negotiations, from the day of the week (Monday as opposed to Friday), to the hour of the day (early morning, late afternoon), to "the final hour" of a schedule. If a party has to travel some distance to the site of the negotiation, factors such as jet lag may affect how well the negotiations proceed. If a final negotiating session is scheduled for the hour before a party's plane departs, this may have a strong effect on the outcome. If you are the traveling party, be careful when you are setting up your flights and schedules. In labor negotiations, there may be a pressing time schedule because labor is due to go out on strike at a particular hour, or a plant is scheduled to close. You can take advantage of these situations and manipulate the scheduling to affect the course and outcome of negotiations.

Delays can be a good ploy to force a concession or resolution, particularly if time is not essential for your side but is a strong concern for the other. Stalling and slowing down the process gives you a means for manipulating the other party. Not showing up on time, asking for a rehash of the proceedings, postponing a meeting, talking endlessly about issues, and other such maneuvers can be used to advantage as long as they do not result in the breakdown of negotiation.

Other Competitive Tactics

Some of the following competitive tactics move into the realm of questionable ethics, about which we will have more to say in Chapter 13. While these more aggressive ploys can be successful, it is also possible that the other party will see through them. If a competitive tactic backfires, negotiations may break off because the other side is angry, feels duped and tricked, and is unwilling to deal with you. Unless you are persuasive enough to get the other side to resume negotiations, or have a good Alternative, these tactics can lead to complete negotiation breakdown.

Manipulate the Other Party's Impression of Your Outcome Concerns. Not only can you manipulate information the other party obtains about you, you can manage their view of where you stand:

- Use body language or be emotional to convey your attitude, whether real or feigned. Make them think you are angry when you are not.
- Give the impression that you do not have the authority to make a decision. Use someone else as a team spokesperson, or use a lawyer or agent. They may think the outcome is of less importance than it is.
- Bring up lots of items for negotiation, many of which are unimportant. Increase the "fog index" and confusion in the negotiation. Do not let the other side know which ones are important. This is often easy to do when negotiations are over technical or complex information, or involve "experts"—accountants, lawyers, engineers—who are not good at explaining technical issues to laypeople.
- Present selectively. Give only the facts necessary to your point of view. This allows you to lead the other party to a particular conclusion.
- Misrepresent your information. In some cases, exaggeration and argument lead to outright distortions of facts and misrepresentation of issues. In the extreme, this is outright deception and lying. We are not advocating this (as we will say very strongly in Chapter 13), but it does happen as parties get wrapped up in the competitiveness of the process.

Make the Costs of the Negotiation Seem Higher. Manipulate facts and behavior to make the other party think the proceedings are more costly than they are.

Manipulate the Actual Costs of Delay or Ending Negotiation.
This can be done by prolonging the negotiations, by introducing other issues, or by asking for other parties to be brought in.

Conceal Information.   Omitting information pertinent to the negotiation can manipulate the outcome, but may have dire results.

Use Emotional Tactics.   Negotiators often try to manipulate the other party's emotions to distract them and to get them to behave in a less rational manner. Get them angry or upset, flattered, or amused—then try to get concessions while they are not paying attention. Highly emotional ploys such as threatening to end the negotiations sometimes achieve your purposes. Another tactic is to appear angry when you are not, to get them feeling contrite or guilty. Disruptive actions may have the desired effect but may escalate the emotional climate and thus block your efforts. Refusal to concede sets a tone for the proceedings. So does silence.

Ally with Outsiders.   Political action groups, protest groups, the Better Business Bureau, and other supportive groups may be able to assist you in putting pressure on the other party for a resolution. Simply threatening to talk with such groups may prod the other party to action.

COPING WITH TACTICS

The best way to cope with competitive tactics is to be prepared. Know the various tactics, why they are used, and how they are used. Have a firm understanding of the other party's position, and keep in mind your own Alternative.

There are a number of ways to handle the other party's tactical moves:[4]

- Ignore them. Pretend you did not hear what was said; change the subject; call a break in the proceedings and when you come back, change topics.
- Confront the issue. Discuss what is going on and what you see. Negotiate about how you will negotiate. Suggest changes. Remember to keep the people separate from the problem.
- Retaliate. Respond in kind. This can escalate the emotions, and result in hard feelings. However, it may be useful if you are being tested by the other party.
- Sidetrack it before it happens. For example, start out the negotiations with a discussion of how the negotiations will be conducted. Offer to behave in a different way, and ask them to comply with your request.

SUMMARY

In this chapter, we have discussed the Competitive Strategy and its related tactics. In a Competitive Strategy, your intention is to maximize what you can achieve on the outcome dimension, while not being concerned about the relationship dimension. As a result, you should be willing to use the strategy and tactics we outlined here without any concern for what it might do to the relationship between you and the opposing negotiator. But as you can see from many of the things we have talked about, if someone uses this strategy on you, it is likely that you will not see the other as nice, friendly, or someone you want to deal with in the future. As a result, if you *do* have concerns about the relationship, then this is *not* the strategy to use. In addition, we have suggested a number of things that you can do to protect yourself from an opponent who uses these tactics.

Chapter 7

Implementing a
Collaborative Strategy

This chapter shows how to use the Collaborative Strategy. The word "collaboration" may sound strange to people who are used to viewing negotiation as competitive. But bargaining does not have to be a win-lose proposition—the pie does not have to be fixed. In many cases, conflict and competitiveness between the parties lead them to *believe* that there are only limited resources to be divided between the parties. It is often possible to find solutions to problems that will satisfy all parties by changing or growing the pie instead of fighting over it. The pie analogy, however, leads us to the principal challenge of a collaborative strategy: the parties must somehow learn how to work together. Collaboration, which is an open, sharing, creative process, does not come naturally when you are in a conflict situation or do not trust the other party. Collaboration is therefore difficult for many negotiators to master.

Some negotiators think they are collaborating when in fact all they have done is wrap their competitive strategy in a friendly package. Thus, they put on the "image" of collaboration, only to move in for a competitive "grab" near the end of the negotiation. This is not collaboration—it is competitiveness in a collaborative disguise. True collaboration requires the parties to move beyond their initial concerns and positions and go on a joint quest for new, creative ways to maximize their individual and joint outcomes. Before we examine how the collaboration strategy works, let's see how our demonstration case can be adapted to this strategy. Here are Felice and Sara again, this time taking a cooperative, win-win approach to setting up a partnership to develop their interior decorating business:

"The bottom line is, we need $50,000 in cash, right now, if we want to do this right. I know you have the money—why are you hesitating to use it when we obviously need it?"

"But Sara," Felice objected, "what's the rush? This is a big decision for me. What if things don't work out? I'd be taking all the financial risks and suffering most of the losses. Whatever happened to getting a bank loan?"

"Well, I tried a few banks, but I didn't have any luck—my credit history isn't so great." Sara paused to offer some homemade cookies to Felice. "I'm sorry I'm being so pushy. I know this is something that you need to think through, and I'm not helping. It's just that I've already made some important contacts, and found promising offices for rent; I'm afraid if we don't get started soon, we'll never get going."

Felice thought for a minute as she ate the cookie. "I understand your impatience. I'm impatient, too. I'm excited about working together and I don't want to waste more time. Maybe we're going about this in the wrong way. Let's just take a few minutes to go over our situation. We want to start an interior decorating business together. You have a lot of experience, but no money to invest, and I have no experience but possibly a lot of money to invest. However, I'm reluctant to sink all my savings into something that may not work out, partly because I'd lose everything I have, but mostly because I'm afraid of ruining our friendship if it doesn't work out. I could probably get a bank loan, but then I'd still be responsible for all the finances, so it seems to me that we should consider bringing in a third party in some capacity."

"Hey—that's not a bad idea. But we would need someone who'd only help us financially—we still need to have control of the business." Sara absently picked crumbs off her sweater. "You know, that reminds me—an old friend of my dad is an architect in a very respected firm. I wonder if we could hook up with them somehow, maybe exchange the rent for an office in their building with a percentage of our business. They could refer customers to us, and eventually we could do the same for them. It's a beautiful old business—you'll love it. It would be a terrific showplace for our work. Do you think I should call him?"

"Well, let's think for a minute," said Felice. "What percentage would we offer them? How about 20 percent? That gives them enough to feel it's worthwhile without taking away our control. Then I could invest $20,000 in the business to get us started and we'll each keep 40 percent of the ownership."

"That sounds great! Let me try it—I'll call my dad right now and get the architect's phone number."

When Sara and Felice proposed the deal to the architect, he was very enthusiastic about their work and the potential for the fit with his business. He offered them office space in his building, and they moved into an office the following week. Within a month, they had landed several jobs that generated a cash flow and helped to establish their reputation as creative, reliable decorators. Over time, the business flourished. They eventually bought the 20 percent back from the architect (with a handsome profit) and their friendship remains strong.

CHARACTERISTICS OF THE COLLABORATIVE STRATEGY

As described in Chapter 5, in the Collaborative Strategy both the relationship *and* the outcome are important to both parties. The two parties usually have long-term goals that they are willing to work for together. Both parties are committed to working toward a mutually acceptable agreement that preserves or strengthens the relationship. Because each party values the relationship, they will attempt to find a mutually satisfying solution for both parties. Working together effectively in a Collaborative negotiation process can itself enhance the quality of the relationship. This approach is very different from the Competitive Strategy, where both sides want to win so badly that they pursue their goal at all costs and ignore all the factors that might allow a Collaborative process.

In addition, in the Collaborative model, intangibles are important and accounted for. These include such items as each party's reputation, pride, principles, and sense of fairness. Because these concerns are important, the negotiations must stay on a rational, reasonable, and fair level. If the parties get angry at each other, the collaborative atmosphere will degenerate into a competitive one. Allow for plenty of venting time if you or the other party begins to get irritated, and be sure to listen to complaints about your behavior with an open mind to avoid conflicts that can derail collaboration. There must be a great deal of trust, cooperation, openness, and communication between the parties to engage in effective problem solving.

Finally, the parties must be willing to make *concessions* to accomplish their goals. These concessions should be repaid with creative win-win solutions, but they represent a risk for each party that the other party must be careful not to abuse.

In the Collaborative Strategy, the constituency (if there is one) plays a very different role from that which it plays in competitive negotiations. Generally, the members of the constituency are supportive and will promote the relationship between the two parties.

The Collaborative Strategy relies on deadlines that are mutually determined and observed. They are not used for manipulation, as we found in the Competitive Strategy. Information flows freely and is not used to control the situation or guarded to maintain power. The objective is to find the best solution *for both sides*. Similarities between the two parties, not differences, are emphasized.

There are four major steps in carrying out a Collaborative Strategy: (1) identify the problem; (2) understand the problem; (3) generate alternative solutions; (4) select a solution. We will examine each in detail.

STEPS IN THE COLLABORATIVE STRATEGY

Identify the Problem

This may sound like a simple step, but in the Collaborative model both sides are involved equally in the process, and both need to agree on what the problem is. When you were gathering information (Chapters 1–4) you focused on *your* point of view, but for the Collaborative Strategy to work, you will need to work closely with the other party to find a common view of the problem.[1]

When defining the problem, try to use neutral language and to keep it impersonal. For example, you might say "We are not able to get our work out on time" rather than "You are preventing us from doing our work and getting it out on time." It is important to define the obstacles to your goals without attacking other people.

Try to define the problem as a common goal. For example, in the Sara and Felice situation, they might say, "Our goal is to find a way to start our business without Felice having to assume too much financial risk." Keep the goal definition as simple as possible. Try not to load the situation with peripheral issues that are not really related to the central concern. Remember how you prioritized issues in the earlier chapters. Stick with the primary issues.

Each party needs to be assertive, but cooperative at the same time: You need to be clear about what you want to achieve, yet not at the expense of dominating the other side. Because the relationship is important, you need to see the problem from the other party's perspective—"to walk a mile in the other person's shoes" as much as possible. Understanding and empathy[2] go a long way to finding the common issues.

Watch out for a tendency to define solutions before you have fully defined the problem. In fact, you should avoid discussing solutions until you have thoroughly defined and understood the problem(s). And remember, the more creative the problem definition, the more likely you are to discover a new, beneficial win-win solution. Throw caution to the wind, brainstorm wildly, and hope for a creative insight that will make it fun and easy to solve the problem.

Understand the Problem

In this step, you try to get behind the issues to the underlying needs and interests[3] as discussed in Chapters 2 and 3. As noted earlier, an interest is a broader perspective that each side has, which is usually "behind" their position. In our example, Felice's position is that she does not want to provide full financial backing for the new business; her interest is to minimize her financial risk while also helping to get the business started and into a profitable mode. You need to learn not only about the needs and interests of each party, but also about their fears and concerns. Felice's fear is that she will lose a large amount of her investment (and her savings) if the business goes bad. The reason for getting behind the positions is that they tend to be fixed and rigid; modifying them requires the parties to make concessions either toward or away from the target point. In contrast, interests define what the parties care about more broadly, and there are often multiple "roads to Rome," or several ways to resolve the conflict between these competing interests. In addition, a focus on interests tends to take some of the personal dimension[4] out of the negotiation and shifts it to the underlying concerns. Since there is bound to be a difference in thinking styles, people will approach even similar issues in different ways. Positions offer only one way to think about an issue; interests offer multiple ways to think about it. Thus, you can find out "where they are coming from" more effectively by discussing interests than by stating positions.

Interests may reflect current or longer term concerns. And parties are likely to have multiple interests. It is also important to realize that each party may have different interests. By using the "why" questions discussed in Chapters 2 and 3, you can dig deeper into the reasons for each party's position. An interest is the why of a position.

Interests[5] may be substantive, as with concerns for prices, rates, and availability of resources. Interests may have to do with the process, as in how we will conduct the actual negotiation. This concern may, in turn, be based on how the process has been completed in the past, or on how we want to change and improve it for the future. Concerns may also center around sustaining and enjoying the relationship. Or, a party may have a strong interest in principles. They may be concerned about what is fair or ethical, right or acceptable. For example, Felice and Sara have a number of interests at stake in addition to the substantive interest of their specific

103

solution to funding their new business. Because they are starting a business in which they will work together actively, they are trying to get off on the right foot in the way they solve and deal with joint problems. Thus, they want to establish a good problem-solving process, they want to preserve—and even enhance—their relationship with one another, and they probably care a great deal about principles, such as the precedent created by both the outcome and the process of this negotiation or the perceived fairness of their agreement. Felice and Sara have a lot riding on this deliberation, and it is most important that they work it out in a way that creates a good outcome and strengthens their working relationship.

Remember that even if you define interests carefully, they can change. Since the negotiation process is an evolving one, you may need to stop from time to time to reconsider interests. If the conversation begins to change in tone or the focus seems to shift, this may be a signal that interests have changed. Since the Collaborative Strategy is one of openness, the parties with changing interests should be encouraged to share their shifts in needs. The other party may facilitate this by being willing to expand resources,[6] extend the time frame, or change the details of the negotiation to accommodate the changed interests (we say more about some of these tactics in the next section). As Sara and Felice's business took off and prospered, their interests changed. As the business was successful, Felice was less worried that her financial investment would be seriously at risk. As the new decorating contracts were assured, she became more confident, trusted Sara more, and the two were eventually able to buy the 20 percent investment back from the architect. Both the changed nature of the business and the trust level between Sara and Felice had a lot to do with changing the interests of these two negotiators.

Generate Alternative Solutions

Once you have defined the issues to the satisfaction of both parties, you can begin to look for solutions. Notice that this is plural: solutions. You want to find a group of possible solutions, then select from among them the best solution for both parties.

There are two major ways to go about finding solutions. One is to redefine the problem so you can find win-win alternatives for what at first may have seemed to be a win-lose problem. The second is to take the problem at hand and generate a long list of options for solving it.

Redefining the Problem.   To illustrate the different approaches, we will use an example suggested by Dean Pruitt, about a husband and wife

104

who are trying to decide where to spend a two-week vacation.[7] He wants to go to the mountains for hiking, fishing, and some rest; she wants to go to the beach for sun, swimming, and night life. They have decided that spending one week in each place will not really be adequate for either person, because too much time is spent in packing, unpacking, and traveling between the two locations.

- *Expand the pie.* If the problem is based on scarce resources, the object would be to find a way to expand or reallocate the resources so that each party could obtain their desired end. Knowing the underlying interests can help in this endeavor. For example, the parties could take a four-week vacation, and spend two weeks in each place. While this would require more time and money, each person would get a two-week vacation in the chosen spot.

- *Logroll.* If there are two issues in a negotiation and each party has a different priority for them, then one may be able to be traded off for the other. For example, if Problems A and B are common to both parties, but Party 1 cares most about Problem A and Party 2 cares most about Problem B, then a solution that solves both problems can provide each party with a happy resolution. "You get this and I get that." If there are multiple issues, it may take some trial and error to find what packages will satisfy each party. In our example, if the husband really wants to stay in an informal rustic mountain cabin, and the wife really wants to stay in a fancy hotel, then another resolution is for them to go to the mountains but stay in a fancy hotel (or an informal beach house at the shore).

- *Offer nonspecific compensation.* Another method is for one party to "pay off" the other for giving in on an issue. The "payoff" may not be monetary, and it may not even be related to the negotiation. The party paying off needs to know what it will take to keep the other party so happy that they won't care about the outcome of this negotiation. In a house sale negotiation, for example, the seller might include all window coverings (curtains, drapes, blinds) as part of the deal. The buyer may be so delighted that he decides not to ask for any other price break. In our vacation example, the wife might buy the husband a set of golf clubs, which will make him so happy that he will go anywhere she wants to go (since there are golf courses everywhere).

- *Cut costs.* In this method, one party accomplishes specific objectives and the other's costs are minimized by going along with the agreement. This differs from nonspecific compensation because in this method the other party can minimize costs and "suffering," whereas in the other method, the costs and suffering do not go away, but the party is somehow compensated for them. This method requires a clear understanding of the other party's needs and preferences, along with their costs. In our vacation example, the wife says to the husband, "What can I do to make going to the beach as painless as possible for you?" He tells her that he wants to stay in a beach house away from the big hotels, get some rest, near a golf course, and near several places where he can go fishing. They both go down to their favorite travel agent and find a location that offers all these things.

- *Bridge.* In bridging, the parties invent new options that meet each other's needs. Again, both parties must be very familiar with the other party's interests and needs. When two business partners (Sara and Felice) bring in a third partner who can offer resources neither of them wanted to contribute, this is an effective example of bridging. In our vacation example, the husband and wife go to a travel agent and find a place that offers hiking, fishing, beaches, swimming, golf, privacy, and night life. They book a two-week vacation for Hawaii and have a wonderful time!

Generating a List of Solutions.   The second approach to inventing solutions is to take the problem as defined and try to generate a list of possible solutions. The key to finding answers in this approach is to generate as many solutions as possible without evaluating them. The solutions should be general rather than party-specific—they should not favor one party over the other. At a later stage, each solution can then be evaluated to determine whether it adequately meets the needs and interests of both parties.

What is interesting in this process is that both parties engage in trying to solve the other party's problem as much as they do their own.[8] It is a cooperative endeavor. And, as you have probably heard many times before, two heads are better than one.

If you get to this stage, but the issues still seem murky, you may need to go back to the problem definition and rework that step. It should be easy to generate solutions if the problem is clearly stated in a way that does not bias solutions toward one party or the other. Otherwise, if you are comfortable with the definition of the problem, forge ahead.

There are a number of ways to generate ideas for solutions. Remember that you are only *generating* solutions in this step, not evaluating them or deciding whether to use them—yet. That will happen in the next step.

- *Brainstorming*. This common method for generating ideas usually works best in several small groups rather than one large one, depending on the number of people involved. Write down as many ideas as possible, without judging them. It is best to write or post the ideas on a flipchart, chalkboard, or similar display device, so that everyone can see them and keep track of what has been done. The key ground rule is that *ideas must not be evaluated as they are suggested*. Don't let anyone say, "Oh, that's a dumb idea!" or "That won't work!" Keep ideas flowing, keep focused on the problem and how to solve it, without associating people with the problem or the solutions.

  It often happens that people quickly think of a few possibilities, and then run out of ideas. At this point, it is easy to think you are done because you have a few solutions. Don't stop here—stick at it for a while longer. Otherwise, you may miss some really good ideas, particularly creative ones that no one has considered before. Ask outsiders for ideas, too. Sometimes they bring a fresh approach to the problem.

- *Piggybacking*[9] can be used in conjunction with brainstorming. This technique is simply to build on someone else's idea to produce yet another idea. It's often done by working in a sequence order; one person starts with a brainstormed idea, then the next person has to "piggyback" until possible variations on the idea are exhausted.

- *Nominal groups*. In this method, each negotiator works with a small group—perhaps their constituency—and makes a list of possible solutions. These are discussed within the group, then considered, one at a time, by the group as a whole. They can be ranked in terms of preferences or likely effectiveness. The drawback of this method is that anyone not present at the session will miss offering input or helping to shape the solution.

- *Surveys*. Another useful method is to distribute a questionnaire stating the problem and asking respondents to list possible solutions. In this case, each person works alone on the survey, so people miss out on the synergy of working together. However, the advantage is that a number of people who have good ideas but are normally reticent about getting into a group's conversation, can offer their thoughts and ideas without being attacked or critiqued. Another advantage is that this draws in the ideas of people who may not be able to attend the negotiation or formally participate in it.

Prioritize the Options and Reduce the List. Once you have a list of possible solutions, you can reduce it by rating the ideas, much as we prioritized the issues in previous chapters. In communicating your priorities and preferences to the other party, it's important to maintain an attitude of "firm flexibility."[10] Be firm about achieving your interests, while remaining flexible about how those interests might be achieved. There are a number of tactics to keep the discussion collaborative while being clear and consistent about your preferences:

- Remember that you are only *prioritizing* the list, not yet deciding on the actual solution.

- Be assertive in defending and establishing your basic interests, but do not demand a particular solution.

- Signal to the other party your flexibility and willingness to hear the other party's interests by practicing your listening skills (see Chapter 12).

- Indicate your willingness to modify a position or have your interests met in an alternative way. Perhaps you will be able to trade one point for another. This will demonstrate your openness to suggestions and willingness to work together.

- Show ability and willingness to problem-solve. Skill in problem-solving is valuable here, especially if you get stuck on a particular point and need to find some way to resolve it to everyone's satisfaction. If you can settle this issue, it will help when you get to the next step and are actually deciding on the solution. You will have set the stage for collaboration.

- Keep lines of communication open. If tempers flare, take a break, and talk about it if need be. Also talk with the other party about how you can continue to work on the problem without getting angry or losing control. Make sure both parties feel that they are being heard. Steer discussion away from personalities, and concentrate on the issues; "Separate the people from the problem."[11]

- Underscore what is most important to you by saying, "This is what I need to accomplish," or "As long as I can accomplish _____ , I'll be very happy." Resist the temptation to give in just to get a resolution. Giving in is an Accommodating strategy that will not result in the best outcome for both parties.

- Reevaluate any points on which you disagree. Be sure that both sides agree on the adjusted prioritized list so that you will both feel comfortable as you move to the final step.

- Eliminate competitive tactics by identifying them and either confronting them or renegotiating the process. If the discussion becomes competitive, point out that this is happening. Then try to resolve the problem *before* the entire negotiation becomes competitive.

Select a Solution[12]

Using your prioritized list of potential solutions from the previous step, narrow the range of possibilities by focusing on the positive suggestions that people seemed to favor most. For example, one way to prioritize is to log roll (package each person's first choice together). If parties have the same first choice, but very different preferences for it, try to invent a way for both sides to "win" on this issue.

Try to change any negative ideas into positive ones,[13] or else eliminate them from the list. Stating alternatives as positives keeps the negotiation upbeat and on a positive note. Avoid attributing negative ideas to any particular person or side.

Evaluate the solutions on the basis of quality and acceptability. Consider the opinions of both parties. Do not require people to justify their preferences. People often do not know why they have a preference, they just do.

When you are preparing to select a solution, if you foresee any potential problems with this process, you may want to establish objective criteria for evaluation before you start the selection process.[14] In other words, before you move toward picking among prioritized options, work against a set of objective facts, figures, data, and criteria that were developed independently of the options. There are numerous examples. In our example between Felice and Sara, they might go to a small business assistance agency, such as a local bank or small business development group, to find out how other business partnerships have dealt with this situation. If a car owner and a garage mechanic are having a dispute about how much it should cost to repair a starter motor, there are books available that indicate the "standard" cost for parts and labor for this repair. Finally, if a group of people is trying to pick a job candidate from among a group who applied for the job, their work will be considerably facilitated if they spend time developing criteria by which to evaluate the applicants before they actually look at resumes and interview people. If you can't find objective criteria, another technique is to have a third party help you—we say more about this in Chapter 11.

If necessary, use subgroups. These are helpful if the problem is complex or if the outcome will affect a large group. It may be more efficient to use several small groups than to use one large one. Be sure the subgroups contain representatives from each party.

Fairness and Other Intangibles. Intangibles are often operating in the decisions. For example, gaining recognition or looking strong to a constituency may be important factors in the selection of solutions. Acknowledge the importance of intangibles by building them into the decisions. For example, if the other party needs to maintain esteem with a constituency, they may be willing to settle on a lesser point that still allows them to appear in a favorable light. In fact, it will help them greatly if you work with them to determine how to make them look strong and capable to the constituency.

Fairness is usually one of the most important intangibles. In a win-win negotiation, both parties want to achieve a fair outcome, rather than maximize their outcome—which they might push for in a Competitive negotiation. There are a number of ways to decide what is fair, but three common criteria often apply:[15]

- An outcome that gives each side *equal* outcomes. Thus, it is not surprising that one of the most common ways to solve negotiation problems—particularly win-lose, competitive ones—is for the parties to agree to "divide it down the middle." We will say more about this in Chapter 8.

- An outcome that gives each side more or less based on *equity* (what it has earned or deserves, based on the time or energy committed). In this case, the side that puts in more should get out more. Equity is usually based on the ratio of outcome to input, so that the person who works harder, suffers more, and so on, deserves a proportionately larger share of the results.

- An outcome which gives each side more or less, depending on what it *needs*. In this case, if one side can create a legitimate claim that it needs or deserves a better outcome, there may be a good case to be made for dividing up the resources so that those with greater needs actually gain more.

We can see how the equity versus equality arguments can easily come into play in the discussions between Felice and Sara. Sara—having no money but great creative skills—could argue that they should split all profits from the business equally. In essence, she is arguing that creative contribution and financial contribution to the business should be weighted equally. In contrast, Felice—having few creative skills but a lot of money to put toward the venture—could argue that they should split profits proportionate to the amount of money contributed during the start-up. If the two of them stuck to these positions strongly, they could have an intractable dispute over how to value financial and creative contributions, which would be a major block in their discussions.

Emotional Escalation.   If emotions surface, or if people get angry, take a break. Give people an opportunity to discuss the reasons for their dissatisfaction. Be sure everyone has cooled off before you start again, and try to keep personalities out of the deliberations. If taking a break does not work, seek out a third party to help you (see Chapter 11).

Other Suggestions for Keeping the Decision-Making Process on Track.   You can use logrolling to make combination options. You can also take advantage of risk preferences, differences in expectations, and differences in time preferences. For example, one party may prefer an option with low risk, while the other party is willing to accept an option with a much higher risk; you may be able to combine these so that each party gets its preferred outcome. Likewise, some options may satisfy only short-term concerns, but may be more important to one party than longer-term issues. These, too, can be traded off.

It is very important not to rush the process of selecting solutions, appealing as it may be to do so. If you get to the bottom line too quickly, you may miss some good potential options, and you may fail to assure that both sides participate equally.[16] Collaborative efforts require the participation of both sides; they may also require time to mull over alternatives and think through all the consequences. Good Collaborative negotiation requires time and cannot be rushed.

Remember that *everything is tentative until the very end*. During the solution-generating phase, some people may even object to writing anything down, as this may make them nervous. They may feel they are being railroaded into commitments they have not agreed to. Other than the "working documents" that you may create as you define the problem and invent options, you may want to begin to record decisions only when the group is close to consensus. That way, nothing is set in stone until the very end. This open, fluid approach makes it possible to share creative ideas and suggestions. The minute one party says, "But you said yesterday you'd be willing to . . . ," the collaboration starts to unravel as participants begin to worry about being held accountable for "positions." This difficult and critical rule is violated too often as people revert instinctively to a competitive style without realizing the impact on idea-generation and sharing.

Once the parties have agreed on solutions and prepared a document to outline the agreement, it should be passed around for everyone to read. Some people have suggested that this may even be an excellent way to manage the entire prioritization and decision-making process. Start with a tentative draft of what people agree to, then continue to pass it around,

111

sharpening language, clarifying words, writing out agreements so that all agree with it and pledge to live by it. You may want to make a plan for implementing the agreement, and to set up a time frame in which the parties can try out the solution.[17] This again allows for all to fully participate and to become committed to the plan.

HOW TO BE SUCCESSFUL WITH COLLABORATIVE NEGOTIATION

Researchers have identified several keys to successful Collaboration.[18] They are useful as a checklist for the strategic negotiator in planning and implementing a Collaborative Strategy.

Create Common Goals or Objectives

There may be three different ways the goals will be played out: All parties will share in the results equally; the parties will share a common end but receive different benefits; or the parties will have different goals, but share in a collective effort to accomplish them. In any of these cases, both parties believe they can benefit by working together as opposed to working separately, and that the results will be better than they would be if each party worked separately.

Maintain Confidence in Your Own Ability to Solve Problems

This is more or less a matter of "If you think you can, you can." As we mentioned earlier, it helps to have a strong knowledge of the problem area, but lack of knowledge can be overcome if the desire is there. Probably the most important element is to develop skills in negotiating collaboratively, since it is a less common form of negotiation. The more you do it, the better you will become at doing it.

Value the Other Party's Opinion

Valuing the other party's point of view is difficult if you have been accustomed in the past to focusing only on your own position and maintaining it. In the Collaborative Strategy, you value the other party's position

112

equally with your own.[19] You need good listening skills and openness to hear the other party's point of view.

Share the Motivation and Commitment to Working Together

In the Collaborative Strategy, you are not only committed to the idea of working together with the other party, you take actions to do so. You pursue both your own needs and those of the other party. This means each party must be explicit about their needs.

In Collaborative negotiation, the parties strive to identify their similarities to each other and to downplay their differences. The differences are not ignored, they are simply recognized and accepted for what they are.

The parties are aware that they share a common fate, particularly if they expect to work together after this negotiation has been completed. They know they can gain more if they work jointly than if they work separately. To do this, they focus on outputs and results.[20]

Motivated, committed parties will control their behavior in a number of ways. Individuals will avoid being competitive, combative, evasive, defensive, or stubborn. They will work at being open and trusting, flexible, and willing to share information and not to hoard it for their own use.

A Cautionary Note. Believe it or not, there is such a thing as too much collaboration! The two parties must not be so committed to each other that they do not look out for their own needs. If they begin to subordinate their needs to the other party, they will be moving toward the Accommodating or Lose-Win Strategies and will lose out on the benefits that the Collaborative Strategy can offer.

Trust

Because trust creates more trust—which is necessary to begin and sustain cooperation—it is important to make the opening moves in Collaborative Negotiation in a way that engenders trust.[21] Opening conversations may occur even before the formal negotiations begin, when the parties are just becoming acquainted. If one party finds a reason to mistrust the other party at this time, this may stifle any future efforts at collaboration. The eleventh rule of strategic negotiation deals with the issue of trust (Figure 7.1).

If the parties are new to each other, or if they have been combative or competitive in the past, they will have to build trust. Each party will

Figure 7.1 The Eleventh Rule of Strategic Negotiation

approach the negotiation with expectations based on the research they did on each other (Chapter 3) or on past history. Generally, we trust others if they appear to be similar to us, if they have a positive attitude toward us, or if they appear cooperative and trusting. We also tend to trust them if they are dependent on us. Likewise, making concessions appears to be a trusting gesture, so we are likely to respond in kind.

In contrast, it is easy to engender mistrust. This often begins either with a competitive, hostile action, or with an indication that one does not trust the other. Once mistrust gets started, it is very easy to build and escalate, and very difficult to change over to collaboration. Trust escalation and deescalation have often been compared with the children's game "Chutes and Ladders." In this analogy, it is easy to move down the "chute" of mistrust, rapidly sliding to the bottom, but much more difficult to climb back up the "ladder" that will restore and sustain good trust between parties.[22]

Clear, Accurate Communication

We devote a whole chapter of this book to communication (Chapter 12). Communicating effectively is the bedrock of negotiation, no matter what form the bargaining strategy takes. In the Collaborative Strategy, precise and accurate communication is of the utmost importance. It is crucial to listen well, so that you know what the other party wants and why they want it. This requires more than just superficial listening.

It is through communication that one party shares information[23] with the other party. This communication must be delivered in the most concrete terms so there is no confusion or misinterpretation. Feedback and frequent questions can clarify the message if necessary.

Some of the communication in negotiation may be formal, based on procedural or other rules such as rules of order. Sometimes communication will be informal, as during breaks and after sessions. Or, perhaps the entire undertaking will be informal, depending on the personal characteristics and styles of the participants.

OBSTACLES TO ACHIEVING GOOD COLLABORATION

Collaborative negotiation is a lot of work. But the rewards can be great. Sometimes, however, no matter how much you want to succeed, obstacles may prevent you from moving ahead with a Collaborative Strategy. One (or both) of the parties:

- May not be able to do the required work.
- May have a win-lose attitude.
- May not be able to see the potential for collaboration.
- May be motivated to only achieve their own goals.
- May not be capable of establishing or maintaining productive working relationships.
- May be inhibited by biases.
- May have a constituency that is pressing for competitive behavior or quick outcomes.

Further, the situation may contain elements that require a mix of strategies. Then you need to separate the issues into the component parts and deal with each separately.

Sometimes, you may feel that you do not have the time or energy to push forward with a collaborative strategy, especially if you encounter one or more of the preceding situations.

What If the Other Party Wants to Be Competitive

If the other party wants to be competitive when you want to be collaborative, turn to Chapter 9, where we discuss how to build collaboration. It is a serious wrinkle in your plans, but in many instances you can change the other party's style.

What If There Is a Breakdown?

If there is a conflict, try to move the discussion to a neutral point, and summarize where you are.[24] If there is a total breakdown in communication, and you just cannot get the negotiation back on track, you may need to resort to conflict resolution strategies or to third-party intervention. Conflict resolution by the two involved parties is discussed in Chapter 10, and third-party assistance in negotiation is covered in Chapter 11. And also note that you and the other party can, at any point, reach a mutual agreement to abandon your collaboration and adopt another negotiating style. For instance, you might try collaborating, decide you don't like working together, and decide that you will "agree to disagree" and revert to a conventional Competitive strategy—or toward a more expedient and simple outcome through Compromising. Remember, however, that you will give up the relationship benefits, so do not advocate the Competitive Strategy unless you decide your initial estimation of relationship importance was too high. Also, since you will have shared much information through your collaboration attempt, it can now be used against you in a Competitive negotiation. Therefore, the slide from collaboration to competition is not generally a happy or profitable one because some of the actions you undertook under the assumption that you could trust the other and work with them may now be used against you as weapons.

A CASE STUDY: NEGOTIATING STRATEGIC ALLIANCES

A business example of the use of negotiation is in the area of strategic alliances, which are gaining in importance worldwide, particularly in Europe. Global competition has intensified the scramble for access to markets, products, and technologies. Strategic alliances are one strategy that companies are using to survive or to keep up with the new developments in industry.

Negotiating a strategic alliance presents a challenge. "A bad negotiation tactic may do lasting damage; good negotiation tactics must be repeated a number of times before the partner accepts this as a pattern."[25] In a strategic alliance, the relationship concerns will be very important.

In 1985, Corning and Ciba-Geigy formed Ciba Corning Diagnostics, an alliance based in the United States, designed to enhance Corning's medical diagnostics business. Ciba-Geigy is a global pharmaceutical and chemical company based in Switzerland. Corning, based in New York, is a world leader in glass and ceramics technology. The alliance would combine the strengths of the two partners to develop innovative medical diagnostic tests.

There was synergy in what each partner could offer to the alliance. Negotiation went smoothly, as Ciba was willing to have Corning manage more extensively in the beginning. Corning's managers were willing to concede on points of strong interest to Ciba, and thus they were able to agree on a time line for their work. Each partner appointed its Director of Research and Development to the board of the new alliance, which signaled to the other party a willingness to share technology, while garnering internal support for the alliance as well.

Each side had representatives to build consensus, improve communication, and obtain support for the parent organization. Ciba and Corning actively looked into ways for each partner to gain by opening up possibilities for broadening the product line, marketing, technology, and growth. They were able to negotiate any issues that arose because, as mutual trust grew, they were willing to discuss such problems clearly and openly.

A strategic alliance will not succeed if the two potential partners have conflicting underlying motives. If they are both leaders in their field, it may be difficult for them to collaborate. Likewise, if they have strongly differing views of which activities should take priority or what the time lines should be, the success of such an alliance would be questionable.

To create a successful alliance, each organization must be willing to support the efforts to create an alliance agreement. This means that political support must be generated within the organizations of the potential partners. Building support may take time. For example, the Japanese take a long time to complete this process (at least from the American point of view). Conversely, the Japanese see American firms as too pushy. (We will talk more about global differences in Chapter 15.)

NEGOTIATING WITH YOUR BOSS

Since everyone has had some sort of experience dealing with a boss at one time or another, we will take a moment here to look at ways to negotiate collaboratively with a manager.[26] Although performance review, salary, and benefits are usually the major areas for discussion and possible conflict with one's manager, there are others that arise more often. For example, what if you are asked by your boss to do a project that you realize you cannot possibly complete without working overtime? If you do not mind staying late, go ahead. But if you find yourself doing this frequently and resenting it, maybe you need to consider negotiating about it the next time.

Negotiating with the boss is often viewed as a competitive, win-lose, or fixed pie situation. It can also be viewed as a lose-win situation, in which it is better to Accommodate and let the boss win all the time, rather than try to argue for a preferred outcome and have the boss be angry at your "assertiveness." But if you think about it, both parties might be able to gain something from Collaborative negotiation.

Think about the steps in the Collaborative Strategy we covered earlier in the chapter. Look at your own needs, as well as those of your boss. Remember that the key to collaborative bargaining is to find a way to solve the other person's problem.

So, in our hypothetical situation, your boss may have been asked by her boss to drop everything and get this project out, at any cost. (Your boss may have some bargaining of her own to do.) At any rate, your boss has to have this project done and there is no way for you to complete it during normal hours, given the other work you have to do and the deadlines for those projects. Your boss could ask someone else to do it, but perhaps she knows you can do the job better and more quickly.

First, clarify the situation. Find out the circumstances from your boss. Be sure you understand the details of the project. Gather information you may need about what you are working on at the present time. This research is somewhat like the work you did in Chapters 2 and 3.

When it is time to discuss the project again, you will be prepared. Be sure your boss knows and understands the situation from your side. List what you are currently working on, and make sure she is willing for you to put those things aside to work on this rush project. Or does she prefer to have you give it only part of your attention? We knew one person who, when her boss piled new work on her desk, made a list of all the projects she was currently managing. Then she handed the list to her boss, and asked him to number the list in the order that he wanted things done. It made him decide what his priorities were.

You can make a number of suggestions for how to complete the project given the circumstances. (This means you will have brainstormed for ideas before you meet with her.) One option might be for the boss (perhaps with your help) to find more resources. Two people could perhaps help with the project, thus halving the time it will take to complete.

Another option would be for your boss to get an extension of the time allotted for the project. To do this, she would have to negotiate with her boss.

A third option might be to change the "specs" of the project (e.g., make it less detailed or more streamlined), which would allow you to complete it in less time.

You also could suggest, "If I stay late several nights to do this project, I would like to take compensating time off," or "If I do this project, then I need help to complete my other projects on time, or else an extension." These are compromising strategies, which we will take up further in the next chapter.

This example illustrates that even an apparently simple negotiation can be more complex than we realize. In this case, it involves not just you and your boss, but her boss as well (and who knows who else?). In any situation, it helps to break down a problem into its component parts and try to get at the underlying needs.

SUMMARY

In this chapter, we have outlined the Collaborative Strategy. When using this strategy, your objective is to maximize both your outcome on the substantive issues and sustain or enhance the quality of the relationship between you and the other side. To do so, you need to meet your outcome needs as well as the needs of the other party in a manner that strengthens the trust, mutuality, and productive problem-solving in the relationship.

Good collaboration is a wonderful thing to be able to create and sustain. But it is not an all-purpose panacea and making it work well often requires a large commitment of time and energy. There are times when the parties might be just as well off to Compromise, Accommodate, or even Avoid negotiations. In the next chapter, we take a look at these alternative negotiating strategies.

Chapter 8

Alternative Strategies: Accommodating, Avoiding, Compromising

Because most people only negotiate when the outcome is important to them, they tend to use strategies that are high in concern for the outcome—the Competitive and Collaborative Strategies. However, we often find ourselves in negotiations that are initiated by others, or where we want a fairly quick resolution or where our primary concern is to maintain or strengthen our relationship with the other party. In this case, the other three strategies introduced in Chapter 5—Accommodating, Avoiding, or Compromising—might be most appropriate. In this chapter, we review these strategies and the circumstances in which they might be used.

Even if you do not intend to use them yourself, it is helpful to understand how these strategies work, and their advantages and drawbacks. It is important for you to know how to use these strategies when your Collaborative and Competitive approaches are inappropriate. You will certainly encounter many negotiating situations where alternative strategies are useful. By and large, they will not be the most critical negotiations, but many low-priority negotiations will be best served with one of these strategies. In addition, as you master multiple strategies, you may want or need to switch modes and use one of these alternatives on occasion during the negotiating process. We will revisit this issue in the final chapter, as the evolution of multiple strategies during a negotiation is a more sophisticated topic requiring knowledge of the fundamentals of negotiation.

We term them "alternative strategies" because most negotiators do not think of them when choosing a strategy. One of the distinctive advantages of the strategic negotiator is that he or she recognizes these as viable alternatives, and does not always use the more common Competitive and Collaborative strategies and styles. Why not always use these two strategies? First, *independent* decisions about the importance of the outcome and the relationship should dictate your strategy. Competition, as we now know, is appropriate where the outcome is important but the relationship is *not* important. Collaboration is appropriate when both the outcome and the relationship are important. But in situations in which one of these conditions is not the case, then these strategies are probably less appropriate than others. They may also be less appropriate when you know the strategy your opponent intends to use and you decide to mirror your opponent's choice.

Remember that the strategic negotiator recognizes dozens of negotiating situations in the typical day. But many of them are not very consequential. A strategic approach leads the negotiator to *manage a portfolio of negotiations* by identifying and concentrating on the few that make the greatest difference in the long run. This may mean emphasizing some and de-emphasizing others to optimize the performance of the overall portfolio. We do not suggest a trade-off approach as an alternative to the strategic assessment of outcome and relationship importance. Rather, we suggest the strategic negotiator *evaluate the outcome and relationship importance of any single negotiation relative to the importance of other negotiations* in the current portfolio, and relative to the time, energy, and resources that it may take to execute that strategy well. If there are few negotiating situations at the moment, then perhaps all can be treated as if one or both dimensions are important. But there are practical limits for each negotiator that dictate trade-offs should be made whenever there are many negotiating situations at hand.

This is another of the points obvious to strategists but often overlooked by negotiators. Kenichi Ohmae, in his classic book on Japanese management strategy, observes that successful strategists "are careful not to spread their precious management resources of time, money and people over too many areas. Rather, they typically conquer one key factor for success after another, one at a time."[1] The same strategic principle should apply to negotiations, thus the twelfth rule of strategic negotiation is to invest in negotiations wisely (Figure 8.1). If you are involved in a collaborative negotiation with your boss that may have a major impact on your career path at the company, plus a competitive negotiation with the insurance company that you *thought* was covering the car your teenage son just totaled, then the relative importance of the relationship and outcome results of negotiations over the cost of patching your leaking garage roof, for example, will be

Figure 8.1 The Twelfth Rule of Strategic Negotiation

lower than if this was the only negotiation on your agenda. Even more significantly, we are often involved in multiple negotiations with the same person. For example, my spouse and I may be discussing where to go out to dinner and a movie. I have preferences about where I want to go for both dinner and the movie, but I know that she does too—so I have to decide which one I want to "Compete" on and which one I might want to "Collaborate" or even "Accommodate" on. In addition, if these deliberations take place while we are also discussing where to go on vacation next month and I have clear preferences for that—I might Accommodate on the entire discussion simply to "put her in a good mood" for the vacation discussion. As we can see, therefore, an alternative strategy is often appropriate for lower-priority negotiations, because they meet alternative criteria and accomplish different objectives.

As the negotiation strategy grid from Chapter 5 indicates, if the relationship importance is high but the outcome is not consequential, then an Accommodating Strategy is best. If you rate the outcome and relationship as unimportant (or low in importance relative to other negotiations in your portfolio), then you need to pursue an Avoiding Strategy. Finally, when both the outcome and the relationship scales are moderately high, and the situation does not warrant a "full-blown" competitive or collaborative strategy, the more economical Compromising Strategy is the best alternative. We will examine each strategy in some detail, and then look at some applications for them.

ACCOMMODATING STRATEGY

The Accommodating Strategy, which was introduced in Chapter 5, is used by a party with high relationship concerns and low outcome concerns. Another way of describing this strategy is "lose to win" or sacrifice the outcome for the sake of the relationship.

The primary purpose of the strategy is to keep the other party happy, or to build or strengthen the relationship. A lose-win strategy is usually a passive one,[2] employed by a party that does not want to dominate. Let's look at the Accommodating Strategy in action, as Sara and Felice negotiate to form a new business partnership.

"Felice, could we talk about something?" asked Sara. "I really want to start this business with you, but I've tried four banks and I can't get a loan. I don't know what else to do."

"Sara," said Felice, "you're my best friend. I know you don't have much money, and I don't want you to have to worry about it. I have some money from my inheritance that I could put in. What do you think?"

The two women were discussing the possibility over a lunch at a Chinese restaurant near Sara's apartment. Sara's answer, put very simply, was "Yes!" But they could not agree on the details of the plan.

"Felice, I am really concerned about what happens if the business fails! I don't think it will, but we have to consider that possibility," said Sara.

"I've thought about that too," Felice responded. "Maybe I should have a larger share of the profits at the beginning, at least until the business proves itself and is in the black."

As they began their dessert, Sara plucked a fortune cookie from the bowl in front of her, and opened it up. The little white slip read, "You will receive generous help from a friend." She took a deep breath and said, "Look, Felice, I'll be completely honest with you. I think it could be great to work together, but you don't have professional decorating skills! Although you have great business skills, I'd be carrying you on the business for the first year or two. I'd have to teach you the trade, but I think it is worth it for someone I like and trust. In this business, great skills will make the business in the long run, and they are much harder to come by than money. Given enough time, I know I can raise the money, but the point is, if you put up some cash now, we can get started sooner. In my view, it's worth a quarter of the business to avoid the wait, but no more. And if we can't agree on something reasonable right away, I might as well just wait until I can line up another financial source."

"Wow," Felice sighed. "That was quite a speech. All right; I can see you're serious about this, and I want to help you. I'll put in whatever you think we need to get started for the next three months; we can figure out the rest of the details later, and we can see how we are doing in 90 days and decide what to do next."

Sara jumped up and hugged Felice. "Oh, Felice, you're the greatest!" Sara gushed. "I'm so glad you're willing to do this with me! This is going to be great! I've got to run to meet a client, but we'll talk about this more later!"

And Sara ran out, leaving Felice to pay the bill. Felice shrugged her shoulders and picked up her untouched fortune cookie. She broke it open and the paper tumbled out. It said, "Be careful of hasty decisions in friendship and business."

In this situation Felice accommodates to Sara's concern. She accepts 25 percent of the business while putting up a significant amount of cash to get the business started. For her, preserving her relationship with Sara, her best friend, overshadows the importance of the financial business risk she is taking. Not everyone would make this same decision. For some, the relationship would not be that critical, or the financial risk would be too great.

Because this strategy is used when the relationship concerns are high, we can be more specific about when you should use the Accommodating strategy:

1. In Chapter 4, we discussed some of the major aspects of relationships that we want to preserve or enhance. An Accommodating Strategy should build or strengthen some of these factors:

To build *trust* between the parties, or not to destroy trust by pressing for one's own outcome concerns.

To enhance a show of *respect* for the other's skills, contributions, and assets. In our example, Felice shows that she respects the interior decorating skills that Sara will bring to the business.

To affect the *"scope"* of the relationship—the number of different ways we interact with key people. If we have other negotiations going on in other aspects of our relationship where we *strongly* care about the outcome (our discussion of the two spouses "negotiating" dinner and a movie), we may want to accommodate in this negotiation.

To simply *make the other feel good* because we want to please the person, make the person happy, show empathy, or celebrate an accomplishment. If today is the other person's birthday, we might accommodate to requests that we won't accept tomorrow.

2. A second major reason to use the Accommodating Strategy is that, in complex relationships where there are multiple ongoing negotiations, the parties tend to "keep score." Over the course of time, people generally expect that there is a balance of winning and losing for each side—this time you win and I lose, the next time it will go the other way. Thus, if we have won in the past or want to win in the future, it may be best to use an Accommodating Strategy now.

3. An Accommodating Strategy may be used when a party has a hidden agenda. An example of this might be an employee who is planning to

ask the boss for a raise in six months. In the meantime, the employee does rush jobs or other tasks "beyond the call of duty," without making a big issue of them, in the expectation that the raise will be able to be negotiated in the future. In a sense, Accommodation is a good strategy when you want to build up a supply of "credits" with the other that you can cash in at some point.

4. Finally, sometimes it is appropriate for Party A to let Party B win. This allows the parties to "keep the peace" because the relationship is so important or because the outcome is relatively unimportant. Thus, if we want to keep conflict to a minimum and keep the other in a good mood, trying to pursue a trivial outcome is not worth the effort; the Accommodating Strategy then can be a good choice.

The major drawback of the Accommodating strategy is that the party using it may appear to be condescending toward the other party, or the other party may feel uncomfortable with an "easy win." In addition, it is important to be careful about the extent of use of this strategy. It is not generally appropriate to establish a pattern of *always* giving in. The party that always Accommodates to others may open itself to being taken advantage of. Particularly if the other is not monitoring the give-and-take in the relationship, he or she may take winning for granted. If this becomes a problem in an important relationship, the party who is disadvantaged should actively talk about the problem with the other person.

AVOIDANCE STRATEGY

If weaker numerically, be capable of withdrawing.
—Sun Tzu, *The Art of War*[3]

An Avoiding Strategy is a strategy of inaction. It is used to stall or delay negotiation, or to avoid negotiating completely. There are two different reasons for pursuing this strategy. The first, as indicated by our negotiating strategy grids, is that both the outcome and the relationship are unimportant and therefore there is little to be lost by avoiding the negotiation. The second is that the timing is wrong. Even where an outcome or relationship is of potential importance, it may not make sense to negotiate *right now*.

Sun Tzu was the first, and perhaps is still the most important, military strategist, hailing from China around 500 B.C. His treatise goes on to state, "When the strike of a hawk breaks the body of its prey, it is because of timing."[4] The point is important, even where a Collaborative situation makes the predatory analogy completely inappropriate; if you lack the power and position to obtain a desirable relationship or outcome result right now, temporary withdrawal is the best alternative. Negotiators rarely have such overwhelming strength of position that they can take the risks of negotiation for granted.

In managing your portfolio of negotiations, you may want to prioritize negotiations based on their *likelihood of success*. And where success is unlikely at the moment, a temporary withdrawal is the best alternative. At worst, "temporary" will turn into "permanent," and you will have lost the outcome or relationship result you did not think you could achieve anyway. But in many cases, the other party will still view the negotiation as of potential value, and will permit you to reinstate the negotiation—when *you* decide the time is right to strike.

What does an Avoidance Strategy look and feel like? Once again, our two prospective business partners—Sara and Felice—demonstrate the strategy in action. Here one of them backs away from the deal:

Through a sleep haze, Felice heard an annoying, ceaseless ringing, which she eventually identified as her telephone.

"Hello," she mumbled.

"Hi Felice! Its Sara! I'm so glad I finally reached you. I've been calling you forever, and I keep getting your machine, and I was starting to think you were avoiding me. I hope I didn't wake you!"

"Oh no, how could you think that. I mean, it's already 6:30 A.M.— the day's half over! In fact, I'm ready for my afternoon nap! No, I haven't been avoiding you—I had to go out of town to see my dad for a few days, and got back late last night. I think I should get going . . ."

"Well, now that I've got you on the phone, I wanted to tell you that I've been thinking about the best way for us to get started on our business, and I think that with all that money you inherited from your grandfather, we could really do some great things! I've talked with a financial consultant already, his name is Todd Danport, but he wants to talk with both of us together, so I've set up an appointment for 2 o'clock this afternoon. I didn't know you were out of town. Is 2 o'clock a good time for you?"

"I don't know," Felice said. "I have to check my appointment book, and the other messages that came in while I was away. I'm not sure I am ready to talk to Todd about this idea yet, either. We have other things to talk about in the business before we see a financial consultant. Can I call you back later to talk about this?"

"Oh, don't worry! Seeing Todd doesn't commit you in any way. It will just be a short meeting. How about if you call me back by 11 if you can't make it, so I can change the appointment. Otherwise, I'll meet you down there just before 2:00. His office is in that new office plaza down on Main Street."

"Look, I really want to think about this for a while."

"Oh Felice, please! It will just take a little while! Please . . ."

"Um, sure. I'll talk to you later."

"Great. Have a good morning, Fe . . ." Sara heard a dial tone.

That afternoon, Sara and Todd spoke for about a half hour before she realized that Felice may not have planned to show up. She tried calling Felice a couple of times that evening, but got the answering machine again. She began to realize that maybe she had done something wrong.

For the party using an Avoiding Strategy, neither the outcome nor the relationship is important. There are two ways to use this strategy, *active avoidance* and *passive avoidance*. In active avoidance, the party refuses to negotiate at all, as did Felice in the preceding example. She is half asleep, recognizes that Sara is deep into her enthusiasm without realizing that she has awakened Felice at a very inconvenient time and is being incredibly presumptuous about Felice's willingness to go to see Todd Danport. Rather than "engage" Sara in a dialogue about all of this, Felice simply makes no commitment—but also does not show up at Todd's office, or tell Sara she is not coming. This is the more active or "aggressive" approach to avoidance.

In passive avoidance, the party simply does not show up for the negotiation, or shows up but voices no objections during the negotiation. The other party and the conflict can thus be put off until some future time, or permanently ended. In either case, the other party may be frustrated because efforts to initiate a serious negotiation are stopped or delayed. That is why the strategy is most appropriate where the relationship is not important. If the relationship is important in the long term, then the strategic negotiator will only use avoidance as a short-term strategy and will have to put effort into overcoming the other party's frustration and rebuilding the relationship before reopening the negotiation in another style (accommodation, compromise, or collaboration).

Using an Avoiding Strategy can be effective for the following reasons:

- You may be able to have your needs met *without* negotiation. If you really do not need to negotiate, it makes sense not to spend the time doing so. This would be the case if you have some other way of meeting your needs.
- You have strong Alternative(s) or BATNAs that you can pursue. If you have strong BATNAs, then you may not need to negotiate. For example, if you can do just as well by switching to one of your Alternatives,

then the present negotiation is not necessary. Thus, a strong Alternative is like a trump card that you can play to maintain power and control in the negotiation.

- You have no interest in negotiating on the outcome and you are concerned that if you try to negotiate, you will damage the relationship. Thus, Felice probably believes that telling Sara she is rude and presumptuous will probably lead to a worse outcome than simply not showing up for the meeting.

- A final reason not to negotiate yourself is that someone else in your party needs the experience. If this is the case, you may choose not to negotiate so the other person can have the learning experience. You may, however, assist the person in negotiating. "Not negotiating" with an opponent whom you want to "develop" may not be a good choice, since your refusal to engage may not be the best approach for helping them to learn how to be more effective.

COMPROMISING STRATEGY

Compromise[5] is at the center of our diagram of negotiating strategies in Chapter 5. When implemented, it is most likely a blend of strategies. The approach in the Compromising Strategy is to gain something on the outcome dimension, but not push for completely meeting one's objectives and needs. This often translates into "splitting the difference" in some way between or among the parties; by not pressing for the maximum, everyone gets something. It may not be an even split, but because it is some kind of symmetrical or logical split, it is easier to obtain agreement with the other party than it is through Competing or Collaboration. Moreover, the outcome is likely to be more beneficial than through Avoiding or Accommodation. With the Compromising Strategy, you show some concern for the relationship because you do not insist on a complete "win" (as in the Competitive Strategy) and you demonstrate empathy by assuring that the other party gets "something" on the outcome dimension as well. You are also showing that you care, to some degree, whether the other party achieves their outcomes in the negotiation, demonstrating empathy for the other's concerns. Thus you may enhance your image with the other as someone who is reasonable, fair, and willing to help both sides gain something—key intangibles discussed in Chapter 2.

The low negotiating costs of an agreement through compromise are beneficial, but it is balanced by the higher *opportunity* costs of the strategy. The compromise may result in satisfying some of each party's objectives, but it does not optimize the situation in the way that collaboration can. Basically, compromise often means trading concessions. Although both sides end up with less than they wanted ("50 percent of something is better than 100 percent of nothing"[6]), they also don't maximize. The objective is for the deal to benefit both parties to some degree, so that both are invested in making the agreement work.[7]

Let's look at the compromise strategy in action. Here, Sara and Felice compromise to cut their negotiations short, minimize the personal costs of negotiating, and get right to the job of building their company.

We find Sara and Felice having tea in a teahouse, trying to have a friendly business meeting, but it quickly goes sour.

"What a great idea, to go out and have real 'high tea,'" exclaimed Felice. "I've never been here before."

Sara took a bite out of a beautiful raspberry torte. "Neither have I, but my mother always said negotiations are best approached in a civilized manner and with sweetness, and I thought I'd take her literally. But seriously, we need to discuss our financial strategy. I'd like to bring you into this project essentially as a silent partner, because what I need the most is financial backing. I propose that you invest the start-up costs for the business, for which you will get 30 percent of the profits."

Felice choked on her tea. "You've got to be kidding. You want me to fund the whole project, have no say in what you do or how you spend the money, and get only 30 percent back? You're talking about a huge chunk of my savings, Sara. If I'm going to put in that much money, then I need to have more control over what happens to it. I want 70 percent of the ownership and profits, and I want to have an active role in the day-to-day business."

"Well, now *you're* being ridiculous," fumed Sara. "This business is my idea, and it's based on my talent, experience, and professional reputation. You can't have more importance than I do in the business. Look, why don't we just compromise on this: you can have 40 percent of the ownership and some involvement in the daily affairs."

"I think we should split it 50-50, to be even remotely fair," countered Felice. "Besides, I thought we were friends. Why are we fighting about this?"

Sara drank her tea and tried to calm herself. "I guess you're right, Felice. The most important thing is that we remain good friends. Let's go ahead and split the shares down the middle, so we can get started already. Should we shake on it?"

"Sounds fine," said Felice as she offered her hand. In truth, she still had doubts that the deal was fair, but she didn't want to prolong the discussion and make both Sara and herself mad.

The business did reasonably well. However, Felice grew increasingly resentful. She felt she'd been cheated on the deal because Sara had invested no capital, while Felice had risked most of her savings. Since they both began taking profits as soon as they were available, Felice had to use her profits to rebuild her initial investment, while Sara took them as complete profits right away. After several months of feeling badly about the arrangement, Felice approached Sara with a request to restructure the agreement, hoping Sara would agree to pay Felice half the start-up investment. However, Sara reacted angrily, accused Felice of trying to undermine their partnership, and this led to a huge fight and the eventual dissolution of the business.

In a Compromising Strategy you make a moderate effort to pursue your own outcomes, and make a moderate attempt to help the other party achieve their outcomes. Such a strategy may appear to be a watered-down version of collaboration. In many ways, that is correct—some actually see it as a "lazy" or yielding approach to negotiation.[8] But a Compromising Strategy can be a good approach, for several reasons:

1. The resources are limited, and can't be expanded or creatively shared. Rather than engage in a big argument in which both sides try to compete to win the resources, or try to collaborate but can't find an inventive way to satisfy either objectives or interests, compromise may be a satisfactory solution.

2. Time is limited. Effective competition and collaboration may both take a lot of time to pursue effectively—Competitive Strategy because it may take a long time to wear the other side down, and Collaborative Strategy because it takes an equally long time to find a good solution and preserve the relationship. Compromise is "quick and dirty," with, for now, an emphasis on the "quick."

3. The relationship is maintained and preserved to some degree. This strategy may be used by a party whose position is weaker than that of the other side. It may also be used by a party who wants to show some degree of concern for the other, and sees the other as weaker—but also does not give the other everything. It can help avoid prolonged conflict.

4. If there are good options available on each side, one party might propose a compromise to obtain a concession on one of their more important objectives.[9] This works well, for example, if you know that the other party wants a particular concession badly and you are in a position to trade off for something that you want. When the parties have multiple issues on the table, Compromising often employs a quick and expedient logrolling process (described in Chapter 7).

Some Principles for the Compromise Strategy

The following are some suggestions for how to carry out a Compromise Strategy[10] without either side losing too much and with everyone gaining something:

Do Your Homework. Know what you want. Be sure you have clear goals and objectives. We did this work in Chapter 2, and it becomes very important if you must compromise, because you need to know what you want to fight for and what you are willing to give up. You need to be strongly committed to your objectives, or you may be forced into a position of "giving away the farm"—giving away everything, or at least those things which you wanted most.

Prioritize Your Goals. If you are going to compromise, you need to know what you must have, as opposed to what would be nice to have. The nice-to-haves may be given up for obtaining the must-haves.

Know Your Walkaway and Alternatives. This can give you power in the negotiations, because at some point, you may be better off pursuing your Alternative than settling for a suboptimal agreement. Know your walkaway point, so that if you need to, you can abandon the negotiation. This, too, can give you power.

Know Which Person Will Make the Decision. If the person you are negotiating with does not have the authority to make an agreement, you may be spending a lot of time waiting while he or she consults with the one who does. It may be better and more efficient for you to present the benefits of your proposal to the decision maker.

Show That You Want to Negotiate. Put yourself out as needed to overcome the other party's reticence or distrust. Look at the other party's problems and try to make sure that your proposal effectively resolves some of their key issues. This will give you a reputation for empathy and fairness.

Try Not to Be the First Side to Make a Major Concession. Since making concessions may be interpreted as a sign of weakness, the other party may take advantage of this and become aggressive, pushing you farther than you wish to go. This will escalate the proceedings so that the more you give in the more they will ask for. You will find yourself moved into an Accommodating Strategy, not a Compromising one.

Do Not Wait until the Deadline to Offer a Compromise. Compromises should be offered from a position of strength, not as a last-ditch gesture, which would suggest to the other party that you are in a weaker position. If the deadline is close and you want to offer a compromise, offer it early enough that the other side can truly consider it. If you wait too long, the other party's deadline may have passed; and either they will be very upset, or they may have lost all possibility of advantage and now may simply want to sabotage the negotiation process.

Start with Small Compromises.   A gradual or staged approach can help you to move toward more compromise. If you work in small steps, each party can move toward a reasonable solution. Moving too fast may escalate the demands.

Use Your Concessions to Your Advantage.   When you make a concession, be sure that the other party gets the message that you are interested in a positive outcome and want to deal with them. Ask for a reciprocal concession in return.

Use Your Offers to Communicate Where You Stand.   As you approach the end of your offers, they should be smaller and fewer, to signal the other party that you are near the end. If the other party is alert, the negotiators will understand that they cannot push you to make further offers. The same is true for your side. Watch the other party's offers, and be alert for signs of distress in their negotiators. When they have reached their limit, you should not push for more concessions. You risk breaking off negotiations entirely.

Do Not Push Too Hard.   Try to avoid the classic assumption of negotiation, that you have to win everything you can. Pushing may result in negotiations coming to an abrupt halt.

Remember That the Split Does Not Have to Be Even.   In compromising, it may not be possible, or even desirable, to "split it down the middle," although that is the most frequent way it is done. A compromise is often based on where the two parties currently stand, but that does not mean that they made equal concessions to get to that point. If one party has moved $2,000 from their starting point and the other party has moved $5,000, and they are still $4,000 apart, a "split down the middle" is a compromise, but it yields a deal that means one party only had to concede $4,000 while the other conceded $7,000.

Compromises Can Also Be "Win-Win."   Consider the well-known story of two girls arguing over an orange. They had one orange to divide between them. The girls could have divided the orange in half to "be fair." But each really wanted something different (underlying interests); one girl wanted the rind, and the other wanted the pulp. A fairer way to divide the orange was to give each what she wanted—a "win-win" solution.

Try Not to Close Too Quickly.   Although a scarcity of time is one of the primary motivators of the Compromise Strategy, it does not mean you have to do it with lightning speed! You may be eager to complete the transaction, but if a deal occurs "too fast," people frequently wonder whether they could have done better. If you are selling, make at least one counteroffer so the buyer will be confident of having obtained the best price. If you are buying, offer low at first, and then move up. People like to feel that they have earned what they've won. Resist going for the "1-2-3" deal (offer—counteroffer—split it down the middle).

Promote the Long-Term Benefits. Point out that there can be an ongoing relationship between the parties (if this is true). One benefit of a successful Compromise is that at best, the future is not put in jeopardy (as it was in the Sara-Felice Compromise), and the possibility of future business together remains viable. In fact, a compromise now might lay the groundwork for future collaboration. Looking at it from another angle, a negotiation that does not go well presents the potential of lost future business.

Stay Focused on the Issues. The other side may use dirty tactics in trying to push for more concessions. Try to ignore these if possible, and stay with your established bottom line. In other words, be firm, particularly if the other switches to a Competitive Strategy.

All Deals Are Not Always Winable. Sometimes, a compromise is the best you can do in a bad situation, when neither side can completely get what it wants, or improving the relationship between them. Sometimes, a good test for an effective compromise is that both sides "are doing the best they can under the circumstances."

Some Other Suggestions. Finally, a few suggestions particularly for negotiating with organizations:

- You are often better off to *deal with smaller companies;* they are more likely to make better deals because they need your business. Larger organizations (particularly bureaucracies) are likely to behave as though they do not care whether they have your business or not. The problem here is often one of "legitimacy" (see Chapter 4) in which representatives of the organization have no authority to deviate from established prices or procedures.

- *Watch out for buying under pressure.* This is more likely to occur when you *must* have the item (you're desperate, and the opponent knows it). You are more likely to be able to bargain if you have time to do so, and less likely to be able to compromise when you are in a hurry. If at all possible, give the *impression* that you are not in a hurry. Likewise, avoid buying something that "may not be available" tomorrow—very few things are that scarce!

- Finally, when you don't know the other, *put everything in writing.* If you have agreed to follow through, do so; make sure your word is good.

What to Do if the Compromising Process Gets Bogged Down

If a session in which you are trying to compromise is faltering, you can sometimes apply a "staged" or incremental process that moves beyond Compromise Strategy into true Collaborative Strategy. In the first stage or step, the parties will come to a temporary or interim agreement (which may include a compromise). Having established this compromise, both parties agree that this establishes a "floor" for further negotiation (that while they may be able to improve on the deal, they will each do no worse than their current agreement). They then begin to explore some of the processes outlined in Chapter 7, on Collaborative negotiation. As a result, the agreement may be enriched, broadened, strengthened, or improved for both sides.

WARNING! AVOID COMPLIANCE STRATEGIES[11]

We discuss compliance at this point just to serve as a warning or alert about how you might find yourself maneuvered into Compliance—which is not the same thing as Compromise! Compliance is agreeing to go along with something that you would really prefer not to do or agreeing to something you really did not want to.

Sometimes people comply with requests when they really prefer not to. Why they do this is something that even *they* may not know. For example, in spite of numerous private and public pledges to the contrary, people buy product offers (books, computer software, investments) or make gifts and contributions to telephone marketers and door-to-door solicitors. Often they do this because they can't say "no," even to someone they don't really care about and for a product that they don't care much for either. For example, a solicitor for a charity will call and request a gift of $50. Rather than say "no," people often give a gift of $25, just to "compromise" and get the solicitor to go away. This is *not compromise—it is compliance*. You need to be *aware* of this possibility and take time to evaluate what you really want out of the situation. If you have done careful thinking and evaluation in Chapter 2, this should not be difficult. But because salespeople and marketers often catch you unaware, you have not had a chance to do any of your planning; hence, you comply with at least part of their request.

Strategies in negotiation and other situations can be designed to persuade you to comply. Here are a few possible reasons why people comply with requests, and suggestions for how to combat a request you really do not want to meet.

Reciprocity

This is the theme in the Compromising Strategy: give and take, tit for tat, I give you something and you give me something. People may even offer compliments or favors to get something in return. If the exchange seems fair and appropriate, and you want it, accept the offer, providing it does not have unwanted strings attached. But if it is a favor given with the notion of getting something in return, be sure you *fully* understand what is going to be expected of you. For example, while writing this very chapter, one of the authors was called by a marketing firm. The firm offered a choice of "free" videos; once the author had selected the free video he wanted, he was then told that it was indeed a free gift, but required considering other videos to purchase, one per month, for 12 months. The implication—without ever saying so—was that since the marketing firm had started off doing something for the respondent, it was his "obligation" to reciprocate and do something for them. This is a very popular sales tactic. So what did the author do? What would you do?

If you decide to refuse an offer, be careful how you do it. A person making a genuine offer, with "no strings attached," may be insulted if you attack or impugn the offer (or the person's motives in offering it to you). Also in some cultures, gift-giving may be much more acceptable than in others. For example, in the American public sector, gift-giving is frowned on, but in Japan, presents are part of the early relationship-building process (see Chapter 15).

Commitment

If you are heavily committed to obtaining something that looks unbelievably attractive (on the surface), you may find yourself the object of a "bait-and-switch" tactic. A classic example of this is a store advertisement for a product such as a toaster that looks like a real bargain. When you arrive at the store to buy the toaster, a salesperson tells you that they are "all out," but that they have another toaster "of equivalent quality"—but it is not on sale, and actually retails for $10 more. If you really need a toaster, you may fall for the bait-and-switch tactic. You may end up with a good toaster but wind up paying $10 more for it than you expected. There is also the possibility that it is inferior to the one advertised.

This tactic might be used in negotiation if one party promises to do something, then suddenly switches to a different commitment, saying it is "just the same." To avoid this problem, write down what has been offered. This may increase and "lock in" their commitment to the initial offer, and prevent switching tactics. It is also wise to watch out for becoming over-committed, which puts you in a position where you may not be able to change your mind without losing face.

Social Proof

Endorsements and statements of support from others, especially people whom we see as "experts," tend to help us commit to something. If a person with some perceived expertise on the subject says it is true (e.g., the ancient cigarette advertisement that promised, "Out of 100 doctors, 73 percent prefer _____ cigarettes"), then we think it must be true. Beware of this tactic. It is important to evaluate such claims for yourself—even though it requires time, effort, and often some research. Do not let yourself be railroaded by what looks like strong "expert" proof. Further, even among specialists, people do not always agree. Any body of knowledge is open to interpretation. If you are concerned about a source's qualifications or education, ask for substantiation of the person's background and credentials or get a second opinion. Request more time to consider what has been presented. Ask an "objective" person whom you know, respect, and trust, and who will give you a reality check.

Liking

We also tend to be more easily influenced by someone we like, or find personally attractive. Based on that fact, a negotiating team may be selected for its "likable" qualities—friendliness, congeniality, personableness. In many negotiations, the parties spend some time "getting to know each other" before getting down to business, and in this phase of the process, likability can be critical to "warming the other up." This can also be seen as a variation on the "good guy/bad guy" technique discussed in Chapter 6. It is important to be aware of your personal feelings about the other party, and to be able to separate personalities from the negotiation.

Authority

From the time we first go to school, we tend to respect people who have "formal" authority over us—teachers, principals, police officers, the clergy. Other "authorities" in our lives include those who make and enforce rules, and people with titles (Doctor, Attorney, Vice President, Reverend, Judge).

We are expected to respect these authorities. However, we need to watch out for overbelieving and overrespecting, particularly when they have an agenda to persuade us.

Although some parties have "authority" by virtue of their title, formal position, or expertise, we tend to overgeneralize about their expertise, and those with that authority may tend to overextend its application. For example, in our culture, we tend to view attorneys as smart people who know the law and its applications. Often, lawyers are hired into jobs that have little or nothing to do with their legal training, but they tend to act in those jobs as though they have considerable authority and expertise. For example, lawyers who specialize in real estate may not be as good in criminal law as those who specialize in that area—and may not know much about business, although they are willing to provide advice on the subject!

Scarcity

Scarcity of resources affects our attitude toward them. If you want something, and you learn that the supply is running short, or that only one item remains, or that the merchandise is an "exclusive," are you more tempted to acquire it? Are you more pleased when you manage to get it? Is your curiosity piqued when you are told that something was censored? Some people are willing to pay a lot for one-of-a-kind or limited-offering articles. To guard against this type of compliance, consider your underlying reasons for wanting an item or option. Be aware of the temptation associated with scarcity.

DEALING WITH THE BOSS (AGAIN)

Negotiating with the boss is not always easy or pleasant, but most of us have to do it occasionally. Although salary is a common topic for negotiation, that usually occurs only once a year, at most. What is more frequently an issue for negotiation is a situation where you are asked to do work above and beyond the call of duty—in other words, more than your job description or time will permit. Both managers and employees should consider the issues involved in such negotiations.

In Chapter 7, we looked at ways to use a Collaborative Strategy with a manager, but that is not always feasible. More frequently, employees find themselves entertaining Accommodating, Avoidance, and Compromising Strategies. There are two primary reasons for this. First, we tend to believe that resources are fixed (that is, they cannot be expanded). Money may already be budgeted, the number of employees is limited by a hiring freeze, the machines can only operate a certain number of hours a day, and so forth. Thus, there must be trade-offs. Second, we do not want to make the boss angry or upset by actively pursuing a Competitive or Collaborative Strategy that is high on the outcome dimension (to maximize our own outcomes). Because the boss has great control over us, we want to keep him (or her) happy, and so we pursue the other three strategies.

Employee-manager negotiations, particularly ones that center around discussions about work and getting a job done, tend to focus on three basic components:[12] specifications, time, and resources. When you are asked to do a project (before you engage in any negotiation with your boss), you should evaluate it with respect to these factors so you have a good picture of all three components.

Specifications have to do with the details of a project; in other words, what the actual task is, such as making a product, providing a service, or writing a report. In evaluating a project and whether you can do it, you need to know and understand the exact nature of the project. All your estimates and planning will depend on your specifying the job correctly. If you are not sure, ask for more details.

Time is also of major importance in evaluating a task. Your estimate should include not only the time involved in actually completing the task, but also any administrative time, such as writing a report on completion of a project, or overseeing the production or printing of a report. Estimate as accurately as possible how long the project will take. Your estimate should include enough time to do a good job—not a slapdash one. Also be sure you build in a "contingency" plan, or time buffer in case of problems. Remember Murphy's Law: "If something can go wrong, it will." If your time frame is too tight, you may suddenly have to renegotiate the project when you are in the middle of it.

Resources are the third component of a project or task. Resources are the materials that go into the project, such as human labor, physical materials (such as paper for a report), computer time, or raw materials for the production of a product. It is important to take account of all the resources that you may need for the project, and whether you can make trade-offs among them. For example, if the schedule suddenly becomes tighter, can you hire a consultant or temporary help to complete the project on schedule? Part of your own strategy should be to assure that you will have adequate resources to complete the job.

Once you account for these three factors, they may be traded off, one for another, if necessary. Thus, if your boss wants a project done in 5 days instead of 10, you will need to increase resources to offset the diminished time. You may also need to make clear what jobs are not getting done so that you can devote full attention to this one, and secure additional resources to make sure your other commitments are met. Likewise, if the specifications change on a project, you may need more time to complete the job according to the new specs. Or you may need different labor with different skills.

You will need to know if any of the factors are fixed and therefore unchangeable. This will have considerable effect on the project, especially if another factor changes. Think about what substitutions and trade-offs you can and cannot make.

How to Respond to an "Impossible" Request

When you are asked by your boss to do a nearly impossible task, it is tempting to say "No" immediately. However, it is wise to avoid responding with an immediate "No." This may give the impression that you are lazy, disloyal, or uncooperative.[13] Buy some time by saying that you would like to think about it (use the Avoidance strategy to temporarily withdraw from the boss's invitation to negotiate, since you know that you have no good response to his or her opening position). It is possible that the whole problem will go away, the storm will pass, and you will not have to consider the situation again.

However, the request may well come again, in which case it is a good idea to be prepared. Asking for time gives you an opportunity to look into the situation and evaluate what you want to do. It allows you to try to redefine the problem and initiate Collaboration, or—more likely with directive bosses—to keep exploring the situation and discussing the problem until a Compromise Strategy can be applied effectively.

When you have evaluated the situation as described previously, and can no longer avoid responding to your boss, we recommend that you initiate a Compromise Strategy with a response that is carefully worded to prevent accidental competitive negotiation and conflict. Use the phrase "Yes, and" rather than "Yes, but," which sounds more like "no." Another good phrase to use if you are going to offer a compromise is "if . . . , then . . ." For example, "If I do this, then I need to have you do that for me (or If I do this, then can you help me . . . ?"

"Yes, and . . ." tells the boss you are willing to help with the task. It also adds what you will need—the missing resources—if you are going to be able to do what you are being asked. You are agreeing to do the task, but setting limits on what is possible. For example, "Yes, I will do it, and I will need an assistant for five days." Or, "Yes I can do it, and it will cost $1,000 more than previously budgeted."

If your boss engages in the negotiation in this same spirit, you will be able to implement a Compromise Strategy. You and the boss will have to trade one thing for another. Be sure you understand exactly what the boss wants, what the time frame is, what resources are available, which aspects are fixed, and which are flexible. The trade-offs you make can result in something close to a win-win situation if you plan carefully.

HAGGLING

We turn now to a strategy that is becoming more popular because of the downturn in the economy: haggling,[14] sometimes called "dickering," or "hardball" bargaining. It is a stylized variant of the Compromise Strategy, often with some competitive tactics *and* collaborative tactics thrown in for good measure. This method of settling on the price has been used in a number of other countries for a long time, but is now becoming more common in the United States in retail stores that, because of the economy, are "ripe for making deals." Although we are most familiar with haggling in the case of new car purchases, it is becoming more frequent in other areas as well.

The willingness to haggle varies across cultures. People from Latino, Asian, and Middle Eastern countries tend to be comfortable with haggling as a method of setting price, as it is the usual way of conducting business in many countries, where bargaining is more than just "agreeing on the price." There is a social value to it. It involves relationship-building. In contrast, in the United States, we don't tend to haggle on most items except those with a high price tag. Thus, a second way that haggling varies is on the relative price of an item. For example, there are international differences in the things we haggle over; in the United States, we tend to simply pay what is asked for low-price items (e.g., a fresh chicken for dinner) but haggle on high-price items (cars, houses, boats). In other countries, it is reversed—people pay the sticker price for a high-price item but will haggle for an hour over the price of a chicken. The size of the store often makes a difference too. Although it is possible to bargain on some items at some department stores, it is more common and usually more successful to haggle with the owner of a small store. Sometimes the owner of a small store will not reduce the price, but will throw in a gift or offer a discount to a faithful customer. The goods that are commonly haggled over are sports equipment, jewelry, suits, and shoes. Another area where haggling occurs is in the price for services: everything from cutting the lawn to washing a car to big events such as catering a wedding. It is also common to bargain about the prices of apartments, rental cars, and mortgages.

To haggle over a price, follow these suggestions:

- It is all right to ask for a price break, but be prepared for the possibility of being told "no."
- Haggle only if you plan to buy. Once you begin to haggle with the other party, you usually are creating the expectation that you will consummate the deal if you can agree on the price.
- Be polite but firm. It is poor form to be pushy.
- "Sales" are good places to haggle. Items are on sale because the seller wants to get rid of them. Sometimes they simply want to get them out of inventory so they don't have to pay storage costs—so you may be able to get the price tag down even further.
- Haggle in stores where you are a regular customer, not in ones where no one knows you.
- It is much easier to haggle in a small store, where you can talk with the owner directly. In larger stores, the clerk probably has no authority to make a decision about whether a price or service can be changed (most clerks are not given any authority to make those decisions, for just this reason).
- Pay in cash rather than with a credit card, which costs the owner when you use it.

BARGAINING FOR A NEW CAR

Car buying is an area where haggling is popular. The strategic negotiator may begin thinking about a car purchase and assume that the relationship with an individual car salesperson or dealership is low in importance, while the outcome is highly important, and so will prefer a thorough, lengthy, Competitive Strategy. However, we believe that the best strategy for a car purchase is really a form of Compromise, and so treat it here in the chapter on alternative strategies. A new car negotiation is rarely Collaborative, because you have no interest in a long-term relationship with the dealer or salesperson, and it is unlikely to be Competitive *and effective*, because they negotiate with buyers every day and you negotiate for a car only once every few years. Dealers know every trick in the book and have either used them or had them used on them. Preserving some kind of working relationship with the dealer (in the case of car defects, repairs, etc.) while achieving some kind of fair and reasonable outcome is usually the preferred strategy.

In addition, the conventions surrounding negotiation with U.S. auto dealerships have changed. First, they know that many buyers—particularly women—have a negative reaction to the haggling ethic. In addition, the widespread publication of information on the dealer's cost for the basic car model and options has made it easier for buyers to get good information. Finally, most dealerships make their real profits on service, not new car sales, and a buyer who feels badly treated is unlikely to return to that same dealership for regular service.

In 1991, Saturn began featuring "no-dicker stickers"[15] which have been popular with those who prefer not to haggle over price. Saturn's prices are relatively low, yet still provide dealers with a profit. Other manufacturers are competing with "value pricing." In this system, low-priced cars are equipped with the options that drivers usually want, such as air conditioning and automatic transmissions, and don't require special ordering or a lot of detailed discussion about each option. Dealer margins and sales incentives are minimal. According to Jeff Hurlbert, general marketing manager for Chevrolet, "the company is moving away from rebates and wide margins."[16] And other manufacturers are following suit. However, researchers and industry-watchers are skeptical. They feel it is important to be thoroughly informed before you choose a "value-priced" car.

The first step is research. One of the key issues for such negotiations is that it's hard to plan for your bargaining range (see Chapter 2) when you must disentangle a multitude of prices, fees, and incentives. Obtain pricing and rebate information for the car you are considering. Use car and truck price guides from reputable publications[17] to find wholesale and retail prices, and the weekly *Automotive News* for listings of rebate programs. These publications can be found at newsstands or in libraries. For a fee, you can also obtain dealer cost, price, and rebate data by telephone, fax, or mail.[18]

You'll want to use the dealer-invoice price for your negotiations. The sticker price, usually shown on the window sticker, includes a profit for the dealer, so that number is not particularly helpful. Note the destination charge on the window sticker.

Ask to see the dealer invoice. If they won't show you, this is where your library research and preparation are essential. Add the destination charge. Subtract any rebates you discovered in your research. Add a reasonable markup, usually from 2 to 7 percent. This should be the price to aim for. It will be affected by availability of the model of car you want, as well as whether you are trading in a car, but the figure should be closer to what you pay than what you see on a sticker or on a value-priced car.

Car salespeople are actually a good resource for the strategic negotiator wanting to test his or her mastery of strategies. If you are thinking of buying a new or used car from a dealer (and who wouldn't—*if* you could get a good enough price?), try to open up the negotiation by doing more research than usual, by finding alternative sources of comparable products (the same make and model in a different dealership down the road), and have the courage to make repeated, strong offers and counteroffers. Often, you may need to walk out and come back several times—deal with the same salesperson and sales manager all the time. Dealerships are designed, and salespeople are trained, to minimize buyers' negotiations. They do this by limiting the buyer's responses and creating the fiction of a collaborative approach. They also try to raise your enthusiasm about the car and per-suade you to buy it as quickly as possible (the classic line is, "what would it take for us to close this deal today?"). But the strategic negotiator needs to master the art of changing the context. Use time slowly, keep coming back, and have a great Alternative that you can tell them about—the same car, down the street, for $1,000 less! And you can withdraw, far more eas-ily than they would like you to believe—as long as you don't sign any con-tracts or make any large deposits. Any dealership wishing to move products will consider even an outrageous offer, if you push them to re-spond so that they know you are serious about negotiating from that offer. And remember, if you can master the difficult art of negotiating a good price on a car, you can certainly master most other negotiating contexts.

SUMMARY

In this chapter, we considered the three strategies of negotiation: Avoiding, Accommodating, and Compromising. Each is a viable negotiation strategy to be used under the right circumstances. Refer to Table 5.1 to de-termine which strategy is most useful in the right circumstances. Have them available to you, and use them when you need to.

Chapter 9

Understanding and Dealing with Traps and Biases in Negotiation

As you have probably discovered from your reading thus far, whenever possible, the Collaborative Strategy is often the one to aim for in negotiation. Collaboration has the *potential* for providing the best solution possible for all parties because its win-win, creative approach and orientation can redefine problems and lead to better solutions. This approach is also most likely to sustain, if not enhance, the relationship between the parties. As we have seen, however, achieving a collaborative agreement requires considerable work, skill, and trust. It also requires the commitment of the other party to pursue this strategy as well. As a result, not all efforts at collaboration work. Even under the best of circumstances, with both parties wanting to be collaborative, successful negotiation is still a challenge. And the best of circumstances rarely prevail.

In reality, the strategic negotiator often recognizes the benefits of a Collaborative approach, but finds that the other party does not fully understand the need for, or the methods of, the Collaborative process. The first, and most natural response of most negotiators in this circumstance is to discuss the need for a Collaborative Strategy, and to invite the reluctant party to change their strategy so that Collaboration becomes possible. If only it were that easy! Often the other party takes this invitation at less than face value, suspecting it is actually some devious Competitive tactic. Or the other party may agree in principle to the concept of collaboration, but fall back on Competitive or Compromise styles of negotiating in practice. This is a common problem, because most people are not as experienced or skilled at Collaboration as they are at Competition, Compromise, and the other strategies. The strategic negotiator is therefore required to train others in the Collaborative Strategy. Collaboration requires a certain missionary zeal to sustain it, particularly in a societal or business context where Competition is the prevailing negotiation strategy.

This chapter offers advice on how to detect many of the problems ("traps") and biases that tend to make negotiations competitive, even if you really intend to be Collaborative. Many of these factors are things that you can control in your own behavior, or watch out for in the other party's behavior. We discuss strategies for moving the negotiation in a different direction. We also examine ways to avoid "escalating" negotiations into an unproductive conflict. As conflict increases, so does the tendency to act competitively. If the conflict increases beyond the point where you can control it on your own, then you may need to consider one or more conflict resolution processes, which we discuss in Chapters 10 and 11.

POTENTIAL CAUSES OF CONFLICTS: TRAPS TO AVOID

We need to look at some of the underlying reasons that conflict becomes heightened during negotiation. Being aware of these possible traps may help you avoid falling into them in the first place. We will also offer suggestions for resolving these situations.

Irrational Commitment

Sometimes we commit to something (e.g., an issue) for an irrational reason. Our commitment may be due to a personal bias, or because we feel we have no other choice to save face. We may look for reasons to support this irrational commitment, and ignore perfectly reasonable arguments against the issue. Once our position becomes "set in stone" (or so we think), we feel we cannot change our commitment. For example, a union may expect that management will capitulate in a strike, so they stay entrenched. Or people make threats they believe will result in action; the threats do not work, yet they still carry through on them to preserve their own credibility.

To combat this trap: A good way to avoid excessive commitment is to have an advisor who can provide you with a "reality check." This person can tell you if you appear to be committing to a position or issue in an irrational, unreasonable way. The best advisor is someone without a stake in the outcome or relationship. If you cannot find someone you know to play this role, consider hiring a specialist—an attorney, accountant, counselor, or consultant who is neutral and impartial. Many companies have ombudspersons who can serve this role. Many communities have volunteer mediation services that can usually be located in the telephone book, or through the local chapter of the bar association or chamber of commerce. There are other national organizations that provide dispute resolution specialists.[1] If you find many conflicts arise among people you manage, consider two strategies. First, try helping them "listen carefully" to the other side's views, so they can understand what the other party is saying. In addition, try to find ways to help them get out of their irrational commitments in a way that allows them to save face and not look foolish by backing down. Team training and experience improve communication and group problem-solving skills.

Belief in the Fixed Pie

Although the resources in some negotiation situations are fixed—there is only a finite amount to be divided among the parties to the conflict—you cannot assume that all situations are similar. Competitiveness often allows us to believe that the resources are limited, and there is no way that both sides can achieve their objectives. Often the pie can be expanded, or other options can be invented, to increase the possible outcomes and make the negotiation more collaborative.

To combat this trap: This type of thinking can lead to competitive dynamics. Be sure you have a reality checker. Look again at Chapter 7 for suggestions on ways to expand the pie, such as logrolling, bridging, and inventing other options, or at Chapter 10 for other strategies.

Anchoring and Adjustment

We frequently use an "anchor"—perhaps an initial offer or an intended goal—as a benchmark against which we calibrate and judge everything else in negotiation. While an anchor can be helpful, especially if it is accurate, it can be detrimental to use a randomly set anchor, and then compare everything else with it. We tend to use our own first offer, or the other's first offer, as an anchor from which everything else is judged. But if the other's first offer was extreme or irrational, it is a poor measure by which to judge more reasonable offers.

To combat this trap: Here again, it helps to have someone who can serve as a reality checker to keep you on track. Also, be sure you set your goals very carefully. If you have planned effectively, you will know what a reasonable anchor is, and can use that to judge the other's offer.

Framing

A frame is a perspective from which we see and evaluate something. Based on how we frame an issue, we behave in a certain way. The frame may be positive or negative. It can cause us to be willing to take a risk, or not. If we are unwilling to take a risk, we may quickly accept any reasonable offer from the other party, for fear of losing the whole deal.

Different kinds of frames affect the way the parties view issues. Frames can be determined around gains versus losses (seeking a positive outcome vs. minimizing one's losses of current resources), interests versus positions, characterizations of the other party, the outcome of the dispute itself, or the process that the parties use to resolve a dispute. If the parties have different frames on a dispute, there may be a great deal of miscommunication, and the parties may feel they are talking *past* one another rather than *to* one another. This occurs because each side has a different frame or definition of what the dispute is about and presents all information and arguments from that frame.

If an issue is framed negatively, negotiation is likely to be more difficult.[2] For example, consider the following situation. Your current salary is $25,000. You are being offered $30,000 for a new position. Your minimum desired salary is $32,000. You believe that the offer could successfully be pushed to $35,000, so you ask for $38,000. If you look at the negotiation from the point of view of your first request ($38,000), the first offer from the other side ($30,000) looks very negative. If you look at the situation from the point of view of where you are now ($25,000) it looks very positive. An offer of $35,000 would look negative in comparison to your first request of $38,000; however, it is better than your bottom line of $32,000.

To combat this trap: To avoid framing an issue incorrectly, be sure to obtain good information, analyze it carefully and thoroughly, and protect yourself further by having someone be your reality checker. Psychologist Scott Sindelar advises negotiators to "get the RED out." RED stands for the *rules, expectations, and demands* we carry around as factors and criteria that tend to shape the frames we use. These REDs are not always understood by others, nor do they necessarily have the same set of REDs. Before getting mad at someone who has broken your REDs, stop to ask yourself whether the REDs are reasonable and deserve to be protected at all costs.

They may be inappropriate, and serve as an incorrect frame for the problem that can lead to unproductive conflict.[3]

Availability of Information

Accurate information is essential to negotiation. But think about how information is presented to you. If someone introduces a colorful, eye-catching graph, you will probably pay more attention to it than to a simple list or black-and-white chart, even if the chart contains more accurate detailed information. Poorly presented information often fails to catch our attention at all. Thus, the information we use may be subject to our own bias for "pretty pictures." We may overvalue information presented in an attractive manner, without questioning the accuracy of the data. Even expensive, full-color slides, billboards, or videotapes can be based on incorrect information.

To combat this trap: Be aware of your biases for attractive presentations of information. Try to overcome or offset this by carefully scrutinizing any information no matter how uniquely or attractively it is presented. Think about how the other has presented the information, what their motives are, and hence what their presentation might intentionally highlight or leave out.

Winner's Curse

When you obtain an "easy win"—that is, the negotiation problem is solved faster than you had anticipated—you may feel that perhaps you could have done better (e.g., on price) or that maybe something is wrong with the product. So even if you win, you may feel uneasy about the outcome. This is termed "cognitive dissonance," and also occurs when you buy a product that you were unsure about or paid more than you thought you needed to. After the purchase, you tend to think you may have made a mistake and actually dislike what you have just bought. But knowing the name for this phenomenon does not help prevent it.

To combat this trap: Be sure you are thoroughly familiar with the object under negotiation so you know both its objective value and its value to you personally. You may also want to ask the other party for some sort of guarantee of quality or performance. And note that using the planning process and selecting the best strategy increases your confidence in the outcome. The winner's curse does not afflict the experienced strategic negotiator because he or she has taken much of the uncertainty out of the negotiation.

Overconfidence

Although confidence is important in negotiation, too much confidence can become a trap. If you are overconfident, you may end up taking an inappropriate stance or supporting a point that is incorrect. You may ignore the point of view or information from the other party that is so important in collaborative negotiation.

To combat this trap: Pay attention to your level of confidence. Watch out for being overly confident. Plan carefully. Have others quiz and check you to make sure you can defend your estimates of how likely you are to win this negotiation.

Predictions of the Future, Based on Small Numbers

It is easy to assume that a few past successes mean that you will be successful in the future. And although there is nothing wrong with confidence, you need to avoid using past successes as predictors for the future. For one thing, the circumstances in the two situations you are comparing will never be exactly alike. For another, it is not wise to predict an event from a small sample. If you have had limited experience, you really cannot predict how any future negotiations will go. You should not assume that past successes mean future success, or that past failures doom the current negotiation.

To combat this trap: Avoid basing your expectations for current or future negotiations wholly on past experience. Give yourself support from expert negotiators—learn from them. And use the strategic negotiation process to select and try a different strategy from the one that failed you before.

Biased Reasoning

We frequently make assumptions about what caused an event. These assumptions may be based on accurate, specific information or on more generalized impressions, which may or may not reflect the actual state of affairs. Such assumptions can affect the process by which we negotiate, the content of the negotiation, and the solutions that we create. It is important, therefore, to be sure we are working with accurate information, not just "gut-level" feelings or assumptions.

To combat this trap: Be sure to use accurate information. Watch out for bias. If questioned, double-check your facts and your sources. Avoid assuming anything.

Tendency to Ignore Others' Ideas

If you do not ask, you do not know. There is a tendency to overestimate or overlook our understanding of the other party's points of view. We may thus oversimplify an issue because we have not asked enough questions to fully understand the point of view of the other side.

To combat this trap: Watch for bias. Try to find out and understand the other party's interests and goals. We discuss methods of doing this in earlier chapters, especially Chapter 3. Training may be necessary to help you learn to understand the other party's position.

Minimizing

Often our behavior is a response to someone else's behavior. Responses to others are also directed by our feelings or impressions about the other party. If we do not like the other party or distrust them, we are likely to minimize their concessions, thus devaluing them.

To combat this trap: Try to stay objective about the other party. Have someone alert you if you get off track in this area. Before you offer any concessions, be sure you clarify each side's preferences on options and concessions. If necessary, use a mediator to help you filter your reactions and resulting concessions.

In summary, there are a number of traps that negotiators can fall into. It is impossible to protect yourself against all of them, or even to recognize that they are occurring. At the same time, understanding how they work can make you more sensitive to them and may enable you to correct them when they are detected.

DEALING WITH BIASES AND BUILDING TOWARD COLLABORATION AT EACH STAGE OF THE NEGOTIATION PROCESS

Now that you understand some of the traps, we can look at the kinds of problems that can occur in each stage of negotiation: the opening, middle, and closing stages in the negotiation process.[4] If you are aware of the kinds of problems that can occur, you can make an effort either to avoid them, or to allow for them in forging Collaborative negotiation.

The Opening Stage

The opening stage is full of potential potholes into which you can fall and damage the negotiation. The problems involve the initial activities that revolve around getting to know the other party, sounding them out, and estimating the potential for negotiation. In the opening stage, each side states its starting position, builds its case, and demonstrates its power. Issues, agendas, and bargaining ranges are discussed.

First and foremost, the parties often have a number of assumptions and biases about each other that they bring into the negotiation. If they have expectations about the other, or have heard about the other's "reputation," or have had previous experience with the other, it is difficult to approach the other with an "open mind." Yet these biases predetermine how the parties will behave, and often preclude the parties from really getting together to reach an agreement. In fact, they may be open to collaboration, but the presumptions of both sides don't permit the opportunity to explore it. For example, it is especially common for these problems to occur in the early stages of negotiations where there has been a history of conflict and "bad blood" between negotiating groups: union and management, spouses in a divorce, or between members of different ethnic groups. But difficulties can occur at any stage in any negotiation. Here are some of the *perception pitfalls* in the early stage:

1. In the initial stages, as each side is feeling its way along, *be careful of making judgments or assumptions about the other party*. Particularly if you have negotiated with this party before and have had a bad experience, you are prone to have strong expectations that can create "self-fulfilling prophecies" about what the other will do. Because you expect them to treat you badly, you approach them with defensiveness and mistrust, which they read as hostility on your part, and then treat you badly (and confirm your initial judgment). Approach the other with an open mind— the other party may behave differently in this negotiation than they have in the past. Try to *avoid stereotypes and biases*. These can derail Collaboration rapidly. You need to keep an open mind so that you are able to generate a variety of solutions to the problem.

2. The *halo effect,* positive or negative, can throw off your judgment. For example, the halo effect tends to cause us to continue liking someone we have always liked even if the person does something wrong. Conversely, if you have a negative picture of someone's behavior, you will tend to expect that same behavior again. The halo effect means perpetuating an

151

idea about something *even when it is no longer true*. As we have seen, the Collaborative Strategy requires open-mindedness to succeed.

3. Another troublesome problem is *selective perception,* in which you pay attention to certain aspects of a situation and filter out others. On a simple level, you may miss something that could help you nudge the other party in the direction of Collaboration. In a more complex situation, you may miss some aspect of the negotiation that could be opened up to allow Collaboration. Selective perception can be helped by good listening, which involves trying to understand the underlying meaning of the other party's communications. Listening also includes paying attention to nonverbal cues—body movement, emotions, and emphasis on particular words or topics.

4. Watch out for *projecting* your qualities onto the other party. A prime example of projection is to believe that the other party wants to collaborate (because you do) when in fact they do not.

In addition to perception biases, a number of other *biases affect our reasoning* in the early stages of negotiation. Here are some of the most important ones:

1. When you are trying to get someone to collaborate, try to *avoid negative thinking*. "Reframing" is a technique you can use to change a negative into a positive. With this method, you try to find a positive viewpoint by looking at the current situation in a novel way, by defining it as a "different situation," "different problem," and so on.

2. *Your own needs and desires affect the target.* This is projection again, affecting how you think about and understand what the other wants. Be sure to include in your thinking the needs of the other party as well. If you stay focused on only your own needs, you may lose the opportunity to foster Collaboration.

3. Watch out for *generalizing,* either about the other party or about the issues. When you make assumptions without finding out the full story, you may be missing opportunities for Collaboration. Likewise, if you use small amounts of information to draw large conclusions, you may come to the wrong conclusions. Be sure you have enough information to make reasonable conclusions.

4. Finally, if the negotiation is Competitive, the differences between the parties will be emphasized. In a Collaborative situation, the parties will overlook differences and emphasize similarities. To move the other party toward Collaboration, be sure to *look for and emphasize similarities*

between the parties. Remember that you want to minimize the differences. In this same vein, avoid we/they comparisons.

Finally, sometimes it will not be possible to move the negotiations toward Collaboration. In such cases, the parties may need help with conflict resolution or third-party intervention (see Chapters 10 and 11).

The Middle Stage

In the middle stage of negotiation, problem-solving is the main focus. The parties look for possible solutions. There will be offers that bring about counteroffers. Issues and concerns may change as offers are made. The important thing is to *stay focused on the areas where the parties agree* and to package an agreement that is acceptable to both parties.[5] Research shows[6] that if parties are concerned about both the relationship *and* the outcome, there will be more collaborative solutions than if only one aspect is of concern. This would suggest that in this middle stage, you need to encourage the relationship while you focus on the issues. Discussion helps immensely in finding collaborative solutions. Here are some specific suggestions:

1. *Be sure your offer is attractive to the other party.*[7] If you have understood the other party's needs in the previous stage, you will have more success in this stage of negotiation. If you are not sure how they are responding to your offer, *ask for their reactions,* comments, or critique, and listen carefully to their answers. If you are too wrapped up in your own view to listen carefully, bring a friend with you to listen as well, and then talk with the friend later about what was said.

2. If you sense that the other party is becoming competitive after you make an offer, *reconsider what you offered:* Was it based on a good understanding of the other party's needs? Did you stress the offer's attractive qualities? If the offer has negative qualities, can the offer be changed to make it more attractive to the other party? Remember that the receiver of an offer frequently pays attention only to the negative aspects.[8] This may help you in reframing your offers.

The Closing Stage

The final or closing stage of negotiation is characterized by working toward a joint solution or settlement point that will make all parties happy. But Collaborative negotiation has potential for veering off course even in this stage, so it is important to keep alert and avoid fatal mistakes as you seek closure.

There are a number of traps[9] to watch out for during the closing stage. The following traps can result from wanting to complete the negotiation, being too eager and missing information or issues, or forgetting to stay sensitive to the people and the problems:

1. If you are near agreement, but the negotiations seem to be stalled, try the strategy of getting the other party to say "yes" to one thing.[10] This can create a positive atmosphere, and you may be able to move along and complete the agreement.

2. Don't wrap up too fast or take shortcuts. You may overlook important points. Make sure you cover all the issues, and that all parties know exactly what has been agreed to. Check to be sure you understand what has been said and agreed to. If in doubt, write out a "statement of understanding" about your agreement (see Chapter 12 for more ideas about communication).

3. Be careful of overconfidence. The agreement is not complete until both parties "sign on the dotted line." Particularly if the deal is beginning to look like a very good one for you, there is a tendency to grow overconfident or even arrogant!

4. Avoid oversimplifying the situation to achieve a quick resolution. If you neglect points important to the other party, negotiation can become stalled.

5. Don't let yourself be pressured into accepting or doing something you do not want, just because the end is near. This can often be the other side using the "nibble" tactic described in Chapter 4. Expect that there will be nit-picking toward the end. Frequently, negotiation can become bogged down over a minor trap because people are tired and their emotions get away with them. Be clear about your own objectives, and don't compromise them at the last minute! If you are very tired—even if the end is in sight—don't hesitate to call for a short recess.

6. Watch your language, and don't make careless remarks. When negotiations are closing, people also let down their guards, and may be less thoughtful about what they say. If the negotiations have been tense, being able to sense the end may let parties release tension, get emotional, and discharge some of the negative feelings before everything is really settled. You can sabotage your own effort if you speak without forethought, or if you say something that can be misinterpreted. It is also possible that the other party will make dumb remarks. If so, ignore them.

7. If you tend to be disorganized, the flurry of activity and emotionality of getting close to the outcome can create a lot of confusion. Keep track of decisions and issues so you do not miss any. Don't hesitate to stop and make notes and write things down.

8. Be sure to include everyone who has something to contribute. Resentments can surface even toward the end of the negotiation. Check with all the parties to make sure they are satisfied.

9. If you get to the end of the negotiation and there are still loose ends, you might want to have the parties make an agreement based on the factors they agree on and discard the stumbling points. The issues you discard now can be brought up for separate negotiation at another time. Another approach is to get the other party to make an agreement "in principle." Then, even if details remain to be ironed out, the general feeling is of a successful negotiation.

10. Make sure your agreement has an action plan that everyone understands. Write up the agreement and have all parties read it to be sure you have covered everything. Be clear about who is to do what, by when, and how others will know it will be done. Many good agreements also include a fail-safe mechanism so that the parties have some way to get back together to work out problems that may arise. This is often where third parties can be extremely helpful (see Chapter 11).

Many of the traps listed in this chapter can be avoided if you bring along a "reality checker"—a friend, colleague, or associate who can simply listen to the proceedings and share his or her perceptions with you when negotiations become heated or break down. Such a person can let you know if you are going off track, with the hope of preventing derailment before it is too late. In general, you should trust your gut-level feelings. If you are not sure about something ask your impartial observer/advisor for feedback.

Chapter 10

Conflict Reduction: From Opponent to Collaborator

Jackie Martin and Mimi Ovanessof co-own a children's clothing store in La Jolla, California, called Merry Moppets. Martin says that, as in all partnerships, conflict sometimes arises in their business relationship. To avoid angry responses, the partners use a systematic approach to conflict resolution. Their method starts by allowing each other to state any complaints. The ground rules require them to let each other vent rather than challenging each other's complaints. Next, they use a cooling-off period to defuse any anger. During a set period of time, they think about the conflict but don't try to talk about it. Finally, they meet to try to develop a solution. This three-step process prevents anger from leading them into an escalation of conflict and helps them see each other's positions—an essential prelude to any collaborative solution.[1]

Negotiation *is* about conflict and conflict management. As a result, conflict sometimes "gets out of hand," and the negotiation process breaks down. Most of the time, these breakdowns in judgment and communication occur as a result of the biases identified in Chapter 9. When perceptions become distorted because of poor communication, frustration and resentment arise. Angry emotions begin to creep into the conversation. Biases surface and strengthen becoming self-fulfilling prophecies. As communication decreases, the sides become entrenched in their positions. Each party blames the other for the difficulty. Negotiation may come to a halt. Why does this happen?

Conflict arises when information is not flowing freely between the two parties. If the channels of communication are blocked, the parties look for reasons, and it is easy to blame the other party: "You did not tell us that," "that's not what you said before," and so forth. When the focus moves away from the issues and becomes a contest of wills, the original issues may be forgotten or blurred, and new issues may be introduced.

As the sides lose their ability to focus on issues, the parties may begin to focus on personalities. Negotiation becomes a we-against-them, win-lose contest where differences are emphasized and similarities begin to be overlooked. When this happens, emotional responses dominate rational ones. Plans and strategies are forgotten or never developed in the first place. Anger often dominates conflict-oriented negotiating situations.

According to Scott Sindalar, a psychologist who leads seminars for employees at companies such as Motorola and US West, "When we express our anger, others may back off temporarily—but they may also back off permanently. The result is often the classic win-lose scenario that turns into a lose-lose situation.[2]

In angry conflicts, each party becomes entrenched in its own position and cannot look at the other's point of view. Lies and distortions abound. Threats and counterthreats may be made. People on the same side will move closer to each other and emphasize their own similarities (even if they did not notice or acknowledge them before) in order to present a united front against the other party.[3]

All the good work you have done trying to build a collaborative relationship may appear to be going down the drain. So what can you do if you see this beginning to happen to you during negotiation? First of all, be aware that these things can—and do—occur, but that you can practice prevention as well as learn how to manage conflicts to successful resolutions.

CONFLICT REDUCTION STRATEGIES[4]

Sometimes, even when you have monitored your behavior carefully and have tried to maintain the most open collaborative negotiation, it still goes wrong. What can you do? There are several techniques that you can use to get the negotiation back on track. Of the methods proposed here, some more readily apply to low-intensity conflict, others to high-intensity conflict. The methods you choose will depend on the level of conflict and whether you think you can resolve the differences between the two parties.

If it becomes evident that conflict resolution is not possible using these methods, you may want to call in a third party to assist you. We discuss this approach to conflict management in the next chapter. This chapter is about techniques you can try yourself to reduce the conflict or to move it from a Competitive to a Collaborative process.

There are five different strategies or approaches to reducing conflict:

1. Take the charge out of the emotional climate by *reducing tension* and hostility.
2. Work on *communication skills* to improve the level and degree of communication.
3. Reduce the *number and size of the issues* involved, if they have become too unwieldy and are causing the difficulty.
4. Enhance or improve the *options and alternatives* themselves.
5. Find some *common ground* as a basis for the agreement, usually by calling on the relationship.

We now look at each of these individually.

REDUCE TENSION

There are three major techniques for diminishing the emotional tension between two negotiating parties—tension release, separation of the parties, and GRIT:

1. *Tension release.* Tossing in an occasional joke or funny remark can lighten the atmosphere. Of course, the joke must be appropriate and inoffensive or it will just add to the tension. If the other side makes an anger-provoking remark, it is best to ignore it. If you can resist the urge to retort, you can usually avoid raising the tension level.

2. *Separation of the parties.* This can be a helpful technique if emotions have escalated. The simplest way to do this is to take a break. This may be a 15-minute break, an hour, or a matter of days or weeks, depending on the level of emotional stress and the urgency of completing an agreement. We recommend that you state clearly the reason for the break. This will give everyone a chance to cool off, to think about what is happening, and to resolve to try harder when they return. This is the second step of Jackie Martin and Mimi Ovanessof's method for coping with conflict in their business partnership.

3. *GRIT.*[5] This acronym stands for *G*raduated *R*eciprocation *I*n *T*ension reduction. This method of tension reduction was devised in the context of diplomacy, where tension during negotiation usually escalates rather than

abates. The way GRIT works is that one party makes a small, usually pub-lic, concession and invites the other party to reciprocate. The concession is not so great that the party loses face, and not so small that the concession is meaningless to the other side. The concession may even be a simple apology—something that is calculated to try to change the nature of the relationship as it stands at the moment. The other party then responds with a small concession, and this process goes back and forth as needed until the climate of the negotiation has cooled down and the two parties can proceed. The entire process is designed to restore trust by following an agreed-on procedure for deescalating the dispute, and showing the other side that you truly want to find a mutually acceptable resolution.

WORK ON COMMUNICATION SKILLS

As emphasized throughout this book, successful communication is the key to successful negotiation. When communication bogs down, so does negotiation. We deal at length with communication techniques and resolv-ing them in Chapter 12. For now, we would like to point out some areas where communication can be problematic, and how you can fine-tune communication to improve it.

Active Listening

Active listening was first proposed by Carl Rogers[6] for use in psychother-apy. It was designed to help one party know that the other is listening (and to get the other party to listen carefully). Active listening is important in any negotiation, but especially in Collaborative negotiation. It becomes crucial when the emotional climate has escalated to the point where the negotiation is in danger.

Communication can become emotional as a result of a poorly sent message. If the receiver misinterprets the message, the problem can worsen. In addition, strong emotion can make it difficult for the party to accurately hear the message. So communication can get distorted at both the sending and receiving ends. The charged emotional climate will esca-late rapidly if communication is off target. Active listening can help avoid misinterpretations.

In active listening, you let the other party know that you heard what they said. You may repeat it back to them to be sure there is no misunder-standing. To reflect back what the sender has said, you might say some-thing like, "Let me make sure that I hear you correctly. I think you see the problem this way: . . ." or "It sounds like you are concerned about . . ." This reflection of the message does not necessarily mean that you agree with the other party, only that you listened to what they said and that you heard it. If you misunderstood the message, the other party gets a chance to say it again so that you can repeat it to their satisfaction. This assures that the message can be corrected before further misinterpretations accumulate.

Role Reversal

Another helpful tool for improving communication is *role reversal*. We mentioned this technique in Chapter 3, and we describe it in detail in Chapter 12. The objective in role reversal is to understand and argue the issues from the other party's point of view. Role reversal can give you insight into how the other party might look at an issue or problem. Another way this technique is used is in trying to get the other party to see your point: "If you look at it from my point of view . . ."

When you use role reversal, you usually assume you have something in common with the other party, and you are trying to find the area(s) of overlap in interests and goals. If there are no commonalties, then role reversal will highlight the differences between the two parties. If there are more differences than similarities, you will know that collaboration is probably not possible, but it is better to know this early in the negotiations. However, what often happens is that role reversal reveals similarities that the parties may not know were there, creating the foundation for an agreement.

Imaging

Another technique for improving communication is *imaging*. There are four steps to this process: (1) Each party writes down *how they would describe themselves;* (2) each party *describes the other party;* (3) each party *describes how the other party sees them;* (4) each party describes *how the other party looks at themselves.* The two parties then exchange this information, and analyze it to gain insight into their behavior.

The purpose of imaging is to discuss and correct the shared perceptions. This usually helps to identify important and less important conflicts in the situation. As emotions escalate, the original issues often get lost. Imaging can help:[7]

- Clarify and correct misconceptions and misinterpretations.
- Uncover needs, goals, and priorities to use in problem solving.
- Gain understanding of the other party's true needs.
- Set up a positive tone for problem solving and negotiation.
- Make the needs and concerns of each party heard without interruption.
- Reduce defensiveness.
- Improve listening.

Like many conflict resolution methods, it is a helpful way to defuse anger and share perspectives at the beginning of a negotiation process.

REDUCE THE NUMBER OF ISSUES

Another approach to reducing the tension between two parties is to manage the size of the conflict. To do this, you need to look at the size and number of issues on the table. As conflict increases, not only do the parties believe they are farther apart than they might be, but the number of issues at stake often increases. When frustrated, people tend to throw more and more issues onto the negotiating table.

There are several ways to reduce the size and number of issues.[8] These methods, which can be used alone or in combination, depending on your situation, include reducing the number of parties on each side, reducing the number of issues under discussion, restating the issues in concrete terms instead of as principles (moving from broad interests and principles to specifics), restricting the use of precedents and procedures (resolving only this conflict, rather than trying to deal with every conflict like it that might occur in the future), finding ways to fractionate or break down large issues into smaller ones, and depersonalizing issues (trying to "separate the people from the problem").

Reducing the Number of Parties

As the issues escalate, each side may bring in experts, authorities, lawyers, accountants, "witnesses," and others to prove their own points, back up their claims, and generally support their side's position. As the players increase, so do the number of perspectives and disagreements. Parties tend to band together with others on their side, polarize against others on the other side, and see each other in more negative terms. You will need more time for more people to speak, and more time for discussion of each issue.

If you can reduce the number of people on a side (preferably to only the principal person on each side), you will have a better chance for resolution. If you cannot reduce the number of actors to two, be sure that you establish ground rules, to minimize the escalation of time, perspectives, and other factors. You may need to be specific about who will speak and for how long, and so forth. We often see this in large formal negotiations, such as international diplomacy and labor strikes. While most of the "formal" negotiations take place with a number of people on each side of the table, ultimately, when dealings get sticky, the two key negotiators may go off by themselves and work out the framework for agreement.

Reducing the Number of Issues

When emotions escalate in negotiation, so do the issues. If there are too many issues in a negotiation, it may be difficult to keep track of everything, no less come to a conclusion. You may also encounter difficulties if there are too few issues because there will not be enough left over for trading off concessions so that each side can win.

You can reduce the number of issues by prioritizing them, as we discussed in Chapter 2. This will help you sort out which issues are the most important and which are the least. Low-priority issues may be eliminated or set aside for separate negotiation. If you need to increase the number of issues, you can define a particular issue more broadly, or add related issues to it. But work hard to make sure that only a few key issues are on the table at any one time.

Restating the Issues in Concrete Terms
Instead of as Principles

If an issue is based on a policy or a principle, it will be harder to change. For example, if the policy is that office hours are 8:00 A.M. to 5:00 P.M. and an employee wants to work 7:00 A.M. to 4:00 P.M., that issue will be hard to negotiate because it is based on a "policy." Issues need to be stated in concrete terms, separate from policies or principles. The ideal in this example would be for the individual to negotiate working hours without tying them to the policy. However, management does not want to negotiate hours with every employee individually (a matter of time and energy). In addition, if management prefers the status quo, the policy might be used as an excuse to limit negotiation. The trick is to find a way to separate this individual decision about this employee's hours from the broader policy, without everyone asking for the same exception. The focus might become the number of hours of work, which is eight in either situation (or nine, counting lunch).

Another approach is to examine whether the issue under consideration can be made into an exception to policy. In the example, it might be possible to negotiate 7:00 to 4:00 as an exception, or, as another alternative, the policy might be amended to say "to be decided at the discretion of the manager"—which would allow for exceptions.

Restricting the Use of Precedents and Procedures

If one party fears that settling a particular issue will create a precedent that will have to be followed in the future, you need to get the parties to focus on the issue rather than on the precedent. The party desiring the different hours in the example may argue that this does not necessarily set a precedent; it is only for this employee on certain days and does not have to carry over to other employees. The goal should be to remain focused on the issue of one employee wanting to work from 7:00 to 4:00, without considering *at this time* any others who might want the same privilege. Their requests would be negotiated separately. If other employees learn about it, however, and want the same thing applied to them, the situation can get out of hand.

Finding Ways to Break Down Large Issues

If the issues are large, break them down into smaller parts.[9] This is easier when the issues are based on quantitative amounts such as money, hours, and rates, since a given amount can get divided as well as one can "slice" or divide the issue, (e.g., to the nearest cent, second, percentage point). You also can use time for splitting issues into smaller pieces, for example, by defining *when* a solution will go into effect or *how long* it will last. For issues that appear indivisible, between parties that deal with each other frequently, sharing can mean that one party gets the desired result now, and the other party will get it later. Parents often resolve the classic fight among their children over which TV channel to watch by giving one child the choice for this hour, and another child the choice for the next hour.

Depersonalizing Issues

Because it is people who are negotiating, it is people who become entrenched in issues. They become attached to their ideas, often when they do not even want to. The problem is usually, "How do we withdraw from our position gracefully?"

Likewise, we tend to attach other people to their ideas: *He* wants to do that; *she* will not do so-and-so. Much of the popular literature on managing conflict stresses the importance of "separating the people from the problem."[10] The parties need to consider the issues without relating them to anyone. For example, avoid the idea that this is *his* problem, or that *she* suggested this option. It does not really matter whose problem it is; regardless of what the parties think of each other, it is the issue that needs to be solved.

MAKE OPTIONS MORE DESIRABLE
TO THE OTHER PARTY

If you understand the other party's needs, then you will be in a better position to convince the other party to opt for your solution,[11] especially if your offer takes into account the other side's needs.

Be sure that you make *offers* rather than demands or threats. People do not usually respond well to threats. In fact, they usually respond *in kind* to demands or threats, and the emotional climate escalates. The secret is to move toward them rather than away from them.

Sweeten your offer. We refer to this as "making the carrot more attractive, rather than using a bigger stick." Emphasize the attractive qualities of your offer and minimize the negative. Demonstrate how your offer meets their needs. Reduce the disadvantages of accepting your offer. Find ways to make your offer more credible. Set deadlines on your offer. In contrast, do not threaten the other side with "dire consequences" if they do not comply.

If the other party does not like part of your solution, refine your offer using the techniques discussed earlier: Make it more specific, split it into parts, rephrase it. Reformulate, repackage, reorganize. Offer a variety of options.

Some of these techniques may sound like sales techniques (e.g., sweetening the package, setting a deadline for your offer). Well, they are. Think of yourself as a salesperson who is concerned about the welfare of both parties, not just your own. You want to get the other side to "buy," and that's what a salesperson's job is all about!

FIND COMMONALTIES

We continue to assume that the Collaborative effort is the best possible approach to negotiation, and that parties will want to focus on their common objectives. There are four basic ways to look for commonalties: (1) Establish common goals, (2) focus on common enemies, (3) agree to follow a common procedure, and (4) establish a common framework for approaching the negotiating problem. We will consider each of these individually. You can use any or all of these in any combination—whatever works best in the situation.

Establish Common Goals

Sometimes, when emotions have escalated, we lose track of the original focus. Try to bring the parties back to the mission of finding common goals. Look for the objectives that the sides have in common. This is the basis of Collaborative negotiation. What can we plan in the future to do in common, share in common, own in common, value in common?

One caveat: Watch out for goals that appear to favor one party more than the other.

Focus on Common Enemies

Another approach to creating solidarity is for two parties to join forces against a third. The third party may be a competitor, or perhaps a party that will intervene in the conflict. For example, union and management may prefer to work together rather than have the government become involved in resolving the dispute. Nothing unites two children faster than one of their parents threatening to intervene in their argument! Parties can often become as cohesive in repelling a common enemy as in pursuing a common interest.

Agree to Follow a Common Procedure

Sometimes the conflict can be resolved by simply getting both sides to follow the same procedures in the negotiation. Often, this occurs as the parties develop basic ground rules for negotiation. This may include setting up some or all of the following:

- A formal agenda which the parties will agree to adhere to.

- A list of the people who will attend the negotiations.

- The time frame for the negotiation.

- Rules for speakers, including who is present and the length of time they may speak.

- The way issues will be introduced.

- What facts may or may not be introduced.

- How record keeping will be done.

- How the agreement will be accepted and implemented.

- What clerical or support services may be used.

Sometimes it is helpful to take a periodic "pulse" of the negotiation. Stop and ask how it is going, and how the parties are doing with the process of negotiation. If there are any problems, resolve them before continuing.

Establish a Common Framework for Approaching the Problem

Review what the parties have accomplished together so far. Have the two parties look for commonalties in their objectives, purposes, philosophy, viewpoint, long-term goals, interests, and styles. If the interests appear to be separate and unrelated, see if you can find a common thread that would link them in some way. Try to redefine the dispute to accommodate all the interests. This involves creating an "overarching framework" or "broad definition" or other vehicles that enable the parties to see the general situation the same way.

Change how the parties look at the problem. Have them consider how an ideal solution for both sides would look, and work from there.

Sometimes the conflict may be as simple as how an agreement is worded. If one side is not comfortable with the wording, see if you can change it so that everyone understands the meaning in the same way.

If the other party is dissatisfied with the suggested outcomes, you may be able to change the dimensions of the conflict so that one party wins on one point, the other wins on a second point, and everyone can gain something.

STRATEGIES FOR CHANGING FROM COMPETITION TO COLLABORATION

In their book *Getting to Yes,*[12] Roger Fisher, William Ury, and Bruce Patton discuss three situations in which you can potentially "turn around" a Competitive negotiation. The first strategy is when the other party is more powerful than you are, the second is when the other party will not play by the rules, and the third is when the other party is either being driven by "best price only," or is using dirty tricks. In each situation, you need to analyze the circumstances and decide what you need to do, and whether you will be able to turn things around.

If the Other Party Is More Powerful

The other party's power may come from greater resources, control over the possible outcomes, authority, or time on their side. Any of these factors alone may put you at a disadvantage, and several of them combined can be powerful deterrents to getting the other party to act collaboratively.

If the other party appears to have more power, you have several choices:

- You can try to be Accommodating and "soften the other party up" to the point where they may choose not to exercise that power. Sometimes this may work, but a more powerful other party who is prone to using a Competitive strategy can and will take advantage of this.
- You can try to Avoid the transaction. Make sure that you do not give anything away. Likewise, be sure to mask any of your own vulnerabilities if you can, for the other party will be looking for cracks in your defenses.
- Have a good Alternative. This can give you some power with which to balance the other party's power, because if they want to deal with you, they are going to have to offer you something better than your Alternative. Further, if you announce that you have a good Alternative, you may be able to force the other party to back off from the Competitive stance, especially if they do not have a good Alternative themselves.
- At best, you may be able to persuade the other to not use their power, and instead work together with you by pursuing Compromise or even Collaboration.

If You Hold the Power

If you have more power than the other party and you want to move toward Collaboration, then your goal should be either to *withhold your use of that power,* or to *balance* the power, either by sharing control, sharing resources, or focusing on common interests. If you have more power and the other party is aware of this, they will be likely to mistrust you unless they have some prior working relationship with you and know that you will not use (or abuse) your power. If they have any reason to mistrust you (if you don't know, ask them), they will probably believe you will take advantage of your power. As a result, you may have to symbolically "disarm" yourself in a way that unequivocally signals your desire to work with the other.

Be aware that if the other has read this book, they may be considering the choices we described earlier in this section. They may assume they cannot get a fair deal from you and are planning to exercise their Alternative. So, in addition to signaling that you are willing to work with them on an "equal" basis, you may have to offer a quick concession, or sketch out an outline of the type of agreement you hope to work toward. If you are unsuccessful in this effort, it is wise to cultivate your own Alternative, including other people with whom you can do business, because you may need to exercise it.

Finally, try to keep focused on your real interests. It is easy to lose track of them when you are concentrating on moving the negotiation in a different direction. Do not get sidetracked just because negotiation has become difficult.

If the Other Party Will Not Negotiate

There are two basic options for you to follow if the other party will not negotiate. The first, which you should try before going to the second, is to try to "get behind the lines." The second is to take the dispute to a third party. (We discuss this approach at length in Chapter 11.)

By getting behind the lines, we mean that you need to get underneath what is happening and try to understand the situation from the other party's point of view. Try to identify their interests. To do this, you need to ask open-ended questions. Use the technique of active listening, which is discussed in depth, along with the technique of role reversal, in Chapter 12. This can help you gain perspective on the other party's strategy and the reasoning behind it.

Try to find ways to recast the issues, perhaps by making them broader, so that they encompass the other party's concerns and underlying interests.

Create other options. When you open up the negotiations in this way, you may be able to find commonalties between the parties that will make it easier for everyone to pursue a Collaborative Strategy.

If the Other Party's Only Objective
Is the "Best Price"

If you are the seller and the other party seems intent on getting the best price to the exclusion of all other considerations, you are most likely dealing with a Competitive negotiator. There are a number of things you can do to deflect this strategy. While you may not end up with a totally Collaborative situation, the outcome has potential for being better than if you let the "price grinder"[13] run the negotiations:

- Ask for something in return—"If I concede on price, what can you do for me?"

- Look for interests other than money, such as esteem, winning, or saving face. You may be able to package these with your product to make it more attractive.

- If they say they can get it elsewhere for less (one type of alternative), point out the value or uniqueness of what you are offering.

- Offer a value-added package. There may be some things that go naturally with the product or service, such as wheel balancing with new tires, or installation with an appliance.

- Emphasize the personal relationship. If you have an ongoing relationship, you may be able to move the focus from prices per se (Competitive) to the idea of a good deal for everyone (Collaborative).

- Compare the situation to the other party's own business. Ask whether they could cut their own prices as they are asking you to do and still stay in business.

- Challenge them to adjust as you adjust (Compromise): "I will _____ if you will _____ ."

- Take a reality check. If all the person wants is a low price, is this really someone you want to be doing business with over the long term? Is bargaining worth it?

- Continue to sell value. If the product is always reliable, then they will return. If the negotiation is only about price and nothing else, you will likely always have a difficult negotiation with this party.

If the Other Party Is Engaging in Dirty Tricks

It is difficult to work with a party that insists on being Competitive when you are trying to be Collaborative. If they engage in dirty tricks, then it is even more challenging to be "nice." But if you want to turn the situation around, try to be as pleasant as you can. Put your private feelings about the people on hold while you work to find common ground. One approach is to reinforce the positive and ignore the negative. Acknowledge their good points, support them, compliment their sensitivity to your needs, and applaud their concessions.

However, if you feel that the other side is supplying false information, attempting to deceive or intimidate you, or applying inappropriate pressure, there are a few tactics you can pursue to try to turn the situation around:

Ignore the tricks. By this, we do not mean you should ignore the other party—just overlook the "dirty" behavior. This may be easy to say and hard to do, but sometimes if you ignore the behavior, it will subside. On the other hand, the other party may not get your subtle message, and may continue to engage in dirty tricks. In that case, step up your response tactics.

Identify the behavior. The next step is to point out the bothersome behavior. Do not personally attack the people doing it. Simply tell them where you have a problem with their behavior. This lets them know you are aware of what is going on. Tactfully tell them that you know what they are doing, and be firm in making it clear that the behavior is unacceptable. When you confront inappropriate behavior, try to be as nonthreatening as possible. Define the objectionable behavior in nonevaluative terms. List the tangible effects their actions are having on you and tell them how you feel about it.[14]

Negotiate how to negotiate. A third approach is to take time out to talk about how the negotiation is progressing, and to set ground rules. (Actually, this should be done before the start of negotiations, depending on how familiar you are with the other party.) Even if ground rules were set up at the outset, you may need to review them or augment them at this point.

Issue a warning. If the behavior continues, warn the other party that they are endangering the negotiation with this behavior. They need to understand that you will not put up with the behavior, and that everyone may lose a lot if the behavior continues and the negotiations break off.

We strongly recommend that you resist the urge to retaliate. Although it may be tempting to give them back some of their own "medicine," this is not a good idea. It usually only escalates the tactics, resulting in an increasingly Competitive response. You will have lost the opportunity for a Collaborative negotiation with positive outcomes and relationships for both sides.

WHAT TO DO WHEN THE OTHER PARTY IS BEING "DIFFICULT"

None of us has any trouble recognizing difficult behavior. We have all seen or experienced it at one time or another. Everyone has a bad day occasionally. But if you have to deal with someone whose behavior is consistently difficult, you need to find ways to cope with that person's behavior. For some, it is largely a matter of ignoring the behavior. For others, it is a bit more work.

There are many books and articles on the topic of dealing with difficult people.[15] The basic advice is to understand why the difficult behavior exists and why it persists. Most likely, the difficult person has used this behavior before and achieved the desired results, and so continues to use the same behavior. If we give in to someone's temper tantrums, the person will tend to behave the same way in the future. If we bribe someone to go along with our wishes, the person will come to expect a bribe any time he or she is asked to do something. Although coping with difficult behavior may be a challenge, once you understand the origin of the behavior, it may be somewhat easier.

If you encounter difficult behavior during negotiation, you may not know whether the person behaves in this manner all the time or not. And you may not have the time to fully assess the underpinnings of the behavior. Nevertheless, you can take steps to defuse the behavior. We will first discuss handling a difficult person in formal negotiation, then we will explain how to deal with a difficult person on an interpersonal basis.

The Five Steps

There are five basic steps to breaking through difficult behavior[16] and creating a favorable environment for negotiation:

1. You need to regain your own balance and control your own behavior.
2. You need to help the other party control their behavior.

171

3. Change the tone of the negotiation from Competitive to Collaborative (see specific techniques for this step in Chapter 9).
4. Help the other party overcome their skepticism so you can find a mutually agreeable solution.
5. Achieve closure, which is the ultimate objective in any negotiation (see Table 10.1).

Regain Your Balance and Control Their Behavior. Do not retaliate, although you may be tempted to. Try not to react or strike back. Do not give in, either. The best thing to do is "remove yourself" from the situation to get some distance. This may mean psychological withdrawal, or it may actually suggest physically getting up and leaving the scene for some period of time. If you have space to breathe and you can cool off, you will be in a better position to consider the situation in context.

If the Opponent...	What You're Tempted to Do...	What You Should Do...
Attacks!	Counterattack!	Back off!

Generally, do the opposite of what you are tempted to do. After you cool off, assess the situation calmly and realistically. Decide whether this is typical behavior for this person or whether it is just a bad day. Look at your own reaction. Is it appropriate or out of proportion to the other person's behavior? Figure out, if you can, what triggered the behavior. Was it something you did or said, or was it something else? Decide whether you can discuss the behavior openly with the other person or if you will just have to cope with it. If it is an individual personality conflict, read the forthcoming section "Managing Conflict with a Difficult Person."

Help the Other Party Regain Their Balance—Actively Listen. Disarm the other party by moving toward their side. To place yourself on their side, you will need to engage in active listening. Acknowledge the other party. Acknowledge points made by them without necessarily agreeing, unless you actually do agree. Look for points on which you do agree. Express your views in a calm, nonthreatening manner.

If the Opponent...	What You're Tempted to Do...	What You Should Do...
Insists on their position!	Rebut their position, assert your own position!	Actively listen!

Table 10.1 Techniques for Breaking Through
Difficult Behavior in an Opponent

If the Opponent . . .	What You're Tempted to Do . . .	What You Should Do . . .
Attacks!	Counterattack!	Back off!
Insists on their position!	Rebut their position, assert your own position!	Actively listen!
Gets Angry	Get angry yourself! Escalate!	Stay calm, ignore their emotion!
Says:	*You're tempted to respond:*	*What you should do:*
It's not my idea.	I don't care!	Involve them in the idea.
It doesn't meet my needs.	I don't care!	Make sure you understand their needs and find a way to make sure their needs are met.
I'll lose face.	No, you won't!	Empathize, try to understand, and help them save face.
It's too big an adjustment.	No, it's not!	Propose ways to make changes slowly, gradually, incrementally.

Summary: Make them an offer they can't refuse.

Change the Tone—Stay Calm. Be calm. Intentionally set a calm, placid tone, which is likely to be quite different from the intense, emotional, angry tone that probably existed. Instead of asking questions that may be interpreted as inflammatory, try to ask open-ended questions. Try using the reframing tactics discussed earlier. You may have to renegotiate the rules of the negotiation.

If the Opponent . . .	*What You're Tempted to Do . . .*	*What You Should Do . . .*
Gets angry	Get angry yourself; escalate.	Stay calm, ignore their emotion.

Overcome Skepticism. Make it easy for the other party to say yes to your offer. There are several things you can do if they are resisting. We discussed some of these techniques earlier in this chapter.

If the Opponent Says . . .	*What You're Tempted to Say . . .*	*What You Should Do . . .*
It's not my idea.	I don't care.	Involve them in the design.
It doesn't match my interests.	I don't care.	Make sure you under understand their interests and find a way to make sure their needs are met.
I'll lose face.	No, you won't.	Empathize. Try to understand, and help them save face.
It's too big an adjustment.	No it's not.	Propose ways to make changes slowly, gradually, incrementally.

Closure. The ideal is to "make them an offer they cannot refuse." However, they quite possibly will still refuse, so it is a good idea to strengthen your alternate or BATNA, and be ready to use it if you have to. Let them know the consequences of achieving no agreement. Sharpen their choices and focus on the advantages of the deal. When you achieve an agreement, make sure it is a lasting agreement by making plans for implementation.

Managing Conflict with a Difficult Person

To review the foregoing discussion, and bring conflict resolution to a more personal level, we will now look at how to resolve conflict in interpersonal communication. These techniques may be used between two individuals who are having communication difficulties during negotiation. They may be used by a manager trying to help two employees settle a conflict, or by two employees or friends trying to resolve an interpersonal dispute.

The main points in dealing with a difficult person are to recognize or identify the behavior, to understand it, and to find a way to cope with it, whether it involves confronting the behavior directly or learning to live with it in some way.[17] In interpersonal conflict, as in negotiation, cultural and ethnic differences and resulting underlying values and biases may be operative.

If you find yourself in a conflict situation, once you cool off but before you do anything else, you will need to decide whether it is worth trying to change the other person's behavior. Ask yourself how much work it will take, and whether a positive result is likely. Consider whether there are risks involved. You may have to accept that some people are unwilling to change. If that is the case in your situation, you will need to concentrate on the changes you can make, and the steps to take for coping with the behavior.

If you decide to try for changes, remember that successful conflict resolution depends on effective communication. This in turn depends on two factors: (1) acknowledging, appreciating, and productively using the differences in people, and (2) developing a personal strategy for dealing effectively with difficult people.[18] The following steps are suggested for conflict resolution:[19]

1. *Identify exactly the behavior that bothers you,* not the values that lie behind the behavior (people will throw up all kinds of resistance to changes in their values). Concentrate on the behavior, not the person.

2. *Confront the behavior* in as nonthreatening a way as possible. Keep focused on the behavior and try to avoid attacking the person. Phrase your statement in the following way: "When you do _____ , I feel _____ ." For example, you might say, "When you shout at me, I feel that you think I am incompetent" or "I feel embarrassed when you tell an off-color story in my presence."

3. *Be willing to hear what the other person has to say.* Use your listening skills (Chapter 12) to identify facts and feelings from the other

person. Keep the discussion as impersonal as possible. Let the other person "ventilate."

4. Resolve conflict by trying to *meet the needs of each party*. This is a mini-negotiation and should be collaborative.
5. *Implement the resolution.*

The keys to the process of successful conflict resolution are:

- Separate people from the problems; remember that the problem is the *relationship,* not the people themselves.
- Acknowledge and appreciate differences.
- Be flexible about the other person's viewpoint or work style.
- Accept that a different opinion or approach is simply different, not wrong; remember that there are differences in thinking styles.
- Avoid negative labels.
- Be flexible.
- Stay focused on outputs rather than positions.

FOUR BENEFITS OF SUCCESSFUL CONFLICT RESOLUTION[20]

With all we have said about the benefits of Collaborative negotiation, the reasons for managing conflict well should be fairly clear:

1. Behavior that is perceived as negative is confronted and resolved. This helps the parties move away from stereotyping or assigning negative attributes based on differences.
2. Parties can learn about other people's needs and viewpoints and better understand the reasons for their behavior.
3. Problem-solving skills can be improved and people can learn to find creative solutions.
4. All parties can benefit from improving their understanding of and friendship with others. This builds trust that will help in future encounters.

Chapter 11

When and How to Use Third-Party Help

It may be that you have tried some or all the techniques discussed in Chapter 10 to move the negotiating parties back on track, but the two sides are still stuck, unable to go anywhere. In that case, you should consider asking a third party to step in. A third party is someone who is not directly involved in your negotiation or dispute, but who can be helpful in resolving it. This impartial party may be a friend, in the case of a simple negotiation, or it may be a neutral person whom both parties know and invite to assist, or it might even be someone with professional credentials whose job it is to intervene in such cases.

A third party is likely to use some of the conflict resolution techniques discussed in the previous chapter, engaging you and the other party in activities designed to reduce tension, improve communication, change the options, adjust the number of players or issues, or help find common ground. With outside help, the disputing parties may be able to move back on track and bring the negotiation to conclusion and closure.

WHEN TO ASK A THIRD PARTY TO INTERVENE

In general, it is best to try everything you can to remedy the situation before you move to third-party intervention. Thus, you should employ the techniques suggested in Chapter 10 before seeking intervention. However, when conflict escalates in negotiation, the parties often become suspicious of each other's motives, intentions, and behavior. One of the parties may try to use the tactics in a "partisan" way, with a bias toward achieving

177

a specific outcome. Moreover, even when that party implements the practices in good faith, the other party doesn't see the efforts as genuine. Instead, he or she sees it as a ruse, a ploy, a tactic, or a way for the other to gain advantage. If the parties just cannot find a way to become "unstuck," then both parties should agree on the need for a third party. Although third parties can be very helpful, negotiators often resist using them because they feel they are decreasing the likelihood of achieving their preferred outcome.

Sometimes, a third-party intervention will be imposed by an outside group that has the power or authority to do so, and is anxious to resolve the matter. In an intrafamily dispute, when two children are fighting, a parent may intervene. In other cases, an intervention may be imposed by a constituency, or higher level authority, or it may result from a rule or legal procedure. For example, a number of warranties and contracts now specify that if there is a question as to liability or fault, the dispute will automatically go to an arbitrator or mediator.

When two negotiating parties invite the third party to intervene, then the intervention is usually friendly and progresses smoothly. If the intervention is imposed by an outside authority, then the relationship between the disputing parties and the third party may not necessarily be friendly, and the negotiating environment may become even more hostile.

REASONS TO USE A THIRD PARTY

You may want to consider using third-party help if:[1]

- The emotional level between the parties is high, with lots of anger and frustration.
- Communication between the parties is poor or has completely broken down, or the parties appear to be talking "past" each other.
- Stereotypic views of each other's position and motives are preventing resolution.
- Behavior is negative (e.g., there is intense anger or name-calling).
- The parties have serious disagreements about what information is necessary, available, or required.
- The parties disagree on the number, order, or combination of issues.
- Differences in interests appear to be irreconcilable.
- Values differ greatly, and the parties disagree about what is fundamentally right.

178

- There are no established procedures for resolving the conflict, or the procedures have not been followed.
- Negotiations have completely broken down and there is an impasse.

Many of these situations were discussed in Chapter 10, along with suggestions for resolution. Here, the difference is that the problems are ongoing; the parties are unable to resolve them and cannot enact effective procedures by themselves.

There can be several objectives in bringing in a third party to achieve a resolution. First, the parties want to resolve the dispute; they care about the *outcome* dimension. A second reason is to smooth, repair, or improve the *relationship* between the parties—to reduce the level of conflict and the resultant damages. Finally, third parties are often used simply to stop the dispute—to get the parties to separate and not fight any more, or to make sure that they have as little future interaction as possible (e.g., when the United Nations intervenes in conflicts around the world, its first objective is often to stop warring groups from fighting). Depending on which type of objective is most important—resolving the dispute, repairing the relationship, or separating the parties—different types of third parties with different skills may be needed. The type of third party selected will focus on some or all of these objectives, and it is important to know which ones are most important and in what order they should be pursued.

Each type of third party has advantages and disadvantages, depending on the situation. Which type you choose will depend not only on the situation, but also on what services are available, who specifically is available and, if applicable, what may be required by rules and regulations that govern the conflict and its resolution (e.g., laws, contracts, documents, precedents). After we discuss the types of interventions, we will look at how to select the appropriate one for your circumstances.

The term ADR is used in the literature and elsewhere in reference to third-party resolution of disputes. ADR stands for *A*lternative *D*ispute *R*esolution. ADR procedures are alternatives to taking the conflict into the court system, hiring an attorney, and pursuing litigation. Since the early 1980s, there has been a major social movement to take *civil* disputes (where there is no criminal violation of law) out of the courts and, instead, refer them to third parties. There are a number of reasons for this: The parties have more control over what happens, the process is often quicker and less costly, and it keeps the court system from becoming hopelessly overburdened, particularly when key issues of law are not in question.

There are many people who perform ADR services, including the more formal labor arbitrators, divorce mediators, community mediators, and process consultants. Dispute resolution is also performed informally by ombudspersons, fact finders and referees, ministers, social workers, teachers, managers, or even friends of the disputing parties. There are also quasi-substitutes for formal court proceedings, such as summary jury trials and minitrials, judicial reference, court-annexed arbitration, settlement conferences, tribunals, and judicial committees.

In this chapter, we will define and discuss the formal and informal processes of arbitration, mediation, and process consultation. We will discuss what these people do and how they work to resolve disputes. These methods are separate from the arena of actual litigation, which will not be discussed here, but which will be used as a point of comparison. For example, all the preceding processes are generally of shorter duration and less costly than a court trial.

ADVANTAGES AND DISADVANTAGES OF USING A THIRD PARTY

Some of the advantages of employing a third party to assist in resolving a dispute are:

- The parties gain time to cool off as they break their conflict and describe the problem to the third party.
- Communication can be improved because the third party slows the communication down, helps people be clear, and works to improve listening.
- Parties often have to determine which issues are really important, because the third party may ask for some prioritizing.
- The emotional climate can be improved, as the parties discharge anger and hostility and return to a level of civility and trust.
- The parties can take steps to mend the relationship, particularly if this work is facilitated by the third party.
- The time frame for resolving the dispute can be established or reestablished.
- The escalating costs of remaining in conflict can be controlled, particularly if continuing the dispute is costing people money or opportunity (paying fees for attorneys becomes very costly).
- By watching and participating in the process, parties can learn how the third party provides assistance and in the future may be able to resolve their disputes without this help.
- Actual resolutions to the dispute and closure may be achieved.

Disadvantages of ADR include:

- The parties potentially lose face when the third party is called in, since there may be an image that the parties are somehow incompetent or incapable of resolving their own fight (this is true when those who are judging the negotiators are others who can publicly criticize them or move to have them replaced).
- There is also a loss of control of the process or the outcome or both, depending on which type of third party is called in to help. Relative to what they think they could have achieved had they "held out longer" or "fought harder," parties may be forced to accept less than 100 percent of their preferred target.

In general, when you bring a third party into the negotiations, the two contending parties will have to give up control over one or both aspects of the negotiation: the *process* and the *outcome*. The process is how the negotiation is conducted, the outcome is the result of the negotiation. As we discuss each type of third-party intervention, we will point out what the parties gain or lose in terms of process and outcome. Figure 11.1 depicts types of third-party involvement.

In negotiation without a third party, the opposing parties maintain control over both process and outcome. If they move to mediation, they give up control of the process but maintain control of the outcome. If they move to arbitration, they give up control of the outcome but retain control

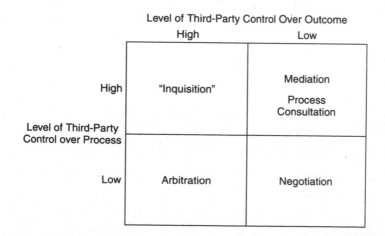

Figure 11.1 Different Types of Third-Party Involvement in Disputes

181

of the process. The fourth area in the diagram reflects a situation where the parties have control of neither process nor outcome—and no negotiation occurs. We now consider the major types of third party behavior individually.

ARBITRATION

Arbitration[2] is the most common form of third-party dispute resolution. When an arbitrator is called into a situation, the negotiators retain control of the process, but the arbitrator takes control of shaping and determining the outcome. Each party presents its position to the arbitrator, who then makes a ruling on either a single issue or on a package of issues.[3] This depends on the rules of the arbitration process, if any, and the request of the parties, if applicable. The arbitrator's ruling (decision) may be voluntary or binding, according to laws or a previous commitment of the parties.

The arbitrator can arrive at a recommended outcome in several ways. Usually, the arbitrator selects one side's position or the other's ("rules" in favor of one party or the other's preferred settlement). But sometimes, third parties may also offer an entirely different resolution. The arbitrator may suggest a "split" between the two parties' positions, in essence creating a Compromise between their positions. In formal proceedings that are governed by law and contract agreements, such as labor and management negotiations, there is usually a very clear and strict set of policies about how arbitration rulings are to be made.

Arbitration is used in business conflicts, disputes between business and union workers, labor relations, contracts (usually in the public sector), and grievances. In the case of grievances, the arbitrator is bound to decide how the grievance should be resolved, whether consistent with the labor-management contract or current labor law.

Advantages of Arbitration

The major advantages of arbitration are:

1. A clear solution is made available to the parties (though it may not be one or both parties' choice).

2. The solution may be mandated on them (they can't choose whether to follow it or not).

3. Arbitrators are usually selected because they are wise, fair, and impartial, and therefore the solution comes from a respected and credible source.

4. The costs of prolonging the dispute are avoided. It is interesting to note that arbitrators' decisions tend to be consistent with judgments received from courts.[4] In a sense, they are "judges without robes," and their decisions are usually governed by public law or contract law.

Disadvantages of Arbitration

There are some disadvantages to arbitration:[5]

1. The parties relinquish control over shaping the outcome; thus, the proposed solution may not be one that they prefer, or are even willing to live with.

2. The parties may not like the outcome, and it may impose additional costs, sacrifices, or burdens on them.

3. If the arbitration is voluntary (they have a choice whether to follow the recommended solution or not), they may lose face if they decide not to follow the arbitrator's recommendation.

4. There is a *decision-acceptance effect*—there is less commitment to an arbitrated resolution, for at least two reasons: They did not participate in the process of shaping the outcome, and the recommended settlement may be inferior to what they preferred. If parties are less committed to an outcome, they will be less likely to implement it. (As we will see when we discuss mediation, there is better commitment to a resolution and its implementation because the parties are fully involved in making the decision.) For example, when divorce proceedings go to arbitration—particularly regarding alimony or child custody issues—the party who "loses" is often uncommitted to the settlement, refuses to follow the mandate, and the parties wind up back in court.

5. Research on arbitration has often shown that it has a *chilling effect*.[6] During negotiation, the parties may behave differently if they expect that the dispute will have to go to arbitration. During the negotiation, they may hold back on compromises so they do not lose anything in arbitration, particularly when they anticipate that the arbitrator will "split the difference." In essence, you might get a better settlement if you refuse to make any concessions, because if the arbitrator splits the difference, you

can do better than if you made concessions and then the arbitrator split the difference. So negotiators may take a hard-line position. To avoid this, parties who expect to go to arbitration often use a method called "final offer arbitration." In this procedure, the arbitrator asks the parties to make their "best final offer," and then the arbitrator rules for one side or the other with no split. This in effect forces the parties to make the best deal they can during negotiation, which reduces the distance between them as they approach arbitration. The more extreme the final offer, the less likely the arbitrator may be to rule in favor of it.

6. In the *narcotic effect*,[7] parties with a history of recurring arbitration tend to lose interest in trying to negotiate, become passive, and grow very dependent on the third party for helping them move toward resolution. Their attitude is, "We're not going to be able to agree, and a settlement is going to be imposed anyway, so why should I work hard to try to negotiate?" Thus, parties become "addicted" to arbitration and take less responsibility for themselves and resolving their own conflict. Further, a party with a strong-willed constituency may be uncompromising and unyielding during negotiation, and then blame the arbitrator for any compromises that have to be made in arbitration.

7. In the *half-life effect*,[8] the results of more and more arbitration are less and less satisfaction with the outcomes. Because the parties have become passive in the process, and have less control over the outcomes as well, arbitration frequently becomes ritualistic and simply loses its effectiveness. Eventually, the parties refuse to participate, take their case elsewhere, or remove themselves completely.

8. In the *biasing effect*, the arbitrators may be perceived not to be neutral and impartial, but to be biased. This is most likely to occur when an arbitrator makes a whole sequence of decisions that favor one side over the other. Interestingly, parties in strong conflict often try to bias the third party, and then reject the third party for being biased. (Witness the harassment that referees and umpires receive in most sporting events!) This shows how insidious and problematic destructive conflict can become. If an arbitrator is seen as biased, the parties will move toward selecting another arbitrator who will be neutral, or preferably, will favor their position.

MEDIATION

Formal mediation[9] is based on established rules and procedures. The objective of the mediator is to help the parties negotiate more effectively. The mediator does not solve the problem or impose a solution. He or she helps the disputing parties to develop the solution themselves and then to agree to it.[10] Thus, the mediator takes control of the process, but not of the outcome.

A major concern for the mediator is to assist the parties in areas of communication. The intent is to improve the parties' skills so they will be able to negotiate more effectively. The assumption in mediation is twofold: First, the parties can and will come up with a better solution than one that is invented by a third party, and second, the relationship is an important one and the parties want to develop their ability to problem-solve about their conflict.

How Mediation Works[11]

There are a number of variations on the mediation process, but in general, it tends to follow a reasonably common process. First, the mediator needs to be selected. The mediator can be a member of a professional mediation center or service, or can be acting informally as a mediator while in some other capacity (minister, manager, social worker, teacher, counselor, etc.).

The mediator begins by taking an active role. Usually, the mediator invites both sides to attend a meeting. The mediator sets ground rules by which the mediation will occur:

- The parties agree to follow a procedure set forth by the mediator.
- The parties agree to listen to each other and follow some rules of civility and respect toward each other.
- The role of the mediator is not to solve the parties' dispute, but to work with the parties to achieve a "negotiated" outcome.

As actual mediation starts, the mediator then takes on a more passive role. He or she meets with each party, to listen to them and learn about the dispute. In most cases, the mediator does this with the other party in the room, so that each can hear how the other sees the dispute. However, if the parties cannot be candid in front of the other, or conflict is likely to erupt, the mediator may hold these meetings with each party separately. Through active listening and questions, the mediator tries to identify and understand the issues. The mediator looks for underlying interests, priorities, and concerns, and finds areas for potential Collaboration or Compromise.

In the next stage, the parties agree on the agenda—the key issues to be discussed, and the order for discussion. The mediator will help them prioritize and package their proposals and counterproposals as needed.

The mediator brings the parties together and encourages exploration of possible solutions, tradeoffs, or concessions. The activities in this stage are likely to be a combination of the mediator facilitating the collaborative negotiation process, and the tactics described in Chapter 10. They are designed to help communication flow more freely, reduce tension, and so forth. The mediator may invent proposals, or suggest possible solutions, but will not impose any of these on the parties.

The final stage is agreement, which may be made public with an announcement of the settlement. There may be a written agreement, and it may or may not be signed. Many mediators push for some form of a written agreement, to help the parties be clear about who is going to do what, and to enhance their commitment.

A long time may be involved in the mediation process, depending on the nature and degree of difficulty between the two parties. However, mediation is still less costly than going to court. The length of the stages may vary. For example, in divorce mediation, the preference is usually for both parties to begin meeting together as soon as possible, rather than having long individual meetings with the mediator. The objective is to move the parties toward communicating and working out their problems, but it will depend on the degree of cooperation of the parties and the skills of the mediator.

How Mediators Help

In addition to facilitating the negotiation process, mediators can help the parties save face when they need to make concessions. They can assist in resolving internal disagreements and help parties deal with their constituencies (e.g., by explaining the agreement to the constituency, or helping the negotiator save face with the constituency by portraying the negotiator as tough, fair, and effective). They may offer the parties incentives for agreement or concession, or offer negative incentives for noncooperation.

Mediators maintain control if the parties are unable to do so, largely by controlling the process (e.g., making sure the conflict between the parties does not escalate again, or that one side does not take undue advantage of the other). Mediators push when needed, and move into the background when the negotiators seem to be able to move forward themselves.

When Mediation Can Be Helpful

Mediation may be used in labor relations, or as a precursor to arbitration in grievance and contractual negotiations. It has also been used successfully in settling malpractice suits, tort cases, small claims, consumer complaints, liability claims, divorce,[12] civil and community disputes,[13] business disputes,[14] business and government cases involving the environment,[15] and international[16] disputes. It is increasingly being used in communities to resolve disputes between landlords and tenants or merchants and customers, and on college campuses to resolve conflicts in residence halls or between students of different genders, ethnic groups, and nationalities.

Most of these types of disputes are self-explanatory. What is interesting is to see the variety of ways that mediation can be taught and used. For example, children are being taught, as early as elementary school age, the art of mediation, and then taught how to use it to resolve conflicts in the classroom, on the playground, and in the home. While the techniques taught to children are probably not as sophisticated as they would be in a major international negotiation, the principles are exactly the same, and the dispute resolution skills children learn at an early age can carry over into their adult lives.

Factors Necessary for Success in Mediation

First, mediators *need to be seen by the disputants* as neutral, impartial, and unbiased. This is critical, because if mediators are seen by one or both disputants as "biased" toward one side or having a preferred outcome, then their actions will not be trusted. It is not enough for mediators themselves to believe they are neutral or can act in an unbiased manner—the acid test is that the *parties must see them as unbiased.*

Second, mediators may need to be expert in the field where the dispute occurs although mediation requires less expertise than arbitration. An arbitrator has to know the key laws or contract issues in the area, and usually has to make a decision that is consistent with previous rulings. In contrast, as long as a mediator is neutral and smart enough to understand the key issues and arguments of both sides, he or she can be effective. Sometimes, in fact, naive mediators have so little biases about the dispute in question that they may discover helpful approaches that experts in this area have become blind to. Expertise is especially important in industrial conflicts, where industry-specific knowledge may be important. In divorce mediation, a knowledge of marital law is helpful. (For an agreement to be legally binding, a lawyer probably has to write the document, but parties can achieve fundamental agreements in principle with almost any kind of a mediator.) It is also useful for the mediator to have experience in mediating similar disputes.

187

Although it is not required by law, certification of mediation training enhances the mediator's credibility. The Federal Mediation and Conciliation Service of the U.S. Department of Labor is one group that certifies mediators. There are also local mediation services and dispute settlement centers that "certify" mediators by having them participate in a mandatory training program, as well as an apprenticeship with an experienced mediator. Mediation centers can assist disputing parties in finding a mediator.

Successful mediation depends to a large degree on timing. Mediation cannot be used as a technique for dispute resolution if the parties do not agree that they need help, or are so angry and upset at each other that they cannot even civilly sit in the same room together. Mediation also depends on the willingness of the parties to make some concessions and find a compromise solution. If they are so committed to their point of view that no compromise is even possible—a problem we see in attempting to mediate value-based disputes around issues like abortion and environmental management—then mediation is doomed to fail. If the parties are not both willing to accept mediation, then it is unlikely that other techniques will work until the parties soften their views.

Success

Mediation tends to be successful in 60 percent to 80 percent of cases, according to statistics. Success of using mediation as an ADR technique is most likely when:[17]

- The conflict is moderate but not high.
- The conflict is not excessively emotional and polarized.
- There is high motivation by both parties to settle.
- The parties are committed to follow the process of mediation.
- Resources are not severely limited.
- The issues do not involve a basic conflict of values.
- The power is relatively equal between the parties.
- Mediation is seen as advantageous relative to going to arbitration (or no agreement).
- The bargainers have experience and understand the process of give-and-take, and the costs of no agreement.[18]

In successful mediation, negotiators tend to be committed to the agreement that is generated.[19] Thus the implementation rate is high.

Disadvantages

Mediation is not effective or is more difficult to use when:

- The bargainers are inexperienced and assume that if they simply take a hard line, the other party will eventually give in.
- There are many issues, and the parties cannot agree on priorities.
- The parties are strongly committed to their positions (and are held to them by an uncompromising constituency).
- There is very strong emotion, passion, and intensity to the conflict.
- A party has an internal conflict, and isn't sure what to do.
- The parties differ on major social values.
- The parties differ greatly on their expectations for what is a fair and reasonable settlement.
- The parties' resistance points do not overlap—the most one party will give is still much less than the minimum the other will accept.

Mediation can be more time consuming than arbitration. The parties have to take a lot of time explaining the dispute to the third party, and then participating in the process of searching for a resolution. Also, because mediation is not binding, there is no impetus for the parties to commit to the settlement or even to settle at all. Thus, there is always the potential for the dispute to reappear and continue—perhaps even for a long time. And it is always possible that the dispute will escalate.

Combining Mediation and Arbitration

Some who monitor third-party interventions have suggested that even better than mediation, in some cases, may be requiring a sequence of dispute resolution events, such as mediation followed by arbitration. This sequence seems to minimize the liabilities of each type of ADR (arbitration and mediation) and to obtain better compromises.[20] If the parties expect that they will have to progress to arbitration, they may be more willing to modify their positions in mediation to improve their chances of a ruling in favor of their side. On the other hand, the expectation of arbitration may make the parties "lazy" in mediation, particularly if they think the arbitrator will ultimately rule in their favor.

Assisting the Mediator

Mediators succeed when both parties are agreeable to the mediation. Further, there are ways you can help the process.

You can help a mediator to help you negotiate by being cooperative with them and giving clear information. Tell them what is important to you, and why you want it. If you do not understand something, speak up. Express your concerns if necessary. Remember that the mediator is there to assist in the negotiation process, not to remake it. Finally, be willing to make concessions or problem-solve. The objective of mediation is to move the dispute from a Competitive solution to a Compromise or Collaborative solution, and this requires the work of all parties. Ultimately, the success of the negotiation is your responsibility. You and the other party need to find, select, and implement a workable outcome. The mediator will assist you in this endeavor, but will not do the work for you.

PROCESS CONSULTATION

Another way of getting help with a stalled negotiation is to use a process consultant. Process consultants serve as counselors who focus on the *process* of negotiation, as their title would suggest. They assist parties in improving communication, reducing the emotionality of the proceedings, and increasing the parties' dispute resolution skills. Their objective is to enable parties to solve their own disputes in the future. Process consultants are thus useful if the relationship between the opposing parties is a long-term one.

A process consultant is somewhat like a mediator in that he or she helps with the steps in the process. But this person differs from the mediator in that there is no discussion of the specific issues or any attempt to solve them. Thus, process consultants are often more like counselors who help the parties to get along better so that they can engage in better negotiation and problem-solving.

The Process

Process consultants (PCs) first interview the parties individually. Then they design a schedule of structured meetings for the parties. At these meetings, the PCs have the disputing parties discuss their past conflicts and perceptions of each other. The PCs remain neutral, guiding the parties as needed. They keep people on track, keep the emotional level from escalating, and move the parties toward problem-solving behavior. Their objective is to change the conflict management climate, improve communication, promote constructive dialogue, and create the capacity for people to act as "their own third party."

PCs have expertise in the areas of conflict and emotions. They provide emotional support to their clients. They confront and diagnose problems while remaining neutral and unbiased. They must also be authoritative to keep the process moving. They control and manage the agenda of how the parties engage each other, but not what actually happens.

Process consultation is used in marital therapy, family therapy, organizational development, and team building. It is also used in labor-management disputes and in international conflict where there are ethical, political, and cultural difficulties to contend with.

Process consultation is less likely to work in the following circumstances:

- There are severe, polarized disputes over large issues.
- The relationship is short-term and the parties have no stake in improving it.
- The issues are fixed (Competitive rather than Collaborative negotiation).
- The party's constituency is not supportive of improving the relationship.
- One or both parties are intent on revenge or retribution.

OTHER, LESS FORMAL METHODS OF DISPUTE RESOLUTION

"Ombuds" and Others

Ombudspersons, fact finders, and referees are employed by various organizations to deal with matters before they turn into disputes. In many cases, their job is to hear and investigate conflicts between employees, or between an individual employee and "the system" (the rules, practices, and policies of the organization). At NCR,[21] as at other companies, ombuds are trained in problem-solving, dispute avoidance, negotiation, and dispute resolution.

Their mission is to limit and resolve problems quickly and informally. They usually are not part of the chain of command in an organization and may report directly to the CEO rather than to a specific department. They often have links with the legal and human resources departments, so they can discuss trends in compliance or legal issues. But it is essential for ombuds to be impartial, and hence they are often unattached to the organizational hierarchy.

When an employee takes a problem to an ombud or the equivalent, the ombud engages in confidential fact-finding, then informs both sides of their rights and the opportunities for resolving the conflict. The ombud may use a combination of counseling, conciliation, negotiation, and mediation. If the complaint involves corporate policy, salary, promotion, tenure, discharge, liability, discriminatory treatment, or the like, the ombud may recommend a settlement, but usually management is involved in the final decision.

The main reason for using an ombuds person is to make sure the process is fair and that the individual employees, with very little power, have a way to get a fair investigation and hearing about their concerns. If you are negotiating within a system or organization, an ombud can make sure you know the channels that are available to you, your rights, and what kind of outside help you may need. Ombuds can often act as "change agents," pushing an organization to change its rules and policies to deal with unfair treatment practices.

Advantages and Disadvantages of Ombuds

Using an ombuds or other type of counselor can be to your advantage, if the power between the two disputing parties is out of balance. This is particularly true when a lower-level employee tries to challenge his or her employer and doesn't want to get fired simply for asking questions or raising concerns about "fairness" and "rights." As with other third-party practices, however, the final outcome may not be what you hoped for.

Some organizations specify a formal process for expressing and hearing problems and disputes in this system. They may require a staged approach, where the first step is an ombuds, the next is mediation, and the final step is arbitration.

MANAGERS AS THIRD PARTIES

Finally, we turn to managers, supervisors, and others whose jobs do not consist primarily of mediating disputes, but who nevertheless often must intervene to get work done or deal with unproductive conflicts in the workplace. It is estimated that managers spend 20 percent of their time in conflict management.[22] Their methods tend to be informal since most work environments do not have established rules or guidelines for how to mediate a dispute. Few managers have any formal training in settling disputes, and many are uncomfortable with conflict. But they need to know that some conflict is all right[23] and to seek assistance themselves if they often find themselves refereeing employee disputes.

Styles

Managers tend to solve disputes along the lines we discussed for other types of interventions—high or low process control, high or low outcome control.[24] The style used will depend on the manager's tolerance for conflict, the time frame, and, to some degree, the personalities of the parties involved.

High Control of Both Process and Outcome. If a manager wants to maintain control of both the process and the outcome (which is the most typical scenario), the manager's style will be inquisitorial or autocratic. The manager behaves more like a judge in a European court, or like the infamous judge on the TV show, "The People's Court." The manager runs his or her own investigation, and then makes a decision. The manager will listen to both parties' stories, structure the process as he or she pleases, asking questions to learn more information, then will decide on the solution. This method tends to be the most common among managers. It is frequently used when the issues are minor, quick decisions are needed, or management needs to implement an unpopular action.[25]

High Outcome Control, Low Process. A manager who wants to retain high control of the outcome, but low control of the process, will use passive listening and then will make a decision. This is most like the arbitration style described earlier. This is somewhat like the "High-High" method, except that the manager listens to both sides; he or she makes little effort to gather more information, ask questions, or structure the process other than to render a decision after hearing the arguments.

High Process Control, Low Outcome Control. This approach is most like Mediation. More managers are learning to use this approach, although not as much as would be hoped. In many disputes, the manager considers the outcome more important than the process, and wants to have some control over it, so this method is used less than it might be.

Low Process and Outcome Control. If the manager does not care about controlling either process or outcome, he or she will either ignore the dispute and let the parties deal with it by themselves, or tell the disputing employees, "You solve the problem yourselves, or I will impose a solution that probably neither of you will like." This may sound like a parent acting as intervenor between two arguing children.

Factors Affecting the Choice of Method

The choice of dispute resolution method will often be based on the time frame. Because outcome-control methods are believed to be quicker by the third party (hence, often ignoring a lot of the "disadvantages" of arbitration and outcome control), high outcome control methods are used when efficiency and saving time are high priorities. Other factors that affect the choice of resolution method are:

- The objectivity (neutrality) of the manager.
- The relationship of the parties (long-term or short-term).
- The effect of how this confrontation is resolved on future negotiations.
- The expected ability of the parties to resolve conflicts for themselves in the future.
- The extent of training of the manager in conflict resolution techniques.

Keys for Managers Helping Employees with Conflict

- Select a neutral site for the meeting.
- Be empathetic; listen as well as you can, and practice listening skills.
- Be assertive, particularly about setting guidelines for how the parties should deal with each other in a more productive manner.
- Ask for cooperation and be cooperative yourself.
- Ask what the parties want you to do to help solve the problem.
- When there is a resolution, if appropriate, get it in writing.
- Help the parties plan for implementation. And do not forget follow-up.

ADR'S USEFULNESS

Since 95 percent of all civil cases are settled out of court, there is room in the area of dispute resolution for ADR.[26] Alternative methods of dispute resolution can save time and money, reduce the number of cases on court dockets, and provide timely solutions to problems. In fact, about one half of state court systems now require that certain civil complaints be referred to arbitration prior to trial. Thirty-three jurisdictions require that family disputes regarding custody and visitation be brought into mediation.[27]

At the federal level, the U.S. district courts increasingly order civil cases into mandatory arbitration or refer parties to moderated settlement conferences, minitrials, and summary jury trials. The U.S. Court of Appeals for the District of Columbia and the U.S. Court of Claims are also experimenting with mediation programs.

As an example of costs, a commercial suit with a $200,000 claim will cost parties almost that much in legal fees, discovery costs, and actual trial costs. Mediation for this situation would cost about $2,500, usually shared between the two parties. So it makes sense to use third-party intervention before taking a case to court. And, as stated previously, mediation has a good track record—70 to 80 percent of all cases are successfully mediated.

Many employers now include in contracts, employment agreements, and other related documents an ADR clause that defines the dispute resolution process. It may specify:[28]

- The rules or laws that apply to the process.
- The ADR methods to use and in what order to apply them.
- The location for the ADR procedure.
- The official language of the ADR process.
- Whether the outcome will be binding.
- How the costs will be allocated among the parties.

In fact, at NCR, ADR is specified as the first, preferred method for dispute settlement.

However, ADR is not always the perfect solution. As an example, in the case of a rate-setting dispute with the Public Utilities Commission of Ohio (PUCO),[29] ADR appeared not to work well for this regulated utility, and was not a viable solution. There were several reasons. First, the intervention was not voluntary, so there was lower commitment to the process. Time constraints for public utilities prohibited the long periods of consideration that tend to be required in mediated situations. Resources were strained because the utility had to prepare for court at the same time as pursuing ADR, in case ADR failed. Statutory requirements added further constraints and costs. Utilities in dispute need to have mediators who are fully aware of industry-specific details (especially in the area of regulation) in order to be effective, and this was not true in this case.

How Some Organizations Solve Disputes

Many organizations follow a "line authority" approach to solving problems: First you go to a supervisor, then to a division supervisor, then to a panel of supervisors, and finally, to top management. If one of the parties is a union, the fourth step is binding arbitration. But there are other, more effective, more proactive ways to solve problems.

One such plan is PGR—peer group resolution[30]—which is used by Northern States Power Company. The purpose of the process is to investigate, review, and resolve disputes; employee peer groups serve on the panel and execute the process. The PGR steps are very specific:

Step 1. The employee with a complaint completes a PGR form and submits a copy of it to the Human Resources department within 10 days of the incident. The employee gives the original form to the immediate supervisor, who completes a meeting with the employee within three working days. The supervisor writes a response to the problem on the form, and returns it to the employee within two working days. The employee then has two days to decide whether the response satisfies the complaint, or whether to progress to Step 2.

Step 2. The employee's second-level supervisor schedules and completes a meeting with the employee within three working days of receiving the form. This person writes a response on the form, and returns it to the employee within two working days of meeting with the employee. The employee has two working days after receiving the written response to complete the appropriate section of the form, either indicating satisfaction with the response and sending it to Human Resources, or going to Step 3.

Step 3. In this step, the employee can select from one of two options listed on the PGR form: Meet either with a third-level supervisor, or with a peer group panel. The supervisor meeting process is similar to that in Step 2. If the employee selects the peer group panel, the Human Resources department coordinates the random selection of panel members and schedules a panel review. The peer group panel consists of five employees, randomly chosen from two panelist pools. If the employee is nonsupervisory, then five panelists are selected from the nonsupervisory pool and four panelists from the supervisory pool. If the employee is supervisory, five panelists come from the supervisory pool, and four from the nonsupervisory pool. In both cases, the employee chooses two names from each pool to discard, resulting in a total of five panelists.

Within 10 working days of the employee choosing the final option, the panel meets with the employee and reviews the documentation and facts. The panel reaches a decision by majority vote to grant, modify, or deny the remedy requested by the employee. The panelists sign the form, adding explanations as appropriate. Human Resources distributes copies of the decision to the employee and supervisors. The decision reached in this manner is binding and cannot be appealed. All materials are kept confidential.

The program is successful in part because all who volunteer to be panelists receive a full day of training for this role. They practice reviewing sample cases using the role-play process.

The results of peer group resolution at Northern States Power Company have been rewarding. Many disputes have been resolved before they get to Step 3. Accountability of management has improved. Communication and problem-solving skills have improved. Concerns can be voiced and dealt with before they become major problems or disputes. The process allows all parties to deal with conflict in an organized manner. Productivity and morale are higher, because employees feel they can be heard. They also learn, as panelists, to better appreciate what goes into management decisions, and participate in a process of resolving disputes.

The company requires everyone to complete an evaluation form to assess the process, and this has provided positive feedback. In addition, each party with a grievance must be interviewed three months after settlement, to ensure that there is no retaliation.

Finding Third-Party Help

There are many organizations for mediators, arbitrators, and other third-party professionals. Among them are the Federal Mediation and Conciliation Service and the American Arbitration Association. There are private organizations which provide professional services, such as Endispute. There are also local mediation services in many communities, as well as consumer protection services available through district attorney's offices. In most communities, you can simply look up "Mediation Services" in your classified telephone directory, and find a list of individuals and organizations providing services.

If you are interviewing a potential candidate for third-party help, you may want to find out about availability, interests, and potential conflicts. Select someone who has a knowledge of the subject area that is the center of your dispute. Do not use a person who is likely to be partisan.[31]

Chapter 12

Communication Skills

You say what you want, I say what I want, and we go back and forth until we find a way to resolve our differences. Is that all there is to negotiation? It would be if all parties could communicate effectively and efficiently. Actually, it is a little more complicated than that.

When negotiations break down, the major reason is usually communication. After all, what is negotiation but communication? In fact, if you keep that point in mind, you can avoid many communication problems and manage the negotiation process far more effectively than most negotiators. The strategic negotiator understands the deceptively simple principle that negotiation is communication, and therefore knows to ask, "Do we have a *negotiation* problem, or is this just a *communication* problem?"

In this chapter, we take a close look at communication—not only how it occurs, but also how we can improve our messages to others, and how we can help others to better communicate with us. We then look at the stages of negotiation and at how communication affects both the process and progress of negotiation through the various steps.

WHAT IS COMMUNICATION?

Most of us tend to think of communication as a two-step process. But on closer observation, we discover that there is more to it than that. A message from you to someone else is not simply *what you say*. Behind the words is *what you mean*. When the other person receives your message, that is not the end of it either. Behind the message that is received is what the person *thinks* you have said. So there are really four parts to even the simplest communication.

WHAT YOU SAY →

    WHAT YOU MEAN→

        WHAT OTHER PERSON HEARS→

            WHAT OTHER PERSON THINKS YOU SAID

Expanding this picture, we need to consider the *method* by which the message is conveyed: Is it written on paper, spoken over the phone, sent via fax, transmitted by telegram, left on an answering machine, or sent by a third party? The vehicle by which the message is sent adds to or detracts from its meaning. This includes messages given in person, where the body language of the sender adds to (or detracts from and confuses) the message.

A message delivered in person generally has an advantage over one sent by some other medium, such as the telephone. If you have a bad phone connection, the message may be garbled. Written communication may also be interpreted incorrectly because of the method by which it is sent. For example, a fax machine may not print clearly, or transmission may be interrupted so that only part of the message is received. Someone may not be able to read your handwriting. Or the sender may inadvertently make the message harder to understand because of his or her choice of words. For example, in trying to keep a telegram or memo short, you may omit important information.

How you create your message, including your choice of words, your tone, the body language you use (if in person), adds positively or negatively to the meaning of the communication. If you do not speak clearly, the message may be unclear. The other person will translate your message through a particular understanding of your words, your tone, and your body language. To add to the complexity of communication, the receiver may have hearing difficulties, or language difficulties, or be affected by distractions such as noise, demands on his or her time, and so forth. So even if you attempt to frame and organize the message very carefully, it may not get through to the receiver in the way that you intended.

Considering all this, it is amazing that communication even occurs! But somehow we send and receive messages regularly, we communicate with one another and we often achieve deep levels of meaning and understanding.

One of us was recently ordering a pizza "to go" from our favorite pizza parlor. The man who answered the phone was familiar with our unusual taste in pizza. (What was really happening in the background of the conversation is shown in parentheses.)

Caller: I would like to order a small pizza with peppers and pepperoni. (The caller thought he had said "jalapeno peppers and pepperoni.")

Pizza man: No jalapenos. (Knowing the caller's preferences well, he was really asking, "Don't you want jalapenos?")

Caller: No jalapenos? Oh no! (The caller thought no jalapenos were available and that we would have to decide on different toppings.)

Pizza man: No, no, no! I have jalapenos! Do you want them?

A simple inflection, where the question mark at the end of the sentence was not understood, made it seem that there were no jalapenos rather than that the caller had unwittingly omitted them from the order.

Feedback

One way we check on the "success" of sending a message is through feedback. In the preceding example, it took several rounds of give-and-take (what did you say, what did you mean) before the caller and the pizza man established that there were, indeed, jalapenos available and the order should include them.

In feedback, the other person, the receiver, may say something like, "Let me see if I understand this correctly. You want me to do _____ on _____ ." The sender now has an opportunity to fine-tune the message to be sure that it is clear. When there is no opportunity for feedback, it is even more important that the original message be as clear as you can make it. As pointed out several times in the preceding chapters, feedback is important in maintaining effective communication in negotiation.

FACTORS THAT AFFECT THE SUCCESS OF COMMUNICATION

In this section, we will review a number of factors that affect the success of communication in negotiation.

Structure of the Message

The *structure* of your message can affect the outcome and influence the other party. Your message generally has a beginning, middle, and end.

Which is the best way to arrange the words for the most impact? Most research says that you should *not* put the important point in the middle.[1] Put it either at the beginning or at the end. If the important information is interesting, put it first, so that it will be remembered. If it is uninteresting or if it conveys bad news, put it at the end. If you are unsure whether the information is good news or bad news, you can put it at both beginning and end.

When you are presenting an *argument,* it is usually more effective to present *both sides,* not just the preferred point of view. The advantage to presenting both sides is that you can demonstrate why the other point of view is weaker.[2] In this case, place the preferred argument last, as a summation.[3]

If you have a complex message to send, break it into smaller, more understandable pieces.[4]

Use repetition to emphasize your point, but be careful not to overdo it.

If you are presenting several points, and you want to draw a conclusion, leave the concluding part open-ended for a sophisticated audience, but draw conclusions for audiences that are strongly opposed to your point of view or are inexperienced in drawing conclusions.[5]

Delivery Style

Your *delivery style*—how you couch your message—can have a positive or negative effect on its acceptance. In some cases, an aggressive approach may work, as for example, if the other party is expected to be belligerent. However, a solicitous or accommodating stance is usually more effective in lowering the defenses of the other party and paving the way for successful communication.

The following points may help you select your method of delivery:

1. *Participation* increases learning. Involve people in the process, physically and intellectually, and they will learn more and respond better.

2. *Metaphors*[6] can help you deliver a message, but be careful not to use them too much. Symbolic words or expressions help the receiver picture what you are saying. But metaphors can pose a problem in cross-cultural communication. For example, there is a story about a soft drink ad that stated, "Come alive, you're in the Pepsi generation!" In Asia, this catchy invitation translated to something like "It brings back your dead relatives."

3. *Arousing fears or making threats.* Playing on people's fears or making threats can frequently get them to respond. However, even if you have

a good sense of the other party from your research, you cannot always be sure how they will respond to a threat. In addition, when you make a threat, you must be ready to follow through on it. What may happen is that the party will respond to the threat, but not be committed to the action. If you offer a fear-arousing message, you should add to it something that "softens the blow"—an alternative action that will reduce or eliminate the object of fear.[7]

4. *Distractions*.[8] Try to offset the tendency of people to start planning their replies while you are speaking. One way to distract the other party is to hand out materials related to the presentation while you are talking. This will draw their attention to the content of your message. The drawback is that you might not have their full attention as you continue talking.

5. *Language intensity*. Research has shown that low-intensity language appears to be more effective[9] than strong language.

6. *Violating expectations*. People usually have expectations about what you say and how you say it. Therefore, you may have more success in communicating if the delivery is not what they expected, or if the content differs from their expectations. Experienced speakers know how to keep listeners attentive by varying the intensity of what they say. A simple example is changing the volume—first speaking softly, then working up to a crescendo, or vice versa. Pounding the table or podium is also an attention-getter, if used sparingly.

Vocabulary and Language

The *words* you use can affect the outcome of the exchange between you and the other person. Thus, the adjectives you use to describe something may be positive or negative in connotation. For example, compare "constructive," "fruitful," "successful," or "useful" negotiations with "serious," "pathetic," "incomplete," or "worthless."

Using *personal* words to convey a message can involve people more than impersonal language. The extent to which you use personal words depends on your objectives. For example, the message, "It is expected that employees will attend a meeting at 3:00 P.M. on Thursday" is impersonal. It may be seen as dictatorial or at least distancing. (It may be intended to be formal.) The active way to say this would be "You are invited to a meeting of all employees on Thursday at 3:00 P.M." or "Please come to a meeting . . ." In either of these latter cases there is more personal feeling, but it is not clear that attendance is required.

The *intensity* of the communication can affect the response. For example, although profanity in some cases may spur some audiences to action, it may totally repel others. Similarly, strong compelling words may produce an unexpected response—some listeners are swayed by them, others are put off by them.

The extent of the speaker's vocabulary may impress some receivers, while it may repel others because it stresses their differences in backgrounds or education. The style of the words may demonstrate either a deference to the other party or a desire to dominate.

The foregoing examples illustrate that what you say and how you say it[10] can affect the outcome of the communication. So it is important to know the intent of your message. Are you trying to tell the receiver what to do, to recommend something, to suggest, or are you sending a message that you are willing to negotiate? Another possibility is that you do not care at all. You need to choose your words carefully so that you convey to the other party exactly what you mean to say. Differences in receivers will affect how they hear your message—all the more reason for the other party to help by giving you feedback.

A word of caution about vocabulary. Be careful with idiomatic expressions, especially in communicating with people of different cultural backgrounds. An expression may be perfectly clear to you, but someone else may interpret it differently. In international negotiations especially, nuances in the language can be lost during translation (see Chapter 15). This generally means it is better to avoid colloquial language. There are often wonderful examples of phrases and colloquialisms that do not translate well across language differences, as in the example of the soft drink ad mentioned earlier. Instances such as this in negotiation can damage effective communication and may be harmful to a relationship.

To carry the idea of meaning one step further, remember that what you mean by a particular word may be a shade different in meaning from what the other person thinks it means. For example, if I say, "No, I do not want to see the movie you suggested," does that mean I do not want to see that particular movie, or that I do not want to go to the movies at all, or that I don't want to see it just because you liked it? Perhaps I prefer to go dancing. Or maybe I want to stay home. Again, feedback can help clarify the content and meaning of the communication.

Body Language

The actual message and the body language that goes with it frequently provide the receiver with conflicting messages. It is important to be aware of this so you do not confuse the receiver of your message. For example, if you ask someone a question but then turn your eyes away or "tune out" while the person is answering, should the person believe you are interested in the answer or not?

Gestures such as snapping fingers, holding thumbs up or down, extending palms up, holding hands up with the palms facing the person, usually have specific meanings that English-speaking people understand. And while people from various regions of the United States may understand them, it may well be that people from other countries may not. So it is important to be careful about the gestures you use.

Impressions

A number of personal factors or characteristics will affect how the receiver of your message is likely to respond personally to you as the sender. In this section, we concentrate on visible impressions because negotiation is usually done in person.

First impressions count for a lot, and they usually endure. Although we do not like to admit it, we do form impressions of people at the first meeting. If the person seems "pushy," we tend to be put off by such behavior. If the person appears spontaneous and relaxed, we usually respond accordingly. A person who seems warm and friendly is very different from a person who appears cold and distant. What is interesting is that this first impression tends to endure. Thus, even if the sender changes behavior, the receiver frequently responds as if the sender were still behaving in the original manner—the first behavior was the "true" behavior, and the current behavior is somehow less true. Thus, it is an advantage in negotiation to make a favorable first impression. And, if your first impression of the other party is favorable, you will usually continue to see that person in a good light even if his or her tactics change. Be alert for differences in behavior and language. They may signal a significant shift in strategy.

When there are disparities, the receiver is less likely to believe the message. Often the receiver can tell if the sender is feigning behavior. It is better to be yourself[11] than to pretend to be someone that you are not.

Dress or clothing makes an impression on the receiver of a message. If you are well-dressed and neat, the receiver is more likely to take you seriously than if you appear in torn jeans and sneakers. This is not to say that a casually dressed person does not have a valid message, only that people tend to filter their reactions to others on the basis of their appearance.

Personal attractiveness also helps the sender of a message. If people like you, they are likely to respond well to you. If they perceive similarities between themselves and you, they are more likely to look for other commonalities. This will be particularly helpful in Collaborative negotiating situations. The wise collaborative negotiator will look for the similarities between the two parties, and deemphasize the differences.

You can emphasize positive qualities in the other party by complimenting them. Compliments, given and received, if sincere and accurate, will add to a pleasant collaborative atmosphere.

The *credibility* of the sender may be intertwined with the sender's attractiveness.[12] Credibility affects believability, trustworthiness, the ability to respect and accept what the other says. Someone with a charismatic personality may thus engender credibility without even demonstrating that he or she is trustworthy or possesses key qualifications. This "plus" occurs almost without having to work for it. This "halo effect," where the other person responds favorably to you because of your personal attractiveness, can be used to advantage in negotiation.

To expand the positive image, the sender of a message can offer to help the other party in negotiation by doing a favor for them, such as agreeing to extend the time limit, or making a concession. Another possibility is to offer to talk with the other party's constituency, to assist in smoothing the way to a conclusion and helping the negotiator look good. Taking advantage of these positive characteristics is associated with the Collaborative strategy more than with the Competitive, although it may be used in a manipulative fashion by the Competitive strategist. Just remember that behavior done under false pretenses is usually discovered.

Other Personal Characteristics

Reputation for honesty is important in evaluating the sender and therefore, the message. Since people generally approach strangers with a positive attitude rather than a negative one,[13] they start out, at least, assuming the best about a person. If you can add to the positive image by telling the truth, being candid and straightforward, and referring to people who can vouch for you, then the other party is even more likely to accept your message.

Likewise, having *associates* can be helpful to the sender of a message, if the associates are known to the other party. You can quietly drop their names or mention references. If necessary, you can arrange for introductions.

Perceived differences in *status* can also affect the success of sending a message. If the sender is prestigious or has a strong or positive image, the message may have a stronger effect. Then again, if the receiver feels that the sender is in a position of much higher status, it may have a detrimental effect on the situation—they may discount the message because of who it came from.

Experience and expertise of the sender are important when a receiver is evaluating a message. Occupation, education, past experience, and competence all help in authenticating the sender and the message.[14] To take advantage of this factor, the sender needs to demonstrate expertise through words and the testimony of others.

Other Differences

Many other personal characteristics affect the success rate of communication: race, ethnicity, religion, class, age, profession, geographic location, language, and international culture. Although we list these here as a group of characteristics—because a particular person represents a combination of such traits—it is important to consider each of these traits in and of itself when you are estimating the ability of the other party to communicate with you successfully.

SUGGESTIONS FOR IMPROVING COMMUNICATION

We have reviewed many of the ways communication can break down, and have pointed out the critical role that communication problems can play in the negotiating process. As a strategic negotiator, you now know to stop, pay attention to, and think about the communication process itself whenever you encounter difficulties. In addition, a proactive approach is helpful. How can the strategic negotiator "stack the deck" in favor of successful communication? Here are some general principles and a set of helpful hints.

Emphasize similarities of goals and objectives. When the goals of the two parties are seen as similar, communication will likely be better. If you and I are on the same "wave length," we are likely to have a framework for our communication and we will be talking the same language. If we can find common ground, communication is likely to proceed more smoothly.

If the two parties have *personal similarities,* then communication is easier. If the differences appear to be great, then communication may be severely limited. To offset this, try to find ways to overcome or diminish the differences, or maximize the similarities.

Styles of communication may affect the outcome. One party prefers to talk a lot, the other is a person of few words. One party prefers to communicate verbally, while another prefers written communication. To work together effectively, the parties will need to accommodate each other's styles.

Gender differences[15] can have a major influence on the success of the communication. This can be caused by differences in vocabulary, conversational styles, and systems men and women use for communication. They may see situations differently and this will affect their interpretation of what is said. Men are generally socialized to be competitive, while women learn to be cooperative. This has significant implications for communication and negotiation. Sara Westendorf of Hewlett-Packard expects a certain amount of sexist behavior in her work as an engineer. But she uses humor to counteract it, and "dishes it right back."[16] She suggests that to combat sexist remarks and conduct, women should establish their technical ability. If your ideas are ignored, you should speak up in private—train those around you to listen to you.

The following suggestions may help you improve communication with others during negotiation:

1. *Know your objectives.* We discussed objectives in Chapters 2 and 3. If you are clear about your goals, you may be better able to communicate them clearly to the other party.

2. *Know the other side.* The more you know about and understand the other side and their position, the better the potential for clear communication about bargaining points, goals, and issues. You also need to understand their background. In Chapter 3, we mentioned role-reversal as one way to understand the other party's point of view in negotiation, and we will discuss this again, as a way of improving your communication with the other party.

3. *Think before you speak.* This (maxim—the title of our book—) is always a good rule to follow. If you have planned carefully, you will be organized and comfortable with your point of view, and this will make it easier to speak.

OTHER SUGGESTIONS FOR SPEAKING

- Practice what you want to say ahead of time, especially if it helps you feel prepared, or if you particularly want to stress a key meaning, a complex idea, or a way of counteracting the resistance you know the other will put up.

- Keep your message simple.
- Make your choice of language plain and clear, unless you specifically want to be ambiguous.
- Be positive rather than negative.
- Watch out for the use of jokes and clichés—while humor can help to release tension, it is often taken the wrong way.
- Maintain eye contact, as appropriate.
- Use visuals (pictures, charts, graphs) to help get the message across.
- Talk slowly and clearly so people can understand you.
- Watch the use of gestures.
- Observe others to see if they are getting your message.
- Watch the body language of the receiver(s) for nonverbal feedback: Frowns, scowls, averted eyes, folded arms can often tell us they don't like what we are saying!

COMMUNICATION TECHNIQUES THAT CAN HELP YOU IN NEGOTIATION

There are three basic techniques you can use to improve the quality of give-and-take during negotiation, and thus decrease confusion and crossed signals. These techniques are (1) questions, (2) active listening, and (3) role reversal.

Questions

Questions, asked of the sender of a message, can help indicate that you have in fact been listening. They can help improve the accuracy of your understanding of the message. Questions can be used either to get information or to give it. It is important to phrase your questions carefully, so that the other party does not become defensive.[17] For example, asking "Where did you ever get that idea?" might get a very negative response. And avoid asking too many questions. Frequent questions can cause the other party to become defensive if they think you are cross-examining or "grilling" them.

Listening, Reflecting[18]

A great deal of research has been done on listening as it pertains to communication. As communicators, we often focus on the constructing and conveying of the message and forget about receiving, which includes listening. In fact, when the other person is talking, many of us are so busy preparing what we are going to say next—to rebut them or argue our own point—that we miss the message coming to us! So, how can we improve our listening skills to improve communication? There are three ways to show you are listening: (1) passive listening, (2) acknowledgment, and (3) active listening.

Passive Listening.   This one is easy. Just let the other party talk. Actually, even though it sounds easy, it may not be. Be sure you are really listening and taking in what they are saying.

Acknowledgment.   In this method of listening, you gesture in some way to indicate that you hear what is being said. This may be a nod, or a murmured "un hunh," or "I see." It may be more openly encouraging: "That is interesting," "Really?" or "Go on." A potential problem with this method is that you may appear to be agreeing with the speaker, when in fact all you are doing is signaling that you are receiving their communication.

In both passive listening and acknowledgment, you need to maintain eye contact, not staring at the speaker, but simply showing that you are paying attention. You can also use other body language such as sitting up straight and turning toward the speaker. For emphasis, body-language gestures should be made at the point of most importance in the message. If you are engaging in multicultural negotiation, be sure you are aware of the customs, for there may be some gestures that are considered impolite or offensive. In Asian cultures, for example, it is a gesture of respect to keep your eyes lowered; in the West, we look directly at the speaker when we want to give them our attention.

Active Listening.   In active listening, you restate the message once it has been given. You might say, "OK. Now let me see if I have this right. You want to have a 5 percent raise, and in return, you are willing to work through your lunch hour three days a week to get the backlog caught up."

The advantages of paraphrasing the message in active listening are:

1. It can help you remember what has been said.
2. It may mean more in your own words.
3. The speaker can correct any incorrect perceptions you may have.

4. It can help move the discussion on (if the speaker is rambling on or repeating, for example).

If the message is long, it may help to reflect after each section or part, rather than to wait until the end.

Active listening sets up a format for listening. If there is give-and-take conversation, you can then ask the other party to rephrase your points to be sure they have understood you.

The following are rules of good listening:[19]

- Respond to the concrete and personal in the message rather than the abstract. This will help the speaker to keep the content of the message concrete and personal.
- Follow rather than lead. If you are really listening, you do not want to be telling the speaker what to think or do.
- Clarify, do not question or tell. The objective is to keep lines of communication open, so you should avoid both confrontational questions and the urge to instruct.
- Respond to the other person's feelings. If you listen carefully, you may be able to also hear the emotions and values under what is being said, and learn about the other's underlying motivations. This is particularly important for the Collaborative negotiator.

Role Reversal

Role reversal involves taking the side of the other person and arguing for that side. Although you can do this mentally and informally, it is more effective to actually do it with a friend or colleague when you are preparing for a communication. The method is to first develop your own point, then to look at the possible counterarguments and develop responses to them[20]—somewhat like walking in the other person's shoes for a while.

Role reversal is a great skill to have when you must focus on someone else's problem, and help them out. Thus, a customer service representative would see what it is like to be a customer frustrated with a product, or a laborer could get a feel for the kinds of decisions management must make. Patients often criticize doctors for having a bad "bedside manner," meaning that the physician fails to listen and really understand how the patient is feeling.

Active arguing of the other person's position as though you really believed it can be very helpful in the following ways:[21]

- It can help you understand the other party's position.
- It can help you see similarities between the two positions.
- It can improve outcomes if the two points of view are basically compatible. However, it is usually less successful when the points of view are fundamentally incompatible.
- It may reduce distortions in communication.

Remember, however, that role reversal, while helpful, does not necessarily result in agreement.

Using these listening/understanding techniques, the receiver of a message may discover a way to alter the response to the message. However, the first impression will frequently remain the continuing impression unless there is a reason to change it.

Understanding the Receiver

If you are sending a message, it is important to understand how a person receives messages, and how he or she usually responds. If you have done your research on the other party (Chapter 3), you may have discovered that this receiver usually responds combatively. In that case, you will likely want to find ways of communicating that defuse a potentially emotional situation. If the other party feels they usually are not listened to, then you need to let them know you hear and understand what they are saying.

If the receiver is usually open-minded and willing to collaborate, then you will likely have an easier time communicating. The listening strategies may help you understand the other point of view better, and may even change your own point of view. The result could be that you are able to find a common ground for collaborative solutions, and you may end up with better results in negotiation.

COMMUNICATION DURING DIFFERENT STAGES OF NEGOTIATION

Let us turn now to the steps in the negotiation process to see how communication affects the success of sending and receiving messages. We will look at beginning, middle, and end stages. Each stage has specific characteristics and potential communication difficulties.

The Beginning Stages

It is in the *beginning* or opening stage of negotiations, when establishing communication, that negotiators are likely to have a lot of trouble communicating. Perceptions are being formed, along with expectations. People will be making assumptions. Biases will cause errors in perceptions. As this stage progresses and the communicators begin to see how the other party will operate, the communication process will usually begin to fall into a pattern. But at the beginning, much social interchange will have to occur so that the parties can understand each other.

Past situations, attitudes, and behaviors will directly affect the progress of this stage. Some of the perceptual difficulties that will complicate communication are the following:

- *Stereotypes*. These come from generalizing about another person. For example, "He is a manager. Managers always want you to work harder than you really need to, and for the least amount of money." Although generalizing may be useful in some cases, it can result in assigning qualities to a party that the party does not in fact possess, or that do not apply in this situation.

- *Halo effects*. If you had a good experience with this person before, you will tend to expect the same this time. This may or may not occur. The halo effect leads you to believe that things will work the same way as in the past.

- *Selective perceptions*. In this filtering of information, only the qualities deemed applicable to the situation are scrutinized. If you think certain information about the person is not applicable, you may discard it, even if it would, in the long run, given you a better overall picture of the person.

- *Projection*. We frequently project onto others qualities we see in ourselves. For example, if I am motivated by money, I tend to assume everyone is.

The Middle Stages

The middle stage of negotiation is a problem-solving phase. In this stage, offers are made and counteroffers are submitted in reply. The objectives and goals of negotiation begin to be focused and narrowed down. Offers[22] and counteroffers are very important in this stage, for they provide a lot of information, even that which is not stated. The process of exchanging offers, which is interactive, causes shifts in the positions of the bargainers. Factors such as the time frame, Alternatives, and constituency pressure all affect the process.

In the middle stages, the issues[23] will undergo some shifts because of the offers and counteroffers. Cases will be made for or against particular positions, and multiple issues will need to be managed. If the parties are successful, they may be able to switch from positions to discussing interests, and exploring commonalities. Careless use of language, or poor listening, may make this transition impossible.

Another feature of the middle stage may be threats.[24] The language used to convey threats may have these characteristics:

- Polarized language in which a party may speak of themselves in a positive fashion and of the other party in a negative tone.
- Immediacy, in which the language is meant to create either urgency and closeness or distance.
- Language intensity, such as profanity or strong language, where high intensity indicates strong feelings and low intensity suggests slight interest.
- Richness in vocabulary, which depends to some extent on education, but which can indicate comfort and competence in speaking, or discomfort and lack of confidence.
- Language style, again somewhat reliant on education, but indicative of a preference either to be aggressive and dominating, or to be polite or subordinate.

In the middle stage, it is important to know whether threats are being used to command, to sell or persuade, or to gain commitment from the other party.

The Ending Stages

The final stage in negotiation is a wrap-up in preparation for closure, when the resolution is at hand. It is important at this point to be absolutely clear. Feedback, active listening, and clear explanations are very important so you do not make any fatal mistakes. The following are possible traps:[25]

- Coming to a conclusion too fast (perhaps because the definition of the problem was incomplete).
- Overconfidence, which results in missing important information.

213

- Solving the wrong problem.
- Coming to a less-than-optimal outcome, to avoid having no outcome at all.
- Short-circuiting the negotiation by accepting incomplete or untrue information.
- Using a careless or undisciplined process, rather than a systematic one.
- Failing to include the group in the process.
- Using feedback incorrectly.
- Poor record keeping.
- Incomplete understanding of one's own position.

Successful Endings

There are a number of stumbling blocks to watch out for at the very end if you are trying to end the negotiation successfully.[26] It is important to know when to keep quiet and let the process work. If you say something irrelevant, you might either give up important information or push the other party away from settlement. And if the other party makes a stupid remark, it is smart to overlook it at this point.

Last-minute requests can be irritating, unless they are planned for. We talked in Chapter 6 about the ploy of the "Nibble"—making "new" requests at the end, to gain an additional concession. Be prepared for this possibility with the other party.

Last, but not least, it is a good idea to write out the final contract. This will give each party an opportunity to review the provisions of the agreement.

EVALUATING THE AGREEMENT—IS IT SOUND?

The following criteria can be used to evaluate the agreement:

1. Is there a preamble that spells out the intent of the agreement?
2. Are all the issues of interest to either side addressed?
3. Are the proposals workable?
4. Have all parties impacted by the agreement been consulted?
5. For each point of agreement, is what you have agreed to absolutely clear, including what is to be done, by whom, by what time, and how?

6. Does the agreement in total make sense?

7. Is the agreement reasonable and equitable?

8. Have you considered the major barriers to fulfilling the agreement? How?

9. Do you have a vehicle for managing disagreements arising out of this agreement? Is it clear to all parties how this vehicle works?

SUMMARY

If the other party disagrees with what you say, is it because they simply disagree, because they did not understand, or are they attacking you, putting you down, challenging you? You need to make sure what is going on before you proceed with a response. This chapter has discussed how to get at the *real* message.

If you know the real message and it is not good, what do you do? If you need help in deescalating an emotional give-and-take, look at Chapters 10 and 11, which cover conflict resolution and third-party intervention.

Chapter **13**

Legal and Ethical Issues

In business in general, and in negotiations in particular, ethics and the law always form two important criteria by which to evaluate our decisions. Why? Because one's strategy needs to be *to achieve one's ends by appropriate behavior*, as judged by *both* these criteria. Legal compliance alone does not insure appropriate and successful negotiations—opponents and stakeholders who know they have been treated unethically hold grudges, look for ways to get even, and spread rumor and gossip that may make it more difficult for the negotiator to achieve future objectives. Similarly, ethical and fair treatment of the other party is of little value if you leave a legal loophole (or landmine) in your agreement due to your ignorance of contract law. Figure 13.1 expresses the four options that arise when legal and ethical criteria are considered in evaluating negotiation strategy and tactics. We will first examine relevant legal issues, and then go on to consider ethics. Both law and ethics define and constrain what can be done in negotiation, but in somewhat different ways. The issues are often similar, but the constraints are different.

LEGAL CONSTRAINTS ON NEGOTIATION

Is it illegal to lie in negotiations? One expert on negotiation writes that "commercial negotiations seem to require a talent for deception. In simple competitive bargaining, when someone asks, 'What is your bottom line?' few negotiators tell the truth." In this book, and in actual negotiations, you have encountered many tactics that are based either on the withholding of some information or the dissemination of misinformation. Are these legal? Could you end up in a court of law from such practices? Legally, where should you draw the line?

216

IS IT ETHICAL?

	YES	NO
YES	Optimal Acceptable legal and ethical zone	Legal but not ethical OK with the law, but may still be unacceptable to people's values
NO	Ethical but not legal OK by ethical standards, but still liable to legal prosecution	Neither legal nor ethical Dual sets of problems make one's tactics very dangerous!

IS IT LEGAL?

Figure 13.1 The Law/Ethics Matrix

Laws related to fraud, misrepresentation, and the nature of contracts are relevant here. Contract law concerns the establishment of legal obligations; so if you enter into a legal contract and then fail to perform, you are exposing yourself to legal problems. Similarly, if you can create a contractual obligation on the part of another party, it doesn't matter whether they intended to perform or not—now you have them over a legal barrel. So it can be helpful to appreciate the subtleties of contract law. However, we will tackle fraud first because it is even more relevant.

Legally, fraud is intentional misrepresentation—the lies that cross over the line from good negotiation tactics into illegal untruths. You had better appreciate this boundary before you negotiate! And misrepresentation, even where a clear intent to lie is not proven, can also be illegal in negotiations. The boundaries between negotiation tactics and fraud or misrepresentation are not always clear. We need to explore them in some depth in order to understand their implications for the negotiator.

Fraud

The first point to understand is that there is no general prohibition against the use of deception and posturing in negotiation. The parties do not *have* to tell the truth—legal precedent recognizes that negotiation is a strange sort of dance with its own rules, and that if you do not like the way another party negotiates, your first legal recourse is to walk away from the negotiation rather than sue. However, the law also recognizes that *some* negotiating behavior is illegal because it is clearly fraudulent. Here are three elements of the acid test: A statement is fraudulent when a negotiator *knows it is untrue,* and the *other party relies on it in a reasonable manner* and *suffers damage as a result.*[1]

What do we mean when we say the "negotiator knows it is untrue"? Exactly that. Let's say you go shopping for a car, but are determined to negotiate hard so as to avoid being fleeced by the salesperson. If you tell him you are not really interested in buying a car today, but are just curious as to what the dealer is selling it for, you are stating something you know to be untrue. Similarly, if the dealer's mechanics fiddle with the odometer to reduce the mileage of a used car, then the business is stating something they know to be untrue (the accurate mileage). You both lied in the opening moments of your negotiation. But are either examples of fraud?

Let's check the rest of the definition. In your opening lie—saying you are not interested when you know you are—will the dealer believe that you are not interested, and hence reveal his true BATNA price to you when he would not have otherwise? Not if he acts "reasonably," particularly by the standards of competitive negotiation. He is unlikely to rely on your statement because it is a conventional bit of posturing that he understands you used to avoid exposing yourself to a hard-core sales pitch right now. On the other hand, the dealer's resetting of the odometer is not something you assume as a prelude to a negotiation over the price of the car. It *would* be reasonable for you to rely on the displayed mileage. This lie now has two strikes against it.

Let's look at the third element of the definition. Will either lie cause damage? Yours won't, because we already decided the salesperson will not reasonably rely on it. Should he claim later that you lied in the negotiation, and he therefore gave you too low a price (damaging himself by cutting his commission), the average judge would just laugh at him for being too naive. However, the reset odometer could indeed cause you some damage if you go ahead and buy the car and pay fair market value for a car with that level of mileage. Should you discover the fraud later on and take the dealer to court, the judge would most likely award you the difference in price between a typical car of that model at the estimated real mileage versus the faked mileage.[2]

You might think that the requirement of "knowing" you are stating an untruth creates an obvious legal loophole. Can the other party *prove* you knew you were lying about an important fact? If you avoided communicating with anyone in writing about this behavior, then there will be no direct proof about what you knew or should have known. Not so fast! The courts often assume you *should* know some facts. A senior manager should know what financial condition his business is in. A salesperson at a car company should know what condition a car is in; witness the "lemon laws" emerging in many states, which hold salespeople responsible for the condition of the cars they sell, even if they really could claim that they didn't know much about who owned them before and what might be wrong with them.

Misrepresentation

Another legal minefield lies in the concept of misrepresentation, a close relative of fraud. Unlike fraud, misrepresentation does not necessarily entail knowing that a statement is untrue. When a used car salesperson chooses to mention the condition of the engine as a way to avoid having to disclose information about the engine that is in the car's file in the dealership office, then we are dealing with misrepresentation. If you don't say anything about a topic as a way to avoid having to lie about it, you are on *somewhat* better ground than with fraud, because it is harder to prove legally. In general, courts punish misrepresentation only in two cases— when superior information is withheld or partial disclosure is truly misleading. Superior information might be, for example, the knowledge that your company is about to file for bankruptcy protection. If you did not mention this to a vendor when you negotiated 30-day terms for a large purchase of supplies—and the vendor was then unable to collect because your firm filed for protection from creditors under bankruptcy laws—then the vendor could make a credible legal claim of misrepresentation. And you as a negotiator should have known that you had gone beyond standard negotiating tactics and breached the legal boundaries of truth in negotiation. Similarly, you ought to know better than to make a partial disclosure that is obviously misleading. Let's say the vendor actually asked you about your company's financial condition, and you answered, "Well, the company posted record profits last year." Even if that is true, it is a misleading answer, and the vendor could claim misrepresentation in this case too.

How do you avoid misrepresentation? Many negotiators believe *silence* is the secret (but note that the problems of partial disclosure and superior information are *not* fully addressed by this traditional rule of thumb). When representing a business or other organization or group, it is not difficult for you to claim ignorance or say you are not authorized to discuss certain topics. The topics in question will involve information you do not

219

want the other party to know about, and therefore information that could materially affect the outcome of the negotiation. While silence is helpful in avoiding fraud, it is still possible that the other party can make some legal claim. For example, they may claim you withheld superior information.

As a general rule of thumb, a negotiator ought to avoid overly tricky strategies and try to negotiate in a fair manner. Disclose as much as you can without giving away key vulnerabilities or your bottom line. A level playing field is probably a legal one. What you want, however, is to tip the playing field just a little bit toward you—but not so steeply that the other party perceives a grave injustice has occurred and decides to pursue a legal remedy under either fraud or misrepresentation laws. If the other party threatens legal action and you have to hire a lawyer, you have probably lost the negotiation, because the extra hassles and costs are doubtless going to negate any advantage won through overly tricky negotiation. Therefore, when in doubt, it is far cheaper to hire the lawyer up front, to give you a one-hour hearing and quick opinion, and thereby avoid stepping over the boundaries of the law.

Contract Law

Contracts often result from negotiations, so we must also consider what negotiation boundaries may be set by contract law. The basic goal of a contract negotiation should be to create a contract that is legally binding on both parties, so let's look at what is required for a contract to be enforceable in a court of law.[3] First, there must be *agreement*. That means one party must make an offer, and the other must accept it. An offer has to meet three criteria: (1) It has to be *serious* (an offhand or humorous offer is no good), (2) it has to include *specific terms* (a vague promise to take care of some problem is not an offer), and (3) it must be *communicated* to the other party in a clear manner.

A landlord might tell a month-to-month tenant (or "tenant at will") that she has to sign a five-year lease, and the tenant might agree in principle to do so. Now suppose the landlord sends the tenant a lease that includes a clause stipulating that the tenant is responsible for 50 percent of the cost of repairs to the building. The tenant signs the lease quickly, but then reads the small print and sets the lease aside on her desk because she is uncomfortable with it. She forgets to follow up and talk with the landlord about it. In the interim, the landlord replaces the roof, and invoices the tenant for half the cost of the work. The tenant argues that the landlord doesn't have a signed lease—but the landlord produces it. He has used his passkey to go into the tenant's apartment and take the lease off her desk. Does the landlord have a legally binding contract? No; the offer was not *communicated* to the landlord, since the tenant had not yet chosen to give him the executed contract.

For a contract to be valid, there must also be *consideration*. That means parties need to get something for what they give up. An *exchange* has to take place. This is rarely an issue in negotiation, but it arises when one party has great power over the other and attempts to force the other to make concessions or agree to perform in exchange for little or nothing. The problem of consideration could also arise if tricky language is used that traps one party into agreeing to do something extra they did not anticipate when the negotiation was taking place—and for which they did not request proper consideration.

Contractual capacity is also necessary. That means the parties must be competent. Negotiating a favorable purchase with the teenage son of your deceased business partner is not going to produce an enforceable contract because he will not be recognized as a competent party. Nor can you negotiate with people who are drunk or ill, and expect the results to be legally binding on them, or on an organization or person they represent.

Legality is also required. The purpose of the contract must be a legal goal that does not run counter to public policy. A contract requiring someone to break the law is not enforceable, for example. This constrains negotiators in terms of the kind of objectives they can pursue. It also constrains employers in the kinds of negotiations they can require their employees to engage in. For instance, imagine that you are a salesperson whose employer tells you to misrepresent the service record of a product to sell more of the product and more service contracts. You refuse; so he pulls out a copy of your employment contract and reads you a clause that states you must use the sales pitch the company has specified. Hold your ground; your employment contract cannot be used to make you do something illegal.

Genuineness of assent is also required; for example, your signature, forged on a contract, does not bind you to the terms of the contract. Similarly, if a low-level employee of your firm signs a highly unfavorable sales agreement with a supplier, you can legitimately claim that the employee was not authorized or prepared to represent the company in such deliberations.

Finally, *form* is important. A clear, written contract is generally required. In some situations, the law stipulates what kind of contract is required, and even what language it must be in; but in general, all that is required is a detailed, clear, written document containing the preceding points, and signed by both parties. Contracts also take the form of a renewable agreement, or one that terminates after some length of time. Despite the requirement of

221

form, many negotiations end in an informal verbal agreement or a short memo from one party to the other confirming their recollection of the outcome. If you want to make a negotiated agreement legally binding, you must take it beyond the level of an informal negotiation process and add one more step: Write and review a formal contract. If it is a complex or important agreement for you, then you need to obtain appropriate legal advice to make sure your contract is complete and binding, and accurately represents the agreement and the parties' interests.

Obligations to Customers and Employees

When negotiating with customers or employees, you must navigate the legal waters of fraud, misrepresentation, and contract law plus any special laws protecting the interests of the other party. For example, imagine you are negotiating with a top job prospect to fill an opening: a professional who has asked for a higher salary than you intended to pay. You tell him honestly that he is your first choice, but that you are not sure you can meet his requirements. Then you ask some questions to explore his requirements in more detail, including some questions about his family, age, and health status that you think are relevant to calculating the cost of employing him. While these may seem like reasonable questions to you, they are illegal to ask in a job interview. The applicant has many legal protections designed to prevent discrimination against prospective employees based on factors such as age and family status. You need to check with your company's human resources department, a law firm, or a text on human resource management before you negotiate in this context.

Similarly, your existing employees have a wide variety of legal protections, and you must avoid crossing legal boundaries in negotiating with them. Sexual harassment, discrimination in promotion, right-to-know issues, and many other legal concerns constrain the employer. The body of law concerning employee-employer relations is large, and you need to check with an expert before trying anything novel in negotiations with an employee.

Most of the legal issues in the area of consumer protection are not directly relevant to negotiating situations because consumer purchases are not negotiated routinely in this country. Consumer protection laws concerning warranties are relevant to customer service issues and need to be considered by negotiators. For example, if a business customer complains that a product your company sold her company is defective and should be replaced at no cost, your position might be to point out that the customer decided not to pay for your extended warranty package, and thus your firm has no obligation to right the problem. Note, however, that the law recognizes an "implied warranty," defined as the expectation that products are fit for normal use; if the customer was able to show that your product was not "fit for normal use," the law would be on her side in the dispute. (Good sense might dictate you retain the customer by avoiding competitive negotiations in this context, anyway. To quote the old adage, "Even when the customer is wrong, the customer is always right!")

The law has a great deal to say about price fixing, unfair or predatory pricing designed to drive a smaller rival out of business, and any other business practices that obviously reduce competition and its downward influence on prices. Should you find yourself in a negotiating situation with a competitor in which an unfair price is an issue, do not bother researching the law—just head for the nearest door! Any such negotiation or discussion of prices with competitors is highly likely to be illegal.

Testing Your Knowledge on a Case

Let's test our newfound knowledge of the legal issues in negotiation with a quick case. Imagine you are a landlord, and you have what you feel is a valuable storefront property. The current tenant has a very favorable lease, which is up for renewal next month. You propose a doubling of the rent to what you think is a fair market price, but she refuses and suggests that a 10 percent increase is more in line with what other retail rents are doing in the community. The difference between the rate you requested and what she proposed is worth many thousands of dollars a year in income for you, so you decide to play hardball and pursue an aggressive competitive negotiating strategy. You ask a real estate agent to publicly list and advertise the space at the higher price, hoping you will receive inquiries from prospective tenants eager to pay it.

The listing process takes longer than it should, and when the time comes to sit down with your tenant again, you still have no alternative tenants lined up. Not to worry—you decide to make the negotiating claim that you have another tenant in the wings who is eager to pay the higher price, and that you intend to evict the current tenant unless she agrees to pay this price too. (Sure, it is an exaggeration, but you still think you *could* find someone if you had the time.) She buckles under the pressure of this strong opening position, signs a five-year lease, and you laugh all the way to the bank. But next year, your tenant runs into the real estate agent at a party and learns that you made up the whole story. Furious, she threatens to take you to court unless you settle by agreeing to cut her rent back to the previous level and extend it at that rate for another five years.

Does she have a strong legal case or not? Let's apply the most rigorous test: the three questions used to define fraud. Yes, you did knowingly misrepresent the situation. Yes, the tenant can argue she reasonably relied on the information you gave her. And yes, there are damages—the extra rent she has had to pay as a result, and the impact that this higher rent may have had on her business. You had better settle with her right away, because the courts may not look favorably on your negotiating technique. And you had better be more honest next time you negotiate!

ETHICAL CONSIDERATIONS IN NEGOTIATION

Having considered the legal questions, we now turn our attention to the ethical ones. Unlike the law, there is no standard, across-the-board written (or even informal) "code of ethics" for negotiators to use as a model. The ethics of a negotiator will depend on such personal qualities as their philosophical and religious training, experience, background, and so forth. But even "expected" standards of right and wrong will vary from person to person. Some of the tactics mentioned earlier in this book are thought to be acceptable to use when trying to negotiate the best settlement possible, particularly in competitive situations. For example, in using the Competitive Strategy, many believe that it is a mistake to be completely open with the other party. After all, the argument goes, if you give away all the information about your bargaining points—particularly your walkaway point, or the least you will take—then you will not have anything left to bargain with. You will be setting yourself up for the other party to take advantage of you. So to be effective in negotiation, particularly in competitive situations, it is to your advantage to be less-than-fully honest with the other. On the other hand, if the parties are completely deceptive all the time, it may be impossible to strike any kind of meaningful agreement.

Some people feel that it is okay to engage in tactics that emphasize the positive aspects of the negotiation, and downplay the negative. For example, if you're selling a used car, it's okay to emphasize the good points about the car, and not tell the potential buyer that the car needs major engine work. Is this truthful and ethical behavior? Some "white lies" may be rationalized, if they are for a particular purpose. Again, this depends on your point of view and your personal ethical code. Because the level of truth-telling and ethics differ from person to person, it is hard to predict what the other party will do in negotiation. There is a further difference between what people *believe* is ethical, and what they *say* is ethical.

In this section, we explore ethical behavior in negotiation. Although we will give examples of sometimes questionable behavior, we do not advocate engaging in such conduct. As stated in Chapter 6, it is important to know how the other party may act, in order to be prepared for such behavior. It is for this reason that we present examples of questionable ethics and explain how to handle them.

WHY PEOPLE ENGAGE IN QUESTIONABLE ETHICAL BEHAVIORS

One of the major motives for using unethical tactics in negotiation is to gain a *power advantage*. This comes from the win-lose attitude. Since information is power, a party who can manipulate information to gain some form of temporary advantage is likely to seek that leverage. One party may withhold information from the other in order to move into a more powerful bargaining position.

Closely related to a concern for power is *ego gratification*. People may desire recognition, esteem, or an enhanced reputation, so they try using deceptive behavior to achieve it. Some people want to be seen as a "winner" and will pay any price to reach their goal.

The drive to gain or maintain a *competitive position* can motivate unethical practices. Competition is a part of our lives. Our capitalistic system thrives on "healthy" competition. We see it in business, in sports, in the struggle to get to the top in careers. This frequently means aiming for the largest market share—the largest piece of the pie—which may in turn produce unethical behaviors. In some areas such as sports, there are rules about what is appropriate and acceptable behavior and what is not. Generally, people agree to abide by the rules.

But in negotiations, there are no written rules. Stretching the limits of acceptable behaviors is seen as a "necessary evil" in competition. The more competitive the situation, the more people try to get away with questionable behavior. If they are caught at it, they can plead ignorance.

A desire for *justice or revenge* is also a strong motivator for unethical practices. A party who feels wronged may respond by engaging in some sort of retaliatory unethical behavior that seems acceptable under the circumstances. "What's fair is fair" may make sense to the wronged party, but how does one define just what is fair?

As an example of "justice-seeking," think for a moment about employees who steal. Why do they do this? Perhaps they did not get a raise this year, so they make off with computer diskettes or use the office photocopier for personal business; or maybe they begin calling in sick more often, even when they are not sick. This may be their idea of how to exact some justice or revenge. And it is easy to rationalize such behavior.

To a large degree, the extent of unethical conduct will be based on the following key factors: (1) whether we believe the other party will also use competitive or unethical practices, (2) whether this is a situation where "everybody does it," (3) how big are the rewards we think we can gain by using the tactic, and (4) whether there are consequences or costs for getting caught.

Information as a Factor in Ethical and Unethical Behavior

We have discussed in earlier chapters how important it is to share information between parties in negotiation. Information was a critical factor in researching the other party—their background, point of view, likely arguments—and in planning negotiation strategies. In the Collaborative Strategy, we have seen that information is crucial to the parties understanding each other and being able to create solutions.

A major factor in ethical behavior in negotiation is information: How much do you have? How accurate is it? How much should you share with the other party? What you choose to share, how you share it, and when you share it will have a major effect on the outcome. If you manipulate the information you give, you can, in effect, manipulate the outcome.

If you share too much information, you may lose ground or give up the negotiating position you have carefully established. If you share too little, the other party may believe you are withholding information to manipulate the proceedings. The problem is how to find a middle ground: As a noted researcher on negotiation has stated:

> . . . to sustain the bargaining relationship, each party must select a middle course between the extremes of complete openness toward, and deception of, the other. Each must be able to convince the other of his integrity while not at the same time endangering his bargaining position.[4]

Relationship between the Negotiators

If the relationship between the two parties is seen as short term, then unethical tactics become easier to use and to rationalize. If the tactic is discovered (and it usually is), the relationship will be affected adversely. The other party may now retaliate in kind, rationalizing that "the other guys did it, so why shouldn't I?" The situation then becomes emotionally charged, as the retaliations and countermoves escalate.

Even if the unethical tactics go undetected in this situation, eventually the perpetrator will be caught. Most negotiators do not want to have a poor reputation. Where relationship concerns are stronger and longer term, there may be less use of unethical actions.

Motives for using dirty tactics can be very subtle. Frequently, the perpetrator does not see the activities as "dirty" but rather as just doing what they are supposed to do. Whether a potential user of an unethical action will go ahead with the action will depend, to some degree, on whether "preventive forces" are at work in the environment. The strength and extent of the consequences for unethical behavior in negotiation may act, to some degree, as a deterrent.

THREE MAJOR WAYS OF LOOKING AT ETHICAL CONDUCT[5]

People tend to confront an ethical decision in three ways:

1. *The ends justify the means.* You have probably heard this expression many times. In negotiation, this belief allows the person to engage in questionable behavior because it results in a preferred resolution, which, after all, is the objective of the negotiation. As you can see, the bigger the stakes or potential outcome for a negotiation, the easier it will be to rationalize using marginally ethical tactics to get it.

2. *Absolute truth versus relative truth.* If you believe in "absolute truth," then you think that rules must be followed with no exceptions. You must go "by the book." If you believe in relative truth, you think that "everything is relative" and therefore, each person must make his or her own value judgments. Your choice of beliefs, whether absolute black-and-white or relative gray, will affect how ethically you behave in each situation. So, for example, if you are an "absolutist," you believe that it is important to tell the truth, even if telling the truth gets you in trouble. If you've made a big mistake, and your boss asks you what happened, telling the truth might mean you will get fired for making the mistake. An absolutist would tell the truth and take the risk, believing that being ethical is more important than the consequences. A relativist, on the other hand, might try to avoid saying anything, be evasive, or—at the extreme—deny any responsibility or blame somebody else, simply to avoid the possibility of being fired.

3. *There is no such thing as "truth."* You may believe that telling the truth is of utmost importance. The difficulty here is in defining "truth." What exactly is "telling the truth"? Where is the line between "truth" and "falsehood"? Some people may believe that bluffing, exaggerating, or concealing are okay if used in the service of the higher good. They may feel that these are within the boundaries of truth, and therefore are acceptable. Are white lies a form of lie or just a stretching of the truth?

EXAMPLES OF UNETHICAL TACTICS[6]

Before we describe some of the questionable tactics that might be used in negotiation, let us repeat that we do *not* advocate using any of these tactics, unless you feel comfortable doing so and understand the possible consequences. Negotiators sometimes use theses tactics just to experiment, or they think that the other party will not be smart enough to discover what has happened. This is usually not the case. Negotiators should not use unethical tactics if:

- They will be dealing with the other party again in the future, and want to have a positive, long-term relationship.
- There is some likelihood that the other party can discover that the tactics are being used.
- The other party has enough power to get revenge or punish the perpetrators of unfair tactics.
- They can't be effective in using them, or their conscience will bother them or give them away.

We primarily offer and describe these tactics here so that you can be aware of possible unethical tactics that may be used against you. Some negotiators will find some of these moves acceptable under certain circumstances; others will not. The more *moderate* tactics are often seen as more acceptable than the extreme ones; these first few tactics, though violations of the truth, are used by negotiators fairly often. It is important to note again that these tactics are more often used in a Competitive negotiation situation than in a Collaborative one.

Moderate Tactics

Selective Disclosure and Exaggeration. There are a number of ways to be selective in what we disclose to the other, or exaggerate the information we share with the other. For one, a party might selectively omit important information—not disclose a defect, problem, or weakness in their argument. For another, the information might be "stretched" to make a point seem more or less important, such as exaggerating the benefits of going through with a particular deal. Further, a negotiator might neglect to report "the whole story" to his or her constituencies, so as to manipulate their impression of the progress and content of the negotiation. The other party may be completely unwilling to move on an issue, but the negotiator chooses not to tell the constituency that, believing that over time, the opponent will "soften up" and begin to move.

Another related type of exaggeration is to start with an opening point that is a lot greater (or less) than you really want. For example, a union might start out by asking for a 15 percent raise when they really will be satisfied with 7 percent. Starting high is frequently used as a tactic to show strength, create tension, and expand the bargaining range so that when concessions are made, we will actually achieve what we want. In general, more exaggerated opening offers tend to lead to better settlements, unless the opening is so extreme as to defeat credibility with the other party.

Hiding the Real Bottom Line.   In this type of behavior, you try to prevent the other party from knowing exactly what you want so you can get there more or less without their knowing. This might involve hiding your starting points and bottom line, or misleading the other party about this information.

More Serious Tactics

This group of tactics has even stronger ethical implications than those we have just discussed, because they involve more outright falsehoods or distortions of the truth.

"Exaggerating" or Disguising Facts.   A party might manipulate the facts to make their position appear more favorable. Or, they might try to make the other party's position appear less favorable. A common tactic is to disguise information about our position, key facts, or what is likely to happen if the deal goes through. For example, in selling a piece of real estate, we may know that the land is not buildable because of the soil conditions, but tell the potential buyer, "We don't know whether the land will support a large office building or not."

Another type of misrepresentation involves a deadline—to act as though we are unhurried and have all the time in the world, when in fact we are anxious to settle. Often we do this when we know that the other has a major deadline, and that if we stall, we can pressure them into giving in first. For example, if we know that the seller of a house is desperate to get out as soon as possible (and we are really anxious to get into the house ourselves), we can nevertheless negotiate as though we have all the time in the world, and hope that they will make a major concession if we agree to close the deal quickly.

Manipulating Power. In this type of falsification, the party makes its reputation seem better than it is, or claims more expertise than it has, the object being to appear to have a more legitimate and stronger position than the other party. Misrepresenting one's credentials or status to fool the other party can backfire if the other party finds out. It can have repercussions in future negotiations if reputations are at stake.

Extreme Tactics

The next group of tactics is considered by most people to be totally unethical; but even so, such moves are sometimes used in negotiation. Note that many of these are controlled by laws preventing their use. These tactics are usually discovered (although the user tends to believe that they will not be), with the result that the negotiator loses face and credibility and, when a formal contract or business is at stake, may be taken to court.

Outright Lying. In this instance, the party gives totally false information to intentionally mislead the other party. Contrast this with a "white lie," in which stretching the truth is dismissed as "necessary under the circumstances." As stated earlier, what you define as a "white lie" may be different from what I define as a "white lie." But usually, there is no argument about whether an outright lie is a lie.

Giving Gifts, Bribes. Giving the other negotiator presents, favors, patronage, or other distractions is often thought to be a way to "soften them up" so that you can get more concessions and a better bargaining outcome. The question is, when is a gift appropriate and when is it just a bribe? Giving of gifts, benefits, and "perks" used to be an extremely popular practice in the sales business, particularly with a company's "good customers." In many cases, the ethical rules governing these practices have tightened considerably, and many companies now have rules that prohibit giving or receiving any gifts at all, or any "large" gift (over $25 in value).

Manipulating the Other Party's Constituency. Sometimes one party will "romance" or coerce the other party's constituency to turn the constituency against its own party. The thinking is, "If the other party's constituency is on my side, I have a better chance for a good outcome." An alternative is that if we don't like our opponent and think we can get him fired, we might talk to the other party's constituency and try to undermine our opponent's credibility and effectiveness.

Making False Threats or Promises. A party may signal its intentions with threats or promises that are actually bluffs. For example, a threat might be, "If you will not go down on your price a little, I am going to stop negotiating with you" (when in fact, you were planning to stick it out a little longer). Or a party might make a false promise, such as, "If you buy this car, I will pay for a complete cleaning and detailing for you" (when you have no intention of doing so). The bluffer may or may not be called on this tactic, but will eventually be discovered. In the long run, this negotiator's reputation and credibility will suffer. In addition, the other party may resort to revenge or even take the issue to court.

Demeaning the Other Party. Another ploy is directly insulting or slandering the other party to undermine his or her confidence. Public accusations may increase one party's power relative to the other, but again may backfire if the other party retaliates."

Deliberately Underpricing. This tactic is used to steal a job or deal from the other party.

Spying, Bugs. Spying on the other party, bugging their phone, or burglarizing their files or offices to get information on them may result in loss of reputation, ending of the negotiations, and litigation.

Stealing. As with spying and bugs, stealing information is a very risky tactic with similar consequences.

Summary

As you can see, there are a broad variety of tactics with varying degrees of "acceptability." The range of what is considered appropriate varies from person to person. There seem to be some tacit rules,[7] however. Consider your reactions to each of the preceding tactics as you were reading about them. If you reacted strongly—saying "Now, I *know* that's not the right thing to do"—it's likely to be unethical. There are some ploys that are just unacceptable by most standards. However, when you are in the situation, and under pressure to get what you want, it's surprisingly easy to rationalize these feelings and use one of these tactics. Remember that the party using such tactics runs the risk of the other party retaliating and thus escalating the emotional climate and ending the negotiation.

CHARACTERISTICS THAT AFFECT THE USE OF UNETHICAL TACTICS

How is it that people can use unethical tactics? Individuals have different ways of deciding whether or not a particular tactic is appropriate and ethical. In business, for example, choices of tactics may be guided by your own moral standards of right and wrong (which vary from person to person). Or, the person deciding on a tactic may simply select what will be most effective to solve a problem. Sometimes the choice will be based on what is easiest, cheapest, or fastest.[8] Each of these methods for choices has pluses and minuses, depending on whether you simply want to get a problem solved, or whether you want to be fair and ethical in doing so.

On a deeper level, personal characteristics, background, motivation, and moral development will tend to guide us in decisions about ethical behavior.

Background Characteristics

Among the background characteristics that affect our level of ethics are our religious upbringing, our age, our gender, our nationality, and our education.

Personality Characteristics

Within the range of personal characteristics, one of the most important predictors of willingness to use unethical practices is Machiavellianism.[9] There are people who tend to believe in a personal philosophy that was outlined in Machiavelli's classic political treatise, *The Prince*. A Machiavellian has a cynical view of people. This person is usually suspicious and mistrustful, and often candid to the point of being tactless. Machiavellians have low standards of morality, honesty, and reliability. They are selfish and unsympathetic to others. They tend to believe that people get what they deserve, and that it is necessary and appropriate to do whatever is necessary to achieve one's objectives. In contrast, people who exhibit high levels of trust in others usually have high moral standards and display higher ethical behavior.

Another personal factor affecting our ethical standards is our view of why things occur in our lives as they do. People tend to differ in the degree to which they believe they can control what happens in their lives, as opposed to everything being the result of luck, chance, or fate. If we feel that we have some control over what happens in our lives, we tend to be more ethical. If we think everything is controlled by something outside ourselves (fate), then we are more likely to engage in unethical behavior because we feel that we need to do whatever it takes to "beat the odds."

Expectations/Motivations of the Other

In Chapter 6, we discussed how one party can be influenced by the other party's expected behavior. That is, if one party expects the other to be competitive, they will take a Competitive stance. (It is much easier to begin to believe this if the other already has some kind of reputation for being very competitive, greedy, unprincipled, etc.). Thus, they are *motivated* to use Competitive tactics (which may contain ethically questionable aspects) when they expect the other side to be Competitive. Further, we will usually rationalize this behavior as being motivated by something or someone outside ourselves. It seems to be easier to be unethical when you believe that "the other party started it."

The trouble with this way of thinking is that if I am Competitive because I expected you to be, then, even if you were prepared to be Collaborative, you may switch to a Competitive Strategy because of what I do. Then the offers and counteroffers can escalate to a point where the opportunity to collaborate is totally lost, another example of a "self-fulfilling prophecy."

The Role of the Environment and the Situation

When you are forming an impression of the negotiation and the possibilities for unethical behavior, do not overlook the sociopolitical nature of the situation. The environment of the negotiation has a lot to do with the behaviors of each party.

First, consider the *relationship* between the parties. We touched on this earlier in the chapter. You looked closely into relationship in Chapter 3, so you should have a good idea of what to expect from the other party. What is the nature of your past relationships with this party, and of other people's relationships with them? Do you expect your relationship with them to be long term or short term? If it is short term, and there is nothing to lose, then be prepared for the possibility of ethically marginal tactics.[10] If it is long term, then unethical tactics generally should not enter into the situation, for such behavior would put a strain on the relationship.

Next, think about the relative *power* between the two parties. We discussed power in Chapter 4. Power can be intoxicating. The party that has more power may be tempted to abuse that power. The party with less power may engage in activities to increase their power.

Are both parties acting for themselves, or do they have *agents?* Agents may be less ethical[11] when they are negotiating for others than they would be if they were negotiating for themselves. For one thing, agents are usually under great pressure to produce positive outcomes, while those who are putting the pressure on may not know how difficult it is to achieve those outcomes. The pressure may prod them to questionable behavior. For another, agents may not have as much to lose personally as they would if they were negotiating for themselves—or at least, that is the way they tend to see it. (We take up the subject of agents in Chapter 14.)

What are the *group, organizational, and industry norms?* Members of organizations have a certain responsibility to their organization. What is expected of them by the organization, either in a formal way through rules and regulations or informally through verbal, unwritten expectations? What are the proper ends[12] of the organization that they serve? Does the organization ask of them more than is reasonable? What is the reputation of the industry that they are in? For example, many people have a negative image of lawyers; therefore, when they negotiate with a lawyer, they may believe that "all lawyers are unethical anyway!"

Tied to organizational norms is the concept of organizational *loyalty.*[13] Loyalty creates pressure. Difficulties can arise when the personal loyalties and the organizational loyalties are in conflict—the old issue of serving two masters (in this case yourself and the organization). What do you do when the organization stresses loyalty over integrity; that is, do you do whatever it takes to be a loyal member of the company, even if it means breaching your personal ethics?

Closely related to loyalty is *obedience*[14] to the organization. What if you as a negotiator are told by a higher-up to do something in negotiation that requires "blind" obedience, and it is something you would not do if you were operating solely for yourself? Suppose you were told to lie to a customer, or to a government regulator, to protect the company's position. Would you do it? Under what circumstances?

Organizational ethics are a complex subject, somewhat beyond the scope of this book. But it is a good idea to be aware that how a manager behaves can set an example for employees. They take their cues from those higher up. Employees not only listen to what the boss says, they watch what he or she does! If managers are behaving unethically, this may send a clear but unintended signal that it is okay for others to do the same.

CONSEQUENCES

We now take up the issue of how consequences can affect the use of unethical tactics. First of all, you need to know whether there are written or simply tacit consequences. If there are explicitly written consequences for particular unethical behavior—what happens if you are caught lying or being deceptive—then you ought to know them, and expect that if you use the tactic, you might get caught and punished. If the consequences are un-written, then you will have to rely on the honesty and trustworthiness of the other party. If there is good reason to expect unethical behavior, then you may want to negotiate beforehand the consequences if the other party uses unethical behaviors.

Repeats

If a tactic works once, will it be used again? Chances are that it will. If a party gets away with an underhanded tactic and the other party does not notice, then it will likely be used again in the future. A repeat tactic may be ignored the first time. Or, the party on which it is being used may re-quest that the proceedings stop and that the two parties negotiate how they are going to negotiate. Another response is for the other party to switch its own tactics to a more competitive stance. In any of these cases, the relationship will be affected and the other party will be less trusting in the future. They will probably behave more competitively in the future, and at worst, may want to take revenge. Further, there is great potential for damage to the reputation of the unethical negotiator because word will spread about the party that used dirty tactics.

Self-Image

How is one's own self-image affected by the use of dirty tactics? Probably not the way we might hope. If a party has used unethical methods, then that party is usually adept at rationalizing their behavior. To defend the use of a particular tactic,[15] the party might say:

- "It was unavoidable. It could not be helped. I had to do it in order to win."
- "It was harmless. No one got hurt. We all got more or less what we wanted."

235

- "It helped avoid negative results. Look what would have happened if I hadn't done this. . ."
- "It helped accomplish good results. Look at the good things that resulted because I did this. . ."
- "The other party deserved it [the revenge motive at work]."
- "Everybody's doing it. Why shouldn't I do it too [the social context factor]?"
- "It was fair, under the circumstances [the justice motive]."

So we see that when unethical behaviors accomplish the desired ends, similar behavior might be tried again in the future. But continued unethical behavior will eventually damage the reputation of the party using it. Over time, the party will lose power, trust, and credibility. The party will be viewed as exploitative. Word travels. Reputations get around. *Bad reputations are easy to get and hard to get rid of!*

DEFUSING POTENTIALLY UNETHICAL TACTICS

What can you do if you detect unethical behavior or if you anticipate it in upcoming negotiation? In Chapter 10 (pages 167–176), we outlined some of the techniques recommended by Roger Fisher, William Ury, and Bruce Patton,[16] on how to respond to negotiators who were using dirty tricks (mostly competitive bargaining tactics). We will briefly repeat their advice here:

Ignore the behavior. Overlook the "dirty" or unethical behavior. This may be easy to say and hard to do, but sometimes if you simply ignore the behavior, it will subside. The opponent may be trying to goad you, distract you or get you mad, and if the opponent sees that you are not responding, that may be sufficient. On the other hand, the other party may not get your subtle message, and may continue to engage in dirty tricks. In that case, step up your response tactics.

Identify the behavior. The next step is to point out the bothersome behavior. Do not personally attack the people doing it. Simply tell them that you are aware of what they are doing, and have a problem with their behavior. This lets them know you are aware of what is going on. Tactfully tell them that you know what they are doing, and be firm in making it clear that the behavior is unacceptable. When you confront inappropriate behavior, try to be as nonthreatening as possible. Define the objectionable behavior in nonevaluative terms. List the tangible effects their actions are having on you and tell them how you feel about it.[17]

Issue a warning. If the behavior continues, warn the other party that they are endangering the negotiation by continuing this behavior. They need to understand that you will not put up with the behavior, and that everyone may lose if the behavior continues and the negotiations break off.

Negotiate about how to negotiate. Another approach is to take time out to talk about how the negotiation is progressing, and to set ground rules. (Actually, this should be done before the start of negotiations, depending on how familiar you are with the other party. However, since we usually don't expect unethical conduct, we sometimes omit it from our prenegotiation discussion because we assume the other party will behave legally and ethically, and don't even want to raise it for fear of accusing them or suggesting that you think they might behave this way.) Even if ground rules were set up at the outset, you may need to review them or augment them at this point.

Retaliate. Finally, you might retaliate with a very strong scolding, anger, or even a competitive or unethical tactic of your own. We strongly recommend that you resist the urge to retaliate. Although it may be very tempting to give them back some of their own medicine, this is not a good idea. It usually only serves to escalate the tactics, resulting in an increasingly competitive response. You will have lost the opportunity for a collaborative negotiation with positive outcomes and relationships for both sides.

SUMMARY

Ethics is an important aspect of negotiation. Because negotiation is often part of a Competitive process, where parties are competing for scarce resources or for getting the best possible deal, they are often prone to move from the realm of honest behavior into dishonest behavior. In addition, as pointed out in earlier chapters, good negotiating—particularly in a Competitive context—requires a "little bit" of dishonesty. We ask for more than we really think we can get. We don't tell the other party "the truth, the whole truth and nothing but the truth" because it would give away our bargaining position. We exaggerate a bit about the advantages of what we want, and play down the deal we don't want. While these are not completely and absolutely honest, they are a regular part of negotiation. In contrast, if we completely distort the facts, make up information, outright lie, or steal or sabotage our opponent, we have strayed over the line into highly unethical behavior.

The challenge is to make sure that both parties fully understand "where the line is" and to maintain that understanding even when the proceedings get a little "hot and heavy." Good negotiations are conducted when both parties respect the same ethical rules—they agree on their definitions of appropriate and inappropriate behavior. To make the line very clear, some people have called for a "negotiator's code of ethics," perhaps written rules and regulations for negotiation. To establish these standards, however, would be a monumental task, given the variations among people's views of ethics. In addition, since we negotiate every day, usually in an informal manner, it is not clear that the "code" could be extended to apply beyond the more formal negotiations that go on within a particular industry, such as labor relations, real estate, and sales.

To a great degree, negotiators—those who negotiate on a regular basis, anyway—tend to police themselves. This is because they know that a bad reputation can be worse for business than the payoff from any single negotiated outcome. In addition, most of us negotiate with the same people on a regular basis—spouses, suppliers, customers, coworkers, partners—where our tactics will catch up with us quickly. A bad reputation, loss of credibility, and an unwillingness for others to deal with us are far more serious than anything we can gain by taking short-term advantage of our opponent.

Chapter 14

"The More the Merrier": Negotiating through Representatives and Teams

In this chapter, we take up issues you are likely to encounter when negotiating in teams or groups, and where there are three or more parties. We begin with a discussion of "agents"—people who represent you in negotiations (e.g., lawyers and real estate agents)—and "audiences"—people whom you may represent in negotiations, or who have the opportunity to watch you. We talk about how the involvement of these people can affect negotiations, and what you need to watch out for. We then survey the topic of teams and how to manage them. Finally, we discuss how negotiations are different when there are three or more parties at the table and actively involved in negotiations. At the end of the chapter, we discuss the management of multiparty negotiation and how to chair a group meeting.

Groups can make negotiation more difficult. Whether you are managing a group of people on one team or trying to manage a group of teams, as the groups grow larger, the negotiating tasks become more difficult. When there are more parties, there is more of everything: more opinions, more options, more concerns, and more time required to deal with it all. You must take all this into account when you plan for multiparty negotiation. At the outset, you should also be aware that because of these additional layers of activity and complexity, it is usually much harder to achieve collaboration in multiparty negotiation.

An underlying thread of this chapter is tying negotiations to group processes. While we touch here on some of the issues of groups, we also highly recommend reading in the area of group dynamics and group process.

AGENTS

Agents or representatives are often used in certain kinds of negotiations. We may employ an agent to negotiate on our behalf for several reasons. First, the agent may have some expertise in the subject matter that we do not possess. We contract with a real estate agent to negotiate buying a house because the agent has more expertise in the house-buying process than we do. We hire an attorney to negotiate in a bankruptcy because the attorney knows the law better than we do and can protect our rights better than we can on our own. A second major reason to hire an agent is that this individual has more negotiating expertise. For example, in many cities you can now find a "professional buyer" who will buy an automobile for you; companies often hire such experts to conduct major financial transactions. Finally, a third reason to hire an agent is that you are too emotionally involved in the issue to negotiate effectively. Agents can be helpful as somewhat detached, impartial representatives of a party. Because "agents" can represent you in a dispassionate way, they may help to get you a better agreement than if you tried on your own. It is particularly useful to have agents do the bargaining if the principal parties are adversarial.[1] Finally, agents are commonly used when there is a group of people on a side in a negotiation. Because negotiation can get chaotic when many people are trying to speak at once, agents can focus the discussion and keep order in the process.

While using agents can be an advantage, there are also disadvantages. When you add agents to the negotiation equation, you are adding more people. The more people, the more complex the mix. Even a simple negotiation between two people becomes complicated when you add an agent for each of them. Now there are interactions between four people—between each party and their agent, between the two agents, and between the two parties (who may continue to interact directly even if they have agents). Second, agents may not do exactly what you want them to do! While the parties often give their agents clear instructions (what to do, what can be agreed to, etc.), agents often decide that they cannot follow these instructions directly. So while you may gain something by using an agent, it is possible that the agent may not come back with the deal you really wanted. Finally, agents seldom perform their services for free; therefore, adding an agent increases the costs of negotiation, and may mean that you need to get a better deal than if you negotiated yourself.

Communication can be more complicated as agents are added, because the information passes through an additional filter increasing the potential for distorted messages. If the parties have a long-term relationship, they may miss out on opportunities for establishing lines of direct communication. A prime example of this is a divorce case, where the two parties may have to have some sort of relationship after the divorce is over (e.g., joint custody of children) but have relied on their attorneys to do the negotiating. While the attorneys may have negotiated a good deal "in principle," the details of day-to-day coordination are probably best worked out by the parents themselves. Another complication can result if the agents themselves become adversarial and lose their ability to represent their constituents well.

On the other hand, the agents of two or more parties may form an alliance that affects the outcome. In this situation, the agents may "collude" to work out a deal that is good for them, but not necessarily for their clients. Lawyers sometimes have relationships outside the courtroom, beyond the realm of the parties negotiating, and they may act to preserve their relationship rather than to get the best possible settlement for their clients. While we expect such people to act professionally (and there are codes of ethics that govern such things), this is not always the case. An unbalanced representation can be another problem: One party has an agent and the other(s) does not have one, or has an agent who is inexperienced in the job.

Finally, the client and the agent may simply have different aims. For example, the agent might be inclined to behave in a Collaborative or Compromising manner, while the person prefers a Competitive approach. Or vice versa. There may also be differences in their ethical values or their definitions of appropriate behavior.

As noted earlier, agents are frequently used because they are experts. They may be authorities in a *subject* area that is concerned in the negotiation, such as labor in the airline industry. Or they may be *process* experts, who are highly skilled in negotiation itself. Or they may have a sphere of *influence* important to the negotiation, such as a political connection or a circle of influential friends whom they can call on (lobbyists are good examples of this type of agent). If a party is composed of a large group, then an agent is helpful in managing the group and serving as a spokesperson.

The agent may have a fair amount of control over the proceedings, but frequently the client (constituent) controls the agent's effectiveness, either positively or negatively. For example, an agent's access to information may be restricted to prevent "leakage" of data. While this can be a drawback in managing the negotiations, the agent can use the situation to "buy time" for concession making. Because of needing to check back with the client before reaching any decision, the agent cannot be pressured into affirming an agreement that the client does not agree with. However, if the agent has to go back and forth between the negotiating table and the group, the process may take a long time.

Rules for Negotiating through an Agent

If you are going to be negotiating through an agent or are hiring an agent to negotiate for you, you need to attend to the following things:

- If you have the option of picking an agent, find a person you feel comfortable with. Since you are asking this individual to negotiate on your behalf, you need to feel trust and a sense of compatibility with him or her.

- Make sure the agent knows your objectives and interests. You need to spend enough time to help the agent understand what you are trying to achieve, your goals, target, and walkaway. You may need the agent's expertise to help you set these points, and if the person is a professional, he or she will interview you about these issues anyway.

- Discuss whether you wish to be present for some or all of the negotiations, or whether the agent will conduct all the negotiations independently. If you are to be present, also be clear about the conditions under which you will be able to speak and participate, as opposed to letting the agent do all the talking. Make sure you and the agent talk about whether you can conduct any separate and independent discussions with the other party without agents present. Negotiations can get very confused if agents are discussing things at one level while the parties are dealing with each other directly without the agents being aware of it.

- Be very clear about how much authority the agent has to "make a deal" on your behalf. Does the agent need to approve the deal with you before settlement? Can the agent make a tentative settlement? Does he or she understand the "limits" of a possible settlement?

- Make sure you have discussed a schedule for receiving progress reports.

- Finally, make sure you and the agent understand the terms of the agent's compensation for time and services. Again, agents will usually raise this issue and explain their fee structure—whether a percentage of the sale, by the hour, or some other scale. *Remember that these rates are also negotiable!* Particularly if many agents are available, it is often possible to negotiate rates. You should do this if the agent is providing limited services but is trying to charge you the "standard rate."

AUDIENCES AND THEIR EFFECT ON
NEGOTIATORS AND NEGOTIATION

Audiences can affect any negotiation, large or small, simple or complex. We discuss audiences in this chapter because they are more likely to be visible and active in larger, multiparty negotiations. Nevertheless, what we say here applies to audiences in any size or type of negotiation.

We will use the word "audience" to include all the various observers of negotiation: constituencies (people whom the negotiators or agents are directly representing), other agents and representatives, and interested or disinterested bystanders. Audiences may include the customers of a business, or a company's shareholders or suppliers. In addition, the other parties to a negotiation may also be audiences because they also observe the proceedings. In labor negotiations, audiences include the rank and file whose contract is being negotiated, other members of management who are not at the table, customers, suppliers and shareholders of the company, and other labor organizations watching this negotiation to determine what they might achieve in their own upcoming negotiations.

Audiences may be *indirectly* or *directly* involved in the negotiation proceedings. The extent of their involvement, if any, will depend on who they are, what is at stake, how much power they have, and the role they choose to play. In Chapter 4, we discussed constituencies in terms of their power over negotiators. We noted that in Competitive negotiation, constituencies usually exert a lot of pressure on negotiators—pushing them hard to achieve tough goals and holding them strictly accountable for their performance—whereas in Collaborative negotiation, constituencies tend to be supportive and leave the negotiators to their work.

An example of an indirectly involved audience would be the people who shop at a store that is embroiled in a labor dispute with its employees. Pickets outside the store encourage shoppers to boycott, and as a result, some shoppers may choose to boycott. This group would be expressing support for the employees, even though they do not attend the negotiations or have any direct stake in the eventual settlement. The group of shoppers who do not boycott the store may also have concerns about the outcome; they may fear increased prices if a wage increase occurs.

Audiences who are directly affected by the outcome are *dependent* on the negotiator. In the preceding example, the store employees would be dependent on the person serving as negotiator for them (perhaps an attorney or professional negotiator). In addition, some store employees might actually be on the negotiating team. An *independent* audience might be the members of the company's management group, who need to know

243

about the proceedings, who are supportive of the negotiator, but who exert little or no pressure or influence on how that person functions.

Audiences can exert pressure on the negotiator to varying degrees. By merely watching the proceedings, an audience can exert pressure on the negotiator. If you have ever tried to do something while someone else is intently watching you, you understand how self-conscious you can become; the same is true for negotiators, who may become very self-conscious about what they say, how they say it, and how the audience is reacting to their behavior. Audiences may also comment on the proceedings, verbally or in writing. They may require the negotiator to provide frequent reports, which increases the pressure on the negotiator. If the constituency is supportive, the negotiator will feel comfortable giving an accurate report. If the constituency is a bit hostile—believing that the negotiator is not fully and accurately representing them in the way they expected—the negotiator may feel compelled to filter the information in the report.

The audience or constituency may be in a position to decide on the remuneration for the negotiator. Sometimes an audience may hold the negotiator liable for the outcome. As noted earlier, the agent's compensation should be explicitly discussed before he or she begins work.

All these pressures, singly or in combination, can result in the negotiator taking advantage of visibility with the audience. For example, a negotiator might purposely "go public" (by making a case in front of a key audience) to get sympathy for the party's position and to avoid having to make concessions. Or the negotiator may blame the constituency for forcing a strong commitment to a position. Yet another tactic is for the negotiator to claim to have limited authority to make concessions, which may be true or not.

On the other hand, if a negotiator wants to be flexible and compromising in negotiation, it may be desirable for the negotiations to be more private. This often happens in high-level diplomacy, where, after days or weeks of public deliberations, small groups may go off to some private place, to "marathon bargain" without being disturbed until they reach some agreement. The agreement may then be announced jointly avoiding the pressures of audiences—particularly the constituencies, who may want the negotiator to maintain a hard-line position. Another approach is to have informal talks and unofficial discussions during breaks and other moments when the parties are less visible to the public. Sometimes, key concessions and breakthroughs are achieved by key negotiators meeting in the hallway, rest room or at the coffeepot for a few minutes, which they then affirm more formally back at the bargaining table.

Negotiators may also manipulate the situation indirectly, through superiors, intermediaries, or members of the constituency. The only problem with trying to circumvent the established norms for negotiation is that negotiators risk angering the party that they are working around. When "going around" someone rather than through them directly, the negotiator has to plan for the eventuality that this party will be upset and may retaliate for being ignored.

Audiences can influence negotiation effectively if they are well organized and have the financial resources to do so. Various political lobbies, advocacy groups, and public interest organizations are able to garner money and great power to influence politicians for their causes.

The Public and the Media as Audience

Negotiators communicate with the public through the media. Frequently the media is involved whether or not it is desirable; the negotiators often prefer to keep the discussion confidential, but the media "leaks" it to get a story. A negotiator needs to know how to use (and this may mean manipulate) the media to advantage, either to build support for or undermine the other party's position, to maintain privacy or "use" public disclosure to leverage the negotiations.

Use of the media is particularly common in public negotiations, such as intergovernmental, international, and labor-management relations. This occurs because the public has a "right to know" what is going on, because the outcome will be newsworthy and affect a large number of people, or because the negotiators want to use the leverage of public disclosure and accountability. In large public events such as these, managing the media can be a full-time job. Giving this job the time it needs and deserves may detract from the work of negotiation, and as a result, some individuals are put in charge of media relations as a full-time job. However, there is no doubt about the positive effect of a photo session that depicts the party surrounded by supportive constituency members, all of whom are apparently approving of and "backing" the key individual.

The more the public is involved in the outcome, the more support they are likely to offer (assuming they approve of the negotiator's position or the outcome that appears to be emerging). Likewise, the more severe the consequences of no resolution, the more likelihood of the public becoming involved. For example, when a large strike cripples key services such as busses, trains, airlines, sanitation pickup, and so on, the public quickly becomes involved. Sometimes, however, this affected public cannot exert the leverage it would like. In 1994, both professional baseball and hockey experienced long strikes by the players. While relatively few people were directly impacted by the strike—the players themselves, the owners, and those people who worked at or near the ballparks and arenas—millions of fans were directly impacted and angry, but had almost no way to express their dissatisfaction except through letters, newspaper columns and radio talk shows. In 1995, when the President and Congress failed to agree on a budget and the government shut down for several weeks, many citizens exerted "leverage" through their congressmen!

A negotiator's maneuvers during negotiation may be based on anticipated audience response. They may also be calculated to save face personally—especially if the negotiator's reputation is involved. Negotiators usually behave more competitively when they are being watched[2] because they care about a favorable evaluation from their constituency and can best achieve it when they are appearing to make strong, impassioned pleas for what the constituency wants. So, *when negotiations are public, it will be harder to get a negotiator to behave collaboratively,* because being "collaborative" may be seen as selling out to the other side. While there is not a great deal of hard data to prove it, most negotiators believe that "public negotiations" lead to poorer outcomes.

Thus, there is much to be said for holding negotiations in private, where audience pressures can be reduced. The negotiator's dilemma is to balance the push and pull of the constituency with the push and pull of the other side. If at all possible, separate relationships need to be established, one with the constituency, one with each of the other parties. Sometimes negotiators try to play off one against the other (e.g., see the description of the "limited authority" tactic in Chapter 3: "I'd love to give you this, but my constituency won't do it"), but this can be a dangerous game with the potential to backfire.

NEGOTIATING IN TEAMS

Team negotiation occurs when there are two or more people on a side. The members of a negotiating team work together and basically have the same responses and interests, but as the group expands, the process tends to become less manageable. Team members may include the spokesperson or agent, experts who serve as resources, advocates for smaller groups within the group, legal or financial counselors, a recorder, an observer, a statistical analyst, and so forth.

Team negotiation is most common in labor-management negotiations, diplomatic situations, and business deals. In such cases, though there are a number of people in the party, there may be only one spokesperson or agent who represents the group. Most of the "formal" communication between the parties occurs through the spokesperson, and this cuts down on any inadvertent revealing of information. Spokespersons usually insist on strict discipline within the team—particularly when they are at the table with the other team—so that individuals do not speak out of turn, give away confidential information, or make unauthorized agreements.

Because teamwork involves such skills as negotiation, problem-solving, and collaborating, we will look now at negotiating teams and how they can be developed. We will then move on to multiparty negotiation, and apply the information about teams to that discussion.

According to a Conference Board survey,[3] more and more companies are using teams for both short-term and long-term functions. Short-term teams may work on single issues that need quick resolution, whereas long-term teams may deal with more complex issues such as new product development, integration of information and services across different departments or geographic regions, or developing partnerships or strategic alliances. Partnerships and alliances are becoming increasingly important in light of global competition. They may become a necessity for survival or for keeping aware of the latest industry developments.[4] We mention strategic alliances here because they require not only widespread political support from the institutions exploring them, but also strong negotiating skills to create and sustain the alliance.

Teams, as they are used today, are typically cross-functional; they include people with a variety of points of view and with a variety of skills, from different functional areas in the organization. Members of departments who may not have interacted before may come together on a team. Each person may wind up being an "agent" for his or her home department's objectives and interests, as well as for the general objectives of the team. It is important that everyone be trained in team-building skills and conflict management (Chapter 10), because the different departments, perspectives, interests, and personalities are bound to come into disagreement at some point.

Successful Teams

Research on successful teams[5] has suggested that for teams to work, they must have support from all parts of the organization,[6] not just in the area where the team is being formed. In companies such as Ford, Xerox, and Scott Paper, self-managed workplace teams have provided large gains in efficiency.[7] Further, the development of a team must be gradual; teams develop over time, and different issues (e.g., membership, power, inclusion, decision making) surface as the team learns to work together. Teams are more successful[8] when implementation is carefully planned, although it is probably impossible to anticipate all the steps that need to occur, or how they will be executed. Initially, a team needs guidance from a leader who understands how to coach team members. The roles of the individual team members as well as the team as a whole will change and evolve as the team matures.

The team must have authority and adequate information to do its work. Xerox Corporation has a successful teamwork relationship with its 6,200 unionized copier assemblers. Xerox shares internal financial documents with union officials and teaches them how to read and interpret key company documents.[9] Their purpose and sense of direction or mission must be clear. Their boundaries[10] must also be defined. The members of the team must be willing to participate, to be involved, and they need to learn to trust each other and the organization. Feedback skills must be developed. The evaluation system must be compatible with the types of functions represented on the team.

One of the more difficult behaviors for a team to learn is how to work as a team—not simply as a group of individuals—and yet maintain their individual perspectives and the key interests of their respective departments and divisions. Team members need to be able to take risks, argue for what they believe in (particularly when it deviates from what the team seems to want to do), and express their opinions without fear of ridicule or reprisal.

A successful team is cohesive, open, can express feelings, and value the opinions of others (even if they do not agree with the other points of view). You may notice from this description that successful teamwork has strong parallels with successful execution of the Collaborative Strategy, where the parties work together to apply resources more effectively.

A study by Hans J. Thamhain[11] lists 15 factors that are critical to success for teams (from among 50 listed as important by managers):

Task-Related Factors

1. Plans.
2. Leadership.
3. Autonomy.
4. Experience.
5. Visibility.

People-Related Factors

6. Work satisfaction.
7. Mutual trust.

8. Good communications.
9. Minimal conflict.
10. Minimal personal risk.

Organization-Related Factors

11. Stability of the team.
12. Availability of resources.
13. High management involvement.
14. Stable goals and priorities.
15. Ample rewards and recognition.

Just Because You Call It a Team Doesn't Mean . . .

Teams may appear to be easy to form and operate, but it takes hard work by everyone for a team to be successful, especially if the concept of teams is new to an organization. If you are involved with the implementation of a team, watch out for the following pitfalls:[12]

- Using the term "team" without explaining how to do it—assuming that if you name it a "team," it will function as a team. A real team requires a great deal more coordination and integration of its efforts than a "group."
- Not providing a leader. This is especially important in the beginning when the group needs guidance, coaching, and feedback. If the group does not have a formal leader, then it should draft a person from among its members to serve this function.
- Letting a team work alone without support from upper management. If the team becomes isolated, it will lose track of what it is supposed to accomplish, or the ability to implement what it designs. A team will have to work in the system and thus will need support from the system.
- Not providing a sense of direction to the team, or allowing it to develop its own goals and visions.
- Overlooking training for everyone (not just team members), as well as resources that the team can call on if conflict erupts and team functions break down.

One other pitfall of trying to implement teams is overenthusiasm without pulse taking. Organizations climb on the empowerment bandwagon, then forget to monitor how the group is doing, or to check whether the team has the resources, expertise, and authority to carry through its actions. They forget that the idea is for the group to decide as a group, not for one "empowered" person to take over. If this happens, it is probably no improvement over the old process.

Nor does teamwork happen automatically. Training is needed. And the training must take into account that some of the people involved have been operating in one way for years, so it will be hard to change their mode of behavior. It is hard to train people to handle empowerment, especially if they have been complying for years in the workplace.[13]

Growth and Phases[14] of Teams

Getting teamwork started and keeping it going can present a challenge. Many teams seem to follow a distinct "life cycle." At first, there is usually resistance to a new way of doing things. Then comes a period of information sharing and development of expectations, followed by commitment to particular roles and expectations.

As a team grows in experience, there will be a phase of stability. People perform as committed, and the group produces results. The successes provide impetus and exhilaration to propel the group along.

As teams age, they may run into more difficult issues, more conflict, and communication blocks. They may find it hard to be "fair" to everyone. If the members of the group start to make assumptions about what they think and feel, some concerns may be overlooked.

In mature groups, the members may revert to old habits, lose their initial motivation, or become frustrated because they run into other parts of the system that do not give them adequate help, support, and assistance. Turmoil begins to occur. Expectations are disrupted and anxiety and resentment may surface. Fingers are pointed. Anger and disillusionment sinks in.

Some options at this stage would be to disband, to ignore the disruptions (though they will certainly occur again), to start back at the beginning, or to "renegotiate" the role expectation by publicly discussing what is expected of the team and its members, and working to eliminate any breakdowns and blocks. But none of these options really solves the problems. A better way is to expect that difficulties of this sort will occur, to anticipate them, and to prepare for them.

If a group does get stuck, what can be done to move the team back toward productivity? Here are some suggestions:[15]

- Be sure that the corporate culture supports teams.
- Let the group know that "plateaus" are common, and that activity has to be sustained to move beyond them.
- Consider providing some retraining, or bringing in a process consultant.
- Help them work on problem-solving, interpersonal, and technical skills.
- Provide career paths and opportunities for some to transfer out of the team if necessary, so that unresolvable personality clashes between key people do not persist and drag everyone else down with them.
- Expand teams to other parts of the organization, or work on removing external barriers that may be hampering team operations.
- Show members the broader picture (by providing information) to give them more context.
- Make sure personal and team growth is an objective—help them work through the conflict.
- Look at team development as a process to keep refining and improving.
- Recognize the group's successes, and make sure that it receives a great deal of acclaim, approval, and visibility.

Teams composed of upper-level managers tend to be more competitive and less cooperative[16] than teams on lower levels. Further, it is more difficult to get long-time managers and other employees to change to a new set of rules, particularly if they have been operating by different ones for a long time. However, in spite of these conflicts, managers may gain from working together. It is important to stress that individual differences are a strength. Further, groups need to acknowledge their mistakes so they can learn from failure. This is also harder for upper level groups to do.

If There Are Disputes

Disputes within a team[17] can be resolved in two ways: The parties can negotiate directly, or a third party (either a team member, team leader or outsider) intervenes with a mediation process much like the ones described in Chapter 11. When done by a third party, the following process is used:

- The consultant discusses the issues with the parties.
- The parties openly and honestly discuss their expectations.

251

- All expectations are written down.
- Expectations must be understood (though not necessarily accepted) by both parties.
- The parties (with the third party) create an agenda of issues to be discussed.
- Negotiation occurs between the parties, facilitated by the third party.
- Pressures and threats are to be avoided if possible.
- When an explicit agreement is reached, it is written down.
- The parties adjourn, test the agreement, and return to renegotiate if needed.

Training in Group Work or Teamwork

For group work or teamwork of any sort to be successful, the members of the team must be trained for the task. Training is the key to successful teams. However, a 1990 survey showed that only 5 percent of companies gave their employees training in group decision making or problem-solving.[18] While no statistics are available, the amount of explicit training in conflict management and negotiation is often less than this. As teams are used more and more, the need for good training programs will increase.

There are a number of ways to train team members, one of which is role playing or simulations.[19] These provide imaginary or real-life situations that a team figures out how to solve. The advantage of this method over the traditional ways of learning is that the members have an opportunity to try out the actual behaviors as they are learning. They learn about the power of a group working together, as opposed to one person working alone. They learn to trust others, to work together with them, and to give feedback. They learn also to deal with conflict resolution.

What is particularly important in using simulations is the feedback the instructor or facilitator gives to the team members. Although members learn much from the actual participation and results of the role plays, they also need "debriefing," both as individuals and as a group. They need for an objective observer to tell them what they are doing right and wrong.

MULTIPARTY NEGOTIATION

We now turn to our main focus in this chapter—negotiation in which there are more than two parties. When there are three or more parties or negotiators, then you have multiparty negotiation.[20] As parties are added to negotiation, and complexities increase, negotiations are much more susceptible to breakdown. Therefore, the participants in multiparty negotiation need to commit to managing the process very carefully if they want to realize some measure of success. We will turn to the actual management of multiparty negotiation in a moment. First, we look at some of the aspects of negotiation and how they affect multiparty negotiation. These include the number of parties and people, the complexity of information, the social complexity, the complexity of the process, and the complexity of strategies.

Number of Parties and People

When adding new individuals to a negotiation—for example, in moving from one-on-one negotiations to two or more parties on a side—all aspects of negotiation are affected: people, issues, concerns, and time. Each party needs time to be heard. Individuals bring different agendas, concerns, and issues. People are concerned about their "image" in front of others. Sometimes, social and political concerns may surface, and there may be difficulties about status if one person or a few in a group have a much higher status than the others. The higher-status people may dominate, and the low-status person may not receive adequate airtime. An example of this would be a group with four vice presidents and a manager; the vice presidents may make it impossible for the manager to gain sufficient time to express concerns.

Problems may also occur if the number and type of people on each side vary considerably. One party may bring in experts for testimony and other authorities to support their position. Such a show of numbers may intimidate another party. Bringing all the parties to the negotiation may provide an impressive show of force, but can be disruptive and distracting. However, there may be a point of diminishing returns for the party with many participants. The group may become difficult to manage, their organization may fall into disarray, and they may be unable to present their side convincingly in negotiation.

Complexity of Information

As you add parties, you also add issues, perspectives, information, facts, values, and documentation, potentially from each member of the party. As this information base increases, it becomes harder to manage and keep track of. The parties will have to develop and stick to a clear-cut agenda,

253

so that the discussion does not wander from one issue to another (or get manipulated by a small group who want to dominate the proceedings). Special "referees" may need to be appointed to orchestrate the conversation, keep the parties on track, and impose some order on the procedure.

Social Complexity

As the group grows larger, its dynamics change. In a small group, everyone feels free to participate—and usually does. Conformity pressures may exist, but usually they are not too strong. However, as the group gets larger, it also becomes less homogeneous, so there is likely to be more diversity and it becomes harder to find a solution that satisfies everyone. This can be positive or negative. If there is a need for conformity or consensus, it may be difficult to achieve. On the other hand, if everyone conforms to present a "united front" in spite of their differences, important information and input may be overlooked.

Complexity of the Process

When two parties negotiate, the sides can take turns—first one party speaks, then the other does the same. But as parties are added to the negotiation, the process becomes more complicated. As you add people who wish to speak, more time will be required. At the same time, individuals become more intimidated about speaking in a larger group, and hence people speak up less often. If one party tries to influence or take over the negotiations,[21] rules of order may be harder to apply. It becomes easy for the proceedings to get off track.

For these reasons, the parties in multiparty situations should establish specific rules for the process *before* the negotiations get underway. The parties need to agree on how the process will work—who will speak first, second, and so on. Or, as mentioned earlier, it may be useful for someone to take on the role of a referee and facilitator to help the group proceed in an orderly manner.

Complexity of Strategies

In a two-party negotiation, there are usually only two strategies at work, yours and the other party's. In multiparty negotiations, there is much more to keep track of because each party can potentially take a stance with respect to each of the other parties. Parties may deal separately with each other or with the rest of the parties as a group. For example, if you are Party C and you choose to deal with one party at a time, Party B will observe how you interact with Party A, and this will affect your negotiation with Party B. And so forth. Constituencies, especially powerful ones, must also be factored into the equation.

All this strategic complexity usually leads to more competitive behavior. Parties entrench in their positions more easily to show their toughness (especially when they are being observed by multiple parties and by influential audiences). This makes it harder for any party to make concessions, because they are concerned that conciliatory behavior will be viewed as a weakness by audiences or other parties. As in any negotiation, parties that have viable BATNAs will be in a better position than those with no Alternatives.

One strategy for coping with the complexity in multiparty negotiations is for a party to ally with another party. Such a coalition can build strength and power and prove advantageous in multiparty negotiation, but collaborative negotiation will in all likelihood probably be sacrificed. "Strength in numbers" and the ability to muster a dominant coalition is likely to drive out Collaborative processes.

This all suggests that it is to everyone's interest to control the number of people directly involved in the negotiation (if possible), and to carefully manage multiparty negotiation.

MANAGING MULTIPARTY NEGOTIATION

Multiparty negotiation can be very complicated and therefore has to be managed carefully to result in any degree of negotiating success. It is hard enough to manage a large number of people when they are basically aligned, but when they are at odds, the task is even more difficult. In this section, we offer suggestions for managing the group process to give all sides fair and complete representation.

Before the process actually begins, there are many factors to consider. These include the conditions for the meeting, such as lighting, noise level, ventilation, temperature, configuration of space (e.g., where people sit, whether a large table is used), group size, and seating pattern (e.g., random, alphabetical, "chief" negotiators opposite to each other). If the meeting is to be long, larger rooms provide more opportunity for people to spread out and be comfortable. Parties and members need to be identified with cards or name tags. Supplies such as pencils and paper will be needed. A chalkboard or flip chart is an excellent tool for recording ideas, structuring the agenda, and providing a focused place to propose motions, amendments, and wording of documents.

Do You Need a Facilitator?

It is a good idea to have an impartial, neutral person to chair or moderate the negotiation meetings. The chair should be someone who has no stake in the outcome and will not be affected by it, but who can be active in structuring and monitoring the group process. This position may be filled by a consultant or mediator (see Chapter 11).

Make Sure Everyone Knows the Score

First, it is crucial for everyone to understand the costs of a failed negotiation.[22] That is, does the group have a viable Alternative, and are parties willing to move toward it if the possible solution is sufficiently poor? The costs are usually different for each negotiator. It is important for each party to consider what will happen if there is no agreement. Will someone else make the decision? Or will there be none?

Another important area concerns the options available to the group. Everyone needs to understand all the options. Research suggests that this is not usually the case[23] in multiparty negotiation. With more people involved in multiparty negotiation, there is likely to be more confusion and missed information. As a result, it may be useful, as the group begins to work on the problem, to list, review and discuss all the possible available options as well as the Alternatives.

Define How the Decision Will Be Made

Because multiparty negotiation is a complex process, there must be a plan for how negotiations are to proceed. Parties need to know what to expect, and also need to have an opportunity to change the process if necessary. Deciding on how the agreement or decision will be made can be fraught with difficulty. Who should decide? How should the decision be made?

First, group decisions are often made by a minority of the members. If one party is stronger than the other due to greater power or status or just plain persuasiveness, then their preference may, by default, turn into the selected process. Or perhaps one group might convince another to join with them, forming a significant coalition, and the resulting more powerful combined group will promote their views.

The decision may be agreed on by voting on it. But how will it be decided? Simple majority? Two-thirds? Must there in fact be a consensus?

If the goal is consensus, it will be harder with multiple parties than it would be in a two-party negotiation. It stands to reason that two parties in a dispute either agree or do not. But if you have three, four, or more parties, it is a major challenge to get everyone to agree. If implementation of the decision is important, consensus is likely to be more critical, because negotiators will be more committed to a decision reached by consensus than by a simple majority.

The moderator should be sure that all pertinent information is presented to and considered by the group. Diverse information and perspectives should be invited, both from parties and from constituencies if applicable. Make sure that all parties have been effectively heard, and no one feels that they were "shut out" or ignored in the deliberations.

The moderator will need to monitor the discussion to be sure that all parties have a chance to speak, and that they all follow the predetermined rules. People also need to be allowed to vent emotions if necessary.

To assist the moderator in managing the discussion, there are several helpful methods that enhance group decision making, such as the Delphi technique, brainstorming, and nominal group technique. These methods allow many parties with diverse points of view a way to have their ideas heard and entered in the group process. In the *Delphi technique,* the moderator sends out a questionnaire to all parties before the beginning of negotiations. The moderator summarizes the results and sends out questions to all the parties again. This process can continue for as many rounds as needed, with the moderator asking questions to uncover issues, concerns, and options. The advantage of this process is that it is *not* face to face, thus saving on the emotional wear and tear likely to occur in group meetings. In addition, those parties who may be more timid in participating in large group discussions have an equal chance of getting their ideas into the discussion. However, because this method may lead to concessions and compromises, it may result in a Compromise solution rather than a truly Collaborative solution.

Brainstorming can also be used in a group setting. As mentioned in Chapter 7, this usually works best with several small groups rather than one large one, depending on the number of people involved. The groups write down as many ideas as possible, without judging them. Then the lists of ideas are brought back to the whole group where they may be prioritized, discussed, or voted on.

Nominal groups may be used after brainstorming, or can be used separately. In a nominal group, each person prioritizes the previously generated list, then the moderator records the tally. Data are then assembled and redistributed to the group several times, to try to achieve some consensus on priorities.

The Key Role of the Agenda

Especially in multiparty negotiation, it is very important to have an agenda and to *use it*. The agenda can be generated by the moderator, or by the group as a whole, if feasible. The agenda not only keeps people on track, it defines what that track will be. It may include:

- A list of the issues under negotiation.
- A definition of how the issues are going to be discussed.
- The order of the discussion of issues (and perhaps the people to present them).
- The amount of time that will be allocated to the discussion and resolution of each issue.

As with other aspects of multiparty negotiation, with more people involved it will be harder to get consensus on an agenda, but it is important. Agendas can be very strong control mechanisms if used manipulatively. The person who makes up the agenda can dominate the meeting by determining what gets discussed and what does not get discussed, and the order in which it is done. Therefore, if the agenda needs to be changed, this should be allowed for. If you believe that the agenda is manipulative and unfair, do not hesitate to question it and the way it was developed.

Steps in Moderating the Group Process

The mandate for the moderator of multiparty negotiation should be to *manage the process, not the outcome.* (The moderator of a multiparty negotiation resembles the mediator in third-party disputes.) If you find yourself in the position of moderator,[24] you can follow specific steps to make the negotiation run as smoothly as possible, starting with the very opening moments:

- Introduce yourself.
- Describe your role.
- Introduce the agenda and get the group to okay it, or build the agenda with the group.
- Set ground rules for meeting times, type of output the group will generate, recording group activities, breaks, location and frequency of meetings, and consultation with constituencies.

- Review how group decisions will be made and implemented.
- Prepare opening remarks that set the tone for the meeting.
- Be sure everyone has a chance to speak and that no one person dominates.
- Look for common interests, priorities, and concerns.
- Have one person restate another's position (active listening) to assure that people are paying attention to each other.
- "Mirror" the communication. Ask "why?" "Listen with your whole being."[25]
- If you ask a question, wait a while for an answer, even if there is silence. Many people cannot stand silence and will fill the silence with new information.
- Try to maintain your neutrality—do not show bias (by your words or actions) to support or oppose any particular subgroup at the meeting.
- Avoid spending too much time on one issue. Keep the pace moving. If the group bogs down, take a break.
- Bring in supporting information if appropriate.
- Allow simultaneous discussion of several issues at once, to encourage trade-offs.
- Use a chalkboard or flip chart to list issues and interests and map discussions. People are often less competitive when they focus on a display of the issues, as opposed to focusing their comments and criticisms at each other.
- Have the group invent options. Use brainstorming and other methods to generate ideas. Use the chalkboard or flip chart for recording these, discussing each, and recording the pros and cons.
- Summarize often—where the group is, and where it should be going.
- Make sure standards are fair and reasonable.
- As possible, try to move the group toward the selection of a Collaborative solution. Use techniques mentioned in Chapter 7 such as logrolling, bridging, packaging, trade-offs, modifications.
- If an agreement at this point is not possible, aim for some form of "general agreement" or "agreement in principle" or common "statement of goals." Plan to come back later and attempt to make it more specific and applied.
- When you have a tentative agreement, write it down. Keep a good set of notes on what is discussed at each meeting.

- Use a "one-text procedure"[26] as you are trying to assemble a final agreement. Write out a tentative draft of the things that have been agreed to, and circulate it so that people may continually make modifications, changes, additions, and corrections until the language is completely drafted.
- Discuss the steps that need to happen after the meeting concludes, and decide who will do what.
- Thank the participants for their time, energy, and commitment.
- Hold a postmortem to learn from the process and the results.

The final item assumes a resolution. However, this may be difficult to achieve in multiparty negotiations. If consensus appears impossible, try to move *toward* consensus by aiming for a preliminary or tentative agreement first. If this is successful, the parties can proceed to improve on the agreement, moving closer and closer to their goal with each iteration. If a lot of time has been spent getting to the first milestone, tempers may be frayed and people may be tired. In that case, take some time (to cool off), then come back and try to push on. At this stage, conflict management skills may be necessary to keep things moving along (see Chapter 10).

SUMMARY

In this chapter, we have discussed how to manage multiparty negotiations—those situations in which the parties have agents, constituencies, and audiences, or in which there are multiple parties who will be negotiating, such as teams, task forces, and project groups. These negotiations are often much more complex, and often require independent facilitators or group leaders to direct the parties so that the process moves along effectively.

Chapter 15

Mastering Strategic Negotiation

Congratulations! You have just completed a thorough and detailed examination of a very complex process. Now is the time to review what you have learned, and, more importantly, figure out how you will profitably apply it in your work and personal life.

First, a review of the basic principles is in order. Let's return briefly to the beginning, Chapter 1. There we left our fictional Helen as she found herself on the wrong end of a series of negotiation situations. We hope you won't make the same kind of mistakes, now that you are an expert. Or will you?

First, you must make sure you *apply* what you know about negotiation. This means recognizing negotiation situations in time to take a strategic approach to them. Think back over the last week. How many opportunities to negotiate did you encounter? And in how many of these situations did you actually take a systematic, strategic approach? If you are like most of us, you did not recognize some situations as opportunities to use your knowledge of negotiation, at least until you had already said or done some things that considerably limited the possible range of outcomes. In other words, you didn't recognize that you could have negotiated until it was too late! You also might have recognized the opportunity to negotiate in some other situations, but felt that it was not worth the time or effort to really improve your outcomes. Finally, if you are like most of us, you also recognized some other negotiation situations in time to negotiate—but failed to take a careful, strategic approach. Did you use your standard response to a negotiating situation—for most of us it is a knee-jerk Competitive or Compromise strategy—rather than diagnose the situation and pick the best strategy? Or, perhaps you picked an appropriate strategy, but went ahead and implemented it in haste, before you had done your homework and developed your negotiating tactics with care. All these negotiating errors are common, even among people who ought to know better. The following sections review each type of error.

ERROR 1. FAILURE TO RECOGNIZE A SITUATION AS A "NEGOTIATION OPPORTUNITY"

If the other party is negotiating and you aren't, guess who is going to win? Similarly, if the other party simply sees it as a situation where they should "rightfully" get whatever they want, guess who is going to get the lion's share of the payoff?

First, you need to recognize a negotiation situation when you are in one. Negotiation can occur when:

- There are two or more parties.
- The parties depend on each other for a full realization of the best outcomes.
- Each party has a clear preference for what they would like to get or what they want the other to do, and these preferences or priorities may be in conflict.
- The parties are willing to engage in give-and-take to achieve a resolution to their conflict.[1]

Although this definition suggests that negotiation is *possible* in all situations, it does not automatically mean that you *should* negotiate in all situations. Sometimes you *should* choose to avoid negotiating—or accommodate to the other's wishes—either because the conflict required to resolve the problem may be intense, or because the relationship with the other party is far more important than the outcome and if you try to exert influence, you might make the other angry or upset. This is often true in long-term personal and business relationships, and particularly where there is a power difference (e.g., the other party is your boss or one of your parents).

While we have acknowledged that accommodation or avoidance is an appropriate strategy at times, make sure that you have truly given the question a moment's thought and considered your options. Are you certain you should accommodate the other party, or avoid conflict altogether? Or are you just giving in because you did not realize that you had a choice, or don't know how to stand up to the other's demands and requests? And, if you do accommodate to the other party, particularly on a repeated basis, *make sure they are aware of it*. For example, when you are with them in the future, you might remind them of your past accommodation as a rationale for their accommodation to your needs now.

A negotiating situation that seems too trivial to bother with in the present can be of value to you if you step back and view it in terms of the value and importance of a long-term relationship. All relationships are composed of many negotiation opportunities—setting goals, assigning roles and responsibilities, dividing work, coordinating timelines and priorities, and so forth. For example, living together with someone else is an ongoing negotiation—dividing up household chores, sharing common property (cars, television sets), or deciding what to have for dinner. Each "negotiation" can have ramifications for the future of the relationship. It might seem at first thought that many *minor* negotiating situations are too trivial to be worth thinking about in the context of negotiation, but in reality the reverse is true. The strategic negotiator recognizes that any negotiation situation, no matter how small, can have at least four possible results:

1. It can be used to derive immediate benefits in this situation.
2. It can affect the probability of winning or losing subsequent negotiations.
3. It can strength or weaken the relationship between you and the other in the future.
4. It can also be used to learn more about how you and the other party negotiate.

ERROR 2. FAILURE TO TAKE A STRATEGIC APPROACH—OR THE *RIGHT* STRATEGIC APPROACH

If you are like most of our readers, you have applied the concepts and tools of negotiation in a number of cases since you began to read this book. Odds are, you have encountered at least one important or major negotiating situation. For example, you may have found yourself involved in discussion with a boss about future assignments, a review of your performance, or access to resources you need for work. And no doubt you tried to bring in some of the tactics of good negotiation from this book. That is how most of us expand our negotiating skills—by practicing new approaches. For instance, maybe you tried a new, more courageous opening in which you made a somewhat larger opening bid than usual, leaving room for lots of movement toward the other party's position before the outcome could become unfavorable to you. This style of opening can work well in some situations, as it allows you room to back down without actually falling below your Alternative. But was this the right tactic? Not if the *strategy* it applies to was wrong. (Remember the eighth rule of strategic negotiation (page 54): The WRONG strategy guarantees FAILURE!)

Quick. Which strategy does this tactic apply to? Right. This tactic is from the discussion of the sequence of events in *Competitive* strategy, in Chapter 6. And by focusing on tactics, you may have ignored the essential first steps in the negotiating process that help you identify the correct strategy. Remember, you are a better negotiator than most people you will negotiate with when you are a *strategic* negotiator, not just a tactical negotiator. Since many negotiations with the boss call for noncompetitive strategies, your tactic may get you the desired outcome but sour the relationship with your boss. Remember the third rule of strategic negotiation, too: Don't compete unless you are prepared to . . . LOSE! And who wants to risk losing to their boss? It is often safer to leave hard-core Competitive job negotiations to the unions and take a Collaborative, Compromise approach when one-on-one with your boss.

ERROR 3. FAILURE TO CORRECTLY IMPLEMENT THE RIGHT STRATEGY

Now that you have five basic strategies in your negotiation repertoire instead of just one, you need to take extra care to implement each one properly.

Even if you avoid Errors 1 and 2, you can lose many negotiations. Errors 1 and 2 address the fundamental strategic question of effectiveness: Do we recognize negotiation opportunities, and do we recognize which strategy is appropriate? If you make either of these errors, you are going to be ineffective because you aren't even trying to do the right thing. But the third fundamental strategic question is, Are we doing it right? It does no good to recognize that a Collaborative style is appropriate in negotiations with your boss, unless you can implement it well and fully. A sloppy approach to Collaborative negotiation can send the wrong signals or misread the situation, breaking down the trust needed for Collaboration. Remember the eleventh rule of negotiation: *Trust* is easier to destroy than it is to build!

Check if done:

1. Define the Issues:	
2. Assemble the Issues and Define the Agenda:	
3. Analyze the Other Party:	
4. Define Underlying Interests—Yours and Theirs:	
5. Consult with Others who have relevant input:	
6. Manage the Goal Setting process—Openings and Targets:	
7. Identify your Own Limits—Walkaways and Alternatives:	
8. Develop Supporting Arguments and consider possible Options for Settlement:	

Figure 15.1 Negotiation Planning Guide

How do you avoid major implementation errors in a Collaborative or other strategy? How did you guess—we're going to quote another rule (the fifth rule of strategic negotiation): *Follow the eight steps of negotiation planning.* If you follow the sequence, you will have a road map for implementing your strategy, and this will ensure far better results than an unplanned approach. Figure 15.1 is a checklist you can photocopy and use to log what you learn from the planning process.

THE STRATEGIC NEGOTIATION PROCESS REVISITED, OR HOW TO IMPLEMENT THE RIGHT STRATEGY WELL

In Chapters 1 through 4, we introduced the topic of strategic negotiation by showing how important it is to analyze the key strategic issues. The information gathered by following the questions and issues raised in these chapters will help you assess your own position, the other party's position, and the negotiation context. While this is easy to do *after* a negotiation is over, it may not be so easy before one has begun—yet that is the critical skill that must be practiced.

In strategic business planning, we often encourage the parties to focus on the most difficult issues rather than to rely on the information that is easy to obtain. Ask yourself, *of all the information and questions raised* (e.g., the eight questions in Figure 15.1), *which are most critical to your choice of strategy?* Which are hardest to nail down? Which are characterized by the most uncertainty? In strategic planning, information is judged on the strength of its ability to alter and improve decisions. And in any individual negotiation situation, much of the information you gather about yourself, other parties, and the context will *not* have such power. The real skill comes when you develop the experience and insight to sense what the key issues are and explore them in depth *before* choosing your negotiating strategy. The analytical processes of strategic negotiation will help you gain real insight into these questions, instead of just plunging you into a detail-oriented analysis that fails to substantially improve your decision-making process.

For example, suppose you have been approached by your boss and asked to take a one-month off-site assignment to set up a project team at another division. What are the key issues for you to consider? Most likely, there are only two. First, you need to understand your boss's motivation and intentions very carefully. She will no doubt tell you this is a great opportunity that will give you breadth of experience and help your career.

But why did you get this assignment? Is it because she truly values your skills? Is she evaluating you for a possible promotion, based on how you complete this assignment? Does she have specific expectations about how things will be set up or organized that she has not shared with you? Is she asking you to do this because she was asked to do this herself by her boss, and she is simply trying to pass the buck? Or, most problematically, does she want to get you out of the office to find out whether your key assistant can really handle your duties while you are gone? You need to explore the context of her decision, including the pressures on her, so that you understand the consequences for you of good performance at this assignment.

The second key consideration is, what opportunities may flow from a stint on this new project team? Will you receive training in some critical skill or competency, such as reengineering or change management, that will become invaluable in the company because the new CEO intends to roll out a reengineering program next year? Or will you simply become less visible to your boss and other key managers in your own division, and perhaps be more likely to be passed over for promotions? Again, here is a high-priority issue that you must explore from many angles before choosing your negotiating strategy.

Let's say you decide that your boss is probably not in your corner on this one. Perhaps your research revealed a well-substantiated rumor that all the managers in your division have been quietly informed they must cut their staff by 10 percent over the next year. With that as the context for your boss's recommendation—that you leave the office to join a team at another division—you recognize that she may see the situation as an easy way to deal with her downsizing problem. One of the secretaries also tells you she heard your boss ask your key assistant if he would be interested in receiving some training in your area. Your worst suspicions seem to be confirmed!

Because you are angry, your first instinct may be to dig in your heels and take a Competitive stance, in which you refuse to accept the assignment, demand job security in your current position, or demand a transfer to a new position before you agree to work on the team. However, let's further assume that you also followed up on the second critical issue, the impact of the team assignment on your job opportunities. And let's imagine you learned that this was indeed a pilot reengineering project, and that the top brass are planning to reengineer the entire corporation next year. Now you realize there are other things you could get out of this negotiation that might be as good—or even better than—a commitment from your boss that your current job will be secure. For one thing, you realize *no* jobs are secure once reengineering takes hold of a company. Even your boss could lose her department or job, for that matter. But what if you could get your boss to approve some special training in reengineering for you before the team assignment, so that you are positioned as one of the few experts on reengineering in the company? And what if you could use this new expertise to gain access to other opportunities; for example, wouldn't you like to be the person in charge of briefing department heads and the senior management about the progress of the reengineering process? That way, your expertise in reengineering would be visible to managers as they struggled to apply the discipline, making you one of the most promotable people in the entire company! Now you begin to see ways in which a Collaborative approach might work better than a Competitive one. You might be happy to meet your manager's short-term need to cut staff, if she was willing to help you reposition yourself to play a key role in your company's reengineering process. That is truly a win-win process!

Such is the power of strategic issue analysis. The more you think about the other players, your own needs, and the context, the more possible scenarios you can see. Once you have gained strategic insight into the situation—once you can see more of the constraints and opportunities than other parties—you are in a position to provide strategic leadership in the negotiation. You can now reframe the negotiation to shape it toward the strategy you choose.

Chapter 5 reviews the key details for selecting a negotiating strategy. The model that describes the nature of this choice process represents the decision on two dimensions: the importance of the relationship, and the importance of the outcome. And, as you have also realized by now, the model does not tell you which relationship to consider, or what outcomes to pursue. These flow from your problem analysis, and from your strategic imagination. In this example, at first, it is the relationship with your current boss and department that seems most important to you. You don't want to leave your department, and you don't want to anger your boss, but on the other hand, it looks as if your boss is not really leveling with you about why she wants you to take this assignment. So you get angry at what you discover, and decide to take a "tough" position and get even. But as you think about the changes occurring in your firm, you shift your definition of the issues and the values of various relationships. You begin to see that you might use this opportunity to build a broader relationship with the company, in which you are positioned as an expert with skills that will be in great demand in coming months. And you realize that your boss will probably have to define her relationship to the firm in a new way as well, if she is to profit from the sweeping changes that are coming instead of being run over by them (along with other middle managers). Thus, you can reframe the negotiation by pursuing ways to benefit both your and your boss's relationship to the change process. That is a very different way to think about the relationship dimension.

And the outcome dimension is also a variable, subject to the information and insight you gain through strategic analysis. At first, the outcome of importance appeared to be whether *you* would be the one who gets sidelined in your department, and therefore it seemed likely that you should compete for job security. As an Alternative, you also tried to raise the costs of sending you off on the assignment, so that your boss would find it easier to send someone else off instead. And if you thought about it, you might decide that if you gave your boss a really hard time about the transfer, her Alternative might be to decide you were an uncooperative employee, and target you for the first round of layoffs. But when you define the broader context, you see that the outcome you desire is to be positioned as one of the few people in the firm who prosper from the changes brought about by reengineering, instead of being hurt by them. When the situation is redefined in this way, you can Accommodate or Collaborate with your boss, trading with her what she wants for what you want ("logrolling" as we called it), since you have a different outcome in mind than she does. You might even take this further by explicitly proposing a Collaborative process to her, helping each other as the company goes through its changes. Will she shift her focus toward surviving the reengineering process, too? If so, you can join forces to help each other out, creating a win-win strategy. Perhaps you can even convince her to include your department in the reengineering pilot study.

What if your boss does not respond to your Collaborative overtures? If she continues to focus on her short-term staffing problem, then you might Accommodate, do what she asks, and try to get what you can from the team assignment on your own. However, it will probably be more appealing to you to compete with her, in a different way. Now you see your relationship with your boss as less important than your relationship to the company's reengineering process, so you don't mind risking the relationship with the boss. If you *do* end up Competing, it certainly won't be the kind of competition that you would have pursued without your analysis. Instead of demanding job security, you will now demand reengineering training and corporate visibility—things your boss is more likely to concede as they cost her little relative to the benefit they provide to you.

Whatever strategy you decide to pursue—based on your assessment of the relative importance of specific relationships and outcomes—you will now initiate an appropriate negotiation process. Will you wind up using your first strategy choice? It depends in part on your boss's willingness to engage in the style of negotiation you initiate. Chapters 6 through 8 detailed the opening steps and general implementation paths for each of the five strategies of negotiation. Whether you Compete, Collaborate, Compromise, Accommodate, or Avoid (which will be difficult in this context), your success will now depend on the skill with which you use the tactics appropriate to your chosen strategy.

Deep in every strategist's subconscious mind, Murphy's law echoes loudly: "Whatever can go wrong, will go wrong!" The same is true for negotiation strategies: something often *does* go wrong as you try to implement your strategy. That is why implementation and follow-through are such important steps. Collaboration between you and your boss may be difficult to build, or some event may break down trust after you start to collaborate. Perhaps she agrees to help you develop expertise in reengineering, and uses the department's training budget to send you to a one-week program. Then, when you return, you find she has learned that you are circulating your resume to several competing companies and actually interviewed with a manager from one of them while you were away. Can you rebuild the trust needed to continue your collaboration? Will your boss claim you violated company travel policy by interviewing for a job on the company's time and funds? If so, you realize this might provide a convenient excuse for her to terminate you and end your efforts at Collaboration entirely.

Time to manage the negotiation with a heavy hand! Are there things you can do to defuse the tension between you and your boss? Can an intermediary help bridge the gap that has emerged in your relationship (for example, a coworker or HR person)? Are there some communication strategies that might help? How can you defuse this conflict before it explodes? By now you are familiar with the many management techniques and ideas covered in Chapters 9 through 14 and can dip into this management toolbox to find solutions to your problems.

Note that the Collaboration between you and your boss in this example fell apart because she lost faith in your commitment to stay at the company long enough to cover the team assignment for her. She became worried that you would leave and that she would have to fulfill her commitment to staff the team by sending another employee from the department, leaving her one person short at the office. The root of this problem is trust—as it often is in negotiations. And in this book, we reviewed many approaches that help build trust among the parties in negotiations.

SOME COMMENTS ABOUT TRUST

The nature and degree of trust required for each strategy differ, but trust in some form is important to all strategies. For this reason, we want to end by talking briefly about trust and how to maintain or enhance it in negotiations.[2] Trust is an important issue in the management of a Collaborative strategy, but it also is critical to other strategies. First, trust involves *consequences*. When we are in a relationship with the other person, we expect that the other person can help us achieve good outcomes, and also help us avoid bad outcomes. In most situations, we seek out those relationships in which the good outcomes outweigh the bad and we end up with more good things than bad things. When we expect good things from our relationship with other people, and bad outcomes happen instead, we usually try to figure out whether the other side was "responsible" for causing those bad outcomes. If they were, our trust is diminished. At a minimum, therefore, trust is developed in a relationship when we can expect that the other will help us gain good outcomes and avoid bad outcomes.

Second, trust is also developed in your ability to predict how the other party will behave. In a negotiation situation, a sudden, unexpected change in behavior by one party will upset the other party and derail the negotiation, because it reduces their trust in their ability to predict the other's behavior. So, trust also requires *predictability of the other's behavior*. Parties who are truly competitive with each other often go out of their way to be unpredictable, so that their tactics will preempt the other's expectations and lead to victory.

Third, in a healthy relationship, we not only want to be able to predict the other's behavior, but we want to know enough about the other so that we can *understand their needs* and *take actions that further our joint goals*. When we described the Competitive strategy, we suggested that each party wanted to maximize their own outcome—often at the expense of the other—and that each would often engage in tactics designed to bully, mislead, or trick the other. These tactics are hardly ones that build or sustain trust! The predictability of the other is low, and the consequences for us are likely to be largely negative unless we effectively defend ourselves. As we move more toward a Compromising strategy, we recognize that effective compromise requires us to obtain some good consequences, and to be able to predict the other's behavior sufficiently so that we can at least find an effective middle ground.

True Collaboration, however, requires more than this. As we pointed out many times when we discussed Collaboration, effectiveness at this process requires us to fully understand what the other really cares about, so that we can use this knowledge to design outcomes that meet the needs of both parties. Let's take only one example. Suppose a husband and wife go out to dinner several times a month. The husband really likes Italian food and always argues to go to one of several Italian restaurants. The wife really likes seafood, but doesn't argue too strenuously for her preferred choice. The husband can find it easy to "win" each negotiation—by claiming some good reason why they should go Italian that night or not go seafood! But if the husband is not sensitive to his wife's preferences, "winning" each negotiation over time is likely to anger his wife and make her less interested in going out to dinner. Instead, truly understanding her preferences should encourage him to Accommodate some evenings—go to the seafood place—or, if they truly Collaborate, find a restaurant that has both good pasta and good seafood. *A negotiator can't address the interests of both sides, and invent options to meet these interests, without knowing enough about the other to fully understand their needs!* In a relationship, consistently acting as though you don't know—or even worse, know and don't care about—the other's needs is destructive of trust.

Finally, in the most personal and "intense" relationships, trust involves some *positive feelings*—liking, warmth, attraction. Often this occurs because the parties begin to identify with each other; they recognize that they have much in common, like the same things, dislike the same things, think the same way, or hold similar values, ideologies, and beliefs. These are not necessarily romantic feelings—good friends, brothers or sisters, tennis partners, or regular coworkers often have the same feelings for each other. These positive feelings are often the "glue" that holds parties together when other foundations of trust fall apart. When our best friend does something that hurts us; when our brother whom we have known for 30 years starts behaving unpredictably, or when our spouse claims that she hates seafood (after we tell her we are taking her to the best seafood restaurant in town for her birthday), our trust of these individuals is challenged. In simple relationships, these might be actions that would be sufficient for us to walk away from the situation. Were it not for the strong feelings of attraction and commitment that we have to the other, we would not be able to discuss the problem, "ride it out," and sustain the trust that effectively keeps us together.

In summary, effective trust in a relationship requires four things: (1) good consequences that we create for each other; (2) predictability; (3) understanding the other's interests and our own; and (4) in close relationships, positive feelings of liking and attraction. To sustain trust in our relationships, we therefore need to do the following things:

1. For those with whom we want to develop trust, we need to try to provide good consequences for them, and avoid creating negative consequences.

2. We need to behave predictably—do what they expect us to do. If we are going to do something that is "out of character" or unpredictable,

we need to let them know before we do it. Doing this well requires more skill than might be immediately apparent since our own behavior almost always makes sense to us (after all, we're the one doing the behavior). The skill of being predictable often requires us to be able to "stand outside ourselves"—see ourselves as others see us—so we can really understand how our behavior looks to other people. Sensitivity to how others relate to us, and how others see and interpret what we do, is essential to understanding whether others will see us as predictable or unpredictable.

3. We need to try to understand what the other really cares about, and design our actions with them to meet their needs as well as our own. This requires "getting to know them" through conversation and doing things together. It also requires taking them into account when we are deciding what we intend to do. We build trust when we know the others' interests well enough to take them into account in designing our joint activities. Trust becomes even stronger when we go "out of our way" (act Accommodatingly) to do things that explicitly address their interests rather than our own. Often, doing the action itself is more important than the value of the activity. Going "out of one's way" to buy a special gift for a friend, save them a trip, or show them how much we appreciate their help and concern, are the building blocks of a trusting and successful relationship.

4. Finally, we need to tell them periodically how much we value the relationship, and we need to work on relationship "maintenance." If we feel good about it, we should let them know. If we are having problems, we need to raise them so they can be worked out. Like cars and houses, good relationships need periodic care and maintenance! Showing our appreciation and indicating our willingness to work on problems in the relationship is key to building and sustaining trust!

CONCLUSION

In this book, we have reviewed a great deal of what is known about effective negotiation. Negotiation is an incredibly complex human process. Lots of things can affect whether you will be successful or not. We have tried to point out:

- Many more of these things can be under your control than you think.
- The way to bring them under your control is to understand them and to plan and prepare effectively to deal with them.

Congratulations! You are now armed with a state-of-the-art collection of strategies and tactics for your negotiations. The rest is up to you. Good luck—and don't forget the rules of the strategic negotiator:

The Twelve Rules of Strategic Negotiation

Rule 1. Wait. Take it slow. Take time to plan before you act.

Rule 2. Define your bargaining range.

Rule 3. Define your interests.

Rule 4. Pursue and protect your needs, not your position.

Rule 5. Follow the eight steps of negotiation planning.

Rule 6. The OTHER PARTY holds the key to success.

Rule 7. POWER gives you leverage over BOTH the outcome and the relationship.

Rule 8. The WRONG strategy guarantees FAILURE.

Rule 9. Don't compete unless you are prepared to . . . LOSE.

Rule 10. Reciprocate "unfairly".

Rule 11. TRUST is easier to destroy than it is to build.

Rule 12. INVEST in negotiations WISELY.

Endnotes

Chapter 1

1. William R. King, "Using Strategic Issue Analysis," *Long Range Planning,* *15*(4), 1982.
2. R. C. Richardson, *Collective Bargaining by Objectives* (Englewood Cliffs, NJ: Prentice Hall, 1977); I. G. Asherman and S. V. Asherman, *The Negotiation Sourcebook* (Amherst, MA: Human Resource Development Press, 1990); *Negotiator Pro Manual* (Brookline, MA: Beacon Expert Systems, 1992).

Chapter 2

1. Brian Dumaine, "The Trouble with Teams," *Fortune,* September 5, 1994, p. 90.
2. Ibid.
3. R. Fisher and W. Ury, *Getting to Yes* (Boston: Houghton Mifflin, 1981); W. Ury, *Getting Past No* (New York: Bantam Books, 1991).
4. R. Fisher and W. Ury, *Getting to Yes* (Boston: Houghton Mifflin, 1981); R. Fisher, W. Ury, and B. Patton, *Getting to Yes: Negotiating Agreement without Giving In,* 2nd ed. (New York: Penguin Books, 1991).
5. D. Lax and J. Sebenius, *The Manager as Negotiator: Bargaining for Cooperation and Competitive Gain* (New York: Free Press, 1986).
6. Fisher, Ury, and Patton, *Getting to Yes,* 2nd ed., p. 40.

Chapter 3

1. L. Blessing, *A Walk in the Woods* (New York: New American Library, 1988).
2. Margaret Kaeter, "Buddy, Can You Spare a Million?" *Business Ethics,* May/June 1994, pp. 27, 28.

3. H. Calero and B. Oskam, *Negotiate the Deal You Want* (New York: Dodd, Mead, 1983).
4. R. Fisher, W. Ury, and B. Patton, *Getting to Yes: Negotiating Agreement without Giving In,* 2nd ed. (New York: Penguin Books, 1991); R. Fisher and W. Ury, *Getting to Yes* (Boston: Houghton Mifflin, 1981).
5. H. Kelley, "A Classroom Study of the Dilemmas in Interpersonal Negotiation," in K. Archibald (Ed.), *Strategic Interaction and Conflict: Original Papers and Discussion* (Berkeley, CA: Institute of International Studies, 1966), pp. 49–73.

Chapter 4

1. R. J. Lewicki, "Negotiating Strategically," in A. Cohen (Ed.), *The Portable MBA in Management* (New York: John Wiley & Sons, 1992), pp. 147–189.
2. A. E. Roth, J. K. Murnighan, and F. Schoumaker, "The Deadline Effect in Bargaining: Some Experimental Evidence," *The American Economic Review, 78* (1988), pp. 806–823.
3. J. Kotter, *Power and Influence: Beyond Formal Authority* (New York: Free Press, 1985).
4. A. Teger, *Too Much Invested to Quit* (Beverly Hills, CA: Sage, 1980).
5. K. Short, "Watch Where They Sit in Your Class," in P. Jones (Ed.), *Adult Learning in Your Classroom* (Minneapolis, MN: Training Books, 1982), pp. 19–20.
6. G. F. Shea, "Learn How to Treasure Differences," *HR Magazine,* December 1992, pp. 34–37.
7. D. Kolb and G. G. Coolidge, "Her Place at the Table: A Consideration of Gender Issues in Negotiation," in J. Z. Rubin and J. W. Breslin (Eds.), *Negotiation Theory and Practice* (Cambridge, MA: Harvard Program on Negotiation, 1991), pp. 261–277.
8. I. Ayres, "Fair Driving: Gender and Race Discrimination in Retail Car Negotiations," *Harvard Law Review, 104,* pp. 817–872.
9. B. Gerhart and S. Rynes, "Determinants and Consequences of Salary Negotiations by Male and Female MBA Graduates," *Journal of Applied Psychology, 76* (1991), pp. 256–262; G. F. Dreher, T. W. Dougherty, and W. Whitely, "Influence Tactics and Salary Attainment: A Gender Specific Analysis," *Sex Roles,* 20 (1989), pp. 535–550.
10. Bruce Fortado, "Subordinate Views in Supervisory Conflict Situations: Peering into the Subcultural Chasm," *Human Relations, 45,* 11 (1992), pp. 1141–1167.
11. L. Greenhalgh, D. I. Chapman, & S. Neslin, "The Effect of Working Relationships on the Process and Outcomes of Negotiations," paper presented to the Academy of Management, 1992; M. Tuchinsky, J. Escalas, M. C. Moore, and B. H. Sheppard, "Beyond Name, Rank and Function: Construal of Relationships in Business," paper presented to the Academy of Management, 1993.

12. R. J. Lewicki and B. B. Bunker, "Trust in Relationships: A Model of Trust Development and Decline," in J. Z. Rubin and B. B. Bunker (Eds.), *Conflict, Cooperation and Justice* (San Francisco: Jossey-Bass, 1995).
13. M. Neale and M. Bazerman, "The Role of Perspective-Taking Ability in Negotiating under Different Forms of Arbitration," *Industrial and Labor Relations Review, 35* (1983), pp. 378–388.
14. K. W. Thomas, "Conflict and Conflict Management," in M. D. Dunnette (Ed.), *Handbook of Industrial & Organizational Psychology* (Chicago: Rand McNally, 1976), pp. 889–935.
15. M. G. Hermann and N. Kogan, "Effects of Negotiators' Personalities on Negotiating Behavior," in D. Druckman (Ed.), *Negotiations: Social-Psychological Perspectives* (Beverly Hills, CA: Sage, 1977), pp. 247–274.
16. See J. Z. Rubin and B. B. Brown, *The Social Psychology of Bargaining and Negotiation* (New York: Academic Press, 1975); R. J. Lewicki, J. Litterer, J. Minton, and D. Saunders, *Negotiation,* 2nd ed. (Burr Ridge, IL: Richard D. Irwin, 1994).

Chapter 5

1. G. T. Savage, J. D. Blair, and R. L. Sorenson, "Consider Both Relationships and Substance When Negotiating Strategically," *Academy of Management Executives, 3,* 1 (1989), pp. 37–48.
2. G. C. Homans, *Social Behavior: Its Elementary Forms* (New York, NY: Harcourt, Brace & World, 1961).
3. R. Fisher and W. Ury, *Getting to Yes* (Boston: Houghton Mifflin, 1981); R. Fisher, W. Ury, and B. Patton, *Getting to Yes: Negotiating Agreement without Giving 'In,* 2nd ed. (New York: Penguin Books, 1991).
4. R. E. Walton and R. B. McKersie, *A Behavioral Theory of Labor Negotiations: An Analysis of a Social Interaction System* (New York: McGraw-Hill, 1965); A. C. Filley, *Interpersonal Conflict Resolution* (Glenview, IL: Scott, Foresman, 1975); R. Fisher, W. Ury, and B. Patton, *Getting to Yes: Negotiating Agreement without Giving In,* 2nd ed. (New York: Penguin Books, 1991); D. G. Pruitt, *Negotiation Behavior* (New York: Academic Press, 1981); D. G. Pruitt, "Strategic Choice in Negotiation," *American Behavioral Scientist,* 27 (1983), pp. 167–194; P. J. D. Carnevale and D. G. Pruitt, "Negotiation and Mediation," *Annual Review of Psychology,* M. Rosenberg and L. Porter (Eds.), Vol. 43 (Palo Alto, CA: Annual Reviews, Inc., 1992), pp. 531–582; D. G. Pruitt and P. J. D. Carnevale, *Negotiation in Social Conflict* (Pacific Grove, CA: Brooks-Cole, 1993).
5. Fisher and Ury, *Getting to Yes.*
6. K. Thomas and R. Killman, *The Conflict Mode Inventory* (Tuxedo Park, NY: XICOM, 1974).

Chapter 6

1. We are indebted to Hannah Gordon of Alexander Hiam & Associates, Amherst, MA, for her assistance in creating this script.
2. R. Fisher and W. Ury, *Getting to Yes* (Boston: Houghton Mifflin, 1981); W. Ury, *Getting Past No* (New York: Bantam Books, 1991).
3. L. Putnam and T. S. Jones, "Reciprocity in Negotiations: An Analysis of Bargaining Interaction," *Communication Monographs, 49* (1982), pp. 171–191, and G. Yukl, "Effects of the Opponent's Initial Offer, Concession Magnitude, and Concession Frequency on Bargaining Behavior," *Journal of Personality and Social Psychology, 30* (1974), pp. 323–335.
4. R. Fisher, W. Ury, and B. Patton, *Getting to Yes: Negotiating Agreement without Giving In,* 2nd ed. (New York: Penguin Books, 1991), and W. Ury, *Getting Past No: Negotiating with Difficult People* (New York: Bantam Books, 1991).

Chapter 7

1. A. C. Filley, *Interpersonal Conflict Resolution* (Glenview, IL: Scott, Foresman, 1975); G. F. Shea, *Creative Negotiating* (Boston: CBI Publishing, 1983).
2. A. Williams, "Managing Employee Conflict," *Hotels,* July 1992, p. 23.
3. R. Fisher and W. Ury, *Getting to Yes* (Boston: Houghton Mifflin, 1981); R. Fisher, W. Ury, and B. Patton, *Getting to Yes: Negotiating Agreement without Giving In,* 2nd ed. (New York: Penguin Books, 1991).
4. M. Freedman, "Dealing Effectively with Difficult People," *Nursing 93,* September 1993, pp. 97–102.
5. D. Lax and J. Sebenius, *The Manager as Negotiator: Bargaining for Cooperation and Competitive Gain* (New York: Free Press, 1986).
6. T. Gosselin, "Negotiating with Your Boss," *Training and Development,* May 1993, pp. 37–41.
7. D. G. Pruitt, "Achieving Integrative Agreements," in M. Bazerman and R. Lewicki (Eds.), *Negotiating in Organizations* (Beverly Hills, CA: Sage, 1983); R. J. Lewicki, J. Litterer, J. Minton, and D. A. Saunders, *Negotiation,* 2nd ed. (Burr Ridge, IL: Richard D. Irwin, 1994).
8. M. B. Grover, "Letting Both Sides Win," *Forbes,* September 30, 1991, p. 178.
9. G. F. Shea, "Learn How to Treasure Differences," *HR Magazine,* December 1992, pp. 34–37.
10. D. G. Pruitt, "Strategic Choice in Negotiation," *American Behavioral Scientist, 27* (1983), pp. 167–194; Fisher, Ury, and Patton, *Getting to Yes: Negotiating Agreement without Giving In.*
11. Fisher and Ury, *Getting to Yes.*
12. Filley, *Interpersonal Conflict Resolution;* D. G. Pruitt and P. J. D. Carnevale, *Negotiation in Social Conflict* (Pacific Grove, CA: Brooks-Cole, 1993); Shea,

Creative Negotiating; R. Walton and R. McKersie, *A Behavioral Theory of Labor Negotiations* (New York: McGraw-Hill, 1965).

13. Shea, "Learn How to Treasure Differences."
14. Fisher and Ury, *Getting to Yes.*
15. B. H. Sheppard, R. J. Lewicki, and J. Minton, *Organizational Justice* (New York: Free Press, 1992).
16. R. H. Mouritsen, "Client Involvement through Negotiation: A Key to Success," *The American Salesman,* August 1993, pp. 24–27.
17. A. Williams, "Managing Employee Conflict," *Hotels,* July 1992, p. 23.
18. Pruitt, "Strategic Choice in Negotiation"; D. G. Pruitt, *Negotiation Behavior* (New York: Academic Press, 1981); Filley, *Interpersonal Conflict Resolution.*
19. Fisher, Ury, and Patton, *Getting to Yes: Negotiating Agreement without Giving In.*
20. Freedman, "Dealing Effectively with Difficult People."
21. C. M. Crumbaugh and G. W. Evans, "Presentation Format, Other Persons' Strategies and Cooperative Behavior in the Prisoner's Dilemma," *Psychological Reports, 20* (1967), pp. 895–902; R. L. Michelini, "Effects of Prior Interaction, Contact, Strategy, and Expectation of Meeting on Gain Behavior and Sentiment," *Journal of Conflict Resolution, 15* (1971), pp. 97–103; S. Oksamp, "Effects of Programmed Initial Strategies in a Prisoner's Dilemma Game," *Psychometrics, 19* (1970), pp. 195–196; V. Sermat and R. P. Gregovich, "The Effect of Experimental Manipulation on Cooperative Behavior in a Checkers Game," *Psychometric Science, 4* (1966), pp. 435–436.
22. R. J. Lewicki and B. B. Bunker, "Trust in Relationships: A Model of Trust Development and Decline," in J. Z. Rubin and B. B. Bunker (Eds.), *Conflict, Cooperation and Justice* (San Francisco: Jossey-Bass, 1995).
23. M. Neale and M. H. Bazerman, *Cognition and Rationality in Negotiation* (New York: Free Press, 1991).
24. R. H. Mouritsen, "Client Involvement through Negotiation: A Key to Success," *The American Salesman,* August 1993, pp. 24–27.
25. Stephen Gates, "Alliance Management Guidelines," *Strategic Alliances: Guidelines for Successful Management.* New York: Conference Board, Report Number 1028, 1993.
26. T. Gosselin, "Negotiating with Your Boss," *Training and Development,* May 1993, pp. 37–41; M. B. Grover, "Letting Both Sides Win," *Forbes,* September 30, 1991, p. 178.

Chapter 8

1. Kenichi Ohmae, *The Mind of the Strategist: The Art of Japanese Business* (New York: McGraw-Hill, 1982), p. 254.
2. T. A. Warschaw, *Winning by Negotiation* (New York: McGraw-Hill, 1980).

3. Samuel B. Griffith, *Sun Tzu: The Art of War* (New York: Oxford University Press, 1963), p. 80.
4. Griffith, *Sun Tzu,* p. 92.
5. Material in this section comes from a number of sources, including J. Calano and J. Salzman, "Tough Deals, Tender Tactics," *Working Woman,* July 1988, pp. 74–97; D. G. Pruitt and J. Z. Rubin, *Social Conflict: Escalation, Stalemate and Settlement* (New York: Random House, 1986); F. Greenburger with T. Kiernan, *How to Ask for More and Get It* (Garden City, NY: Doubleday, 1978); R. L. Kuhn, *Dealmaker* (New York: John Wiley & Sons, 1988).
6. J. Calano and J. Salzman, "Tough Deals, Tender Tactics," *Working Woman,* July 1988, p. 74.
7. Calano and Salzman, "Tough Deals, Tender Tactics," pp. 74–97.
8. D. G. Pruitt and J. Z. Rubin, *Social Conflict: Escalation, Stalemate and Settlement* (New York: Random House, 1986).
9. Greenburger, *How to Ask for More and Get It.*
10. Kuhn, *Dealmaker.*
11. Most of the concepts in this section are fully presented in R. B. Cialdini, *Influence: Science and Practice,* 3rd ed. (New York: Harper-Collins, 1993).
12. T. Gosselin, "Negotiating with Your Boss," *Training and Development,* May 1993, pp. 37–41.
13. S. M. Pollan and M. Levine, "Turning Down an Assignment," *Working Woman,* May 1994, p. 69.
14. "Bargaining Chips," *Los Angeles Times,* Friday, February 22, 1991, pp. E1, E5.
15. P. Bohr, "Driving a Bargain on a New Car," *Working Woman,* April 1994, pp. 32–33.
16. Bohr, "Driving a Bargain."
17. E.g., Pace Publications or Edmund's New Car Prices.
18. Examples include Consumer Reports Auto Price Service, IntelliChoice, Car Price Network, Automotive Experts, or others in your local area.

Chapter 9

1. E.g., the American Arbitration Association (they maintain an 800-number at their national office and you can get local contact information from there; check the 800-number directory information for the latest contact information on this organization). Or if you have a conflict with your boss or company, try using an Employee Assistance Program specialist, available through the EAP national office (call 703-522-6272).
2. M. H. Bazerman and M. A. Neale, *Negotiating Rationally* (New York: Free Press, 1992).
3. Scott Sindelar, "Temper, Temper," *Entrepreneur,* September 1994, p. 813.
4. M. Holmes, "Phase Structures in Negotiation," in L. Putnam and M. Roloff (Eds.), *Communication and Negotiation* (Newbury Park, CA: Sage, 1992), pp. 83–105.

5. R. J. Lewicki, S. Weiss, and D. Lewin, "Models of Conflict, Negotiation and Third Party Intervention: A Review and Synthesis," *Journal of Organizational Behavior, 13* (1992), pp. 209–252.
6. T. Simons, "Speech Patterns and the Concept of Utility in Cognitive Maps: The Case of Integrative Bargaining," *Academy of Management Journal, 36* (1993), pp. 139–156.
7. S. K. Michener and R. W. Suchner, "The Tactical Use of Social Power," in J. T. Tedeschi (Ed.), *The Social Influence Process* (Chicago: AVC, 1971), pp. 235–286.
8. R. M. Emerson, "Power-Dependence Relations," *American Sociological Review, 27* (1962), pp. 31–41.
9. J. E. Russo and P. J. H. Schoemaker, *Decision Traps: The Ten Barriers to Brilliant Decision-Making and How to Overcome Them* (New York: Simon & Schuster, 1989); R. H. Mouritsen, "Client Involvement through Negotiation: A Key to Success," *The American Salesman,* August 1993, pp. 24–27; G. Karrass, *Negotiate to Close: How to Make More Successful Deals* (New York: Simon & Schuster, 1985).
10. E. F. Fern, K. B. Monroe, and R. A. Avila, "Effectiveness of Multiple Request Strategies: A Synthesis of Research Results," *Journal of Marketing Research, 23* (1986), pp. 144–152; J. L. Freedman and S. C. Fraser, "Compliance without Pressure: The Foot in the Door Technique," *Journal of Personality and Social Psychology, 4* (1966), pp. 195–202; C. Seligman, M. Bush, and K. Kirsch, "Relationship between Compliance in the Foot in the Door Paradigm and Size of First Request," *Journal of Personality and Social Psychology, 33* (1976), pp. 517–520.

Chapter 10

1. Scott Sindelar, "Temper, Temper," *Entrepreneur,* September 1994, p. 176.
2. Sindelar, "Temper, Temper," p. 176.
3. R. R. Blake and J. S. Mouton, *Group Dynamics: Key to Decision Making* (Houston, TX: Gulf Publications, 1961); R. R. Blake and J. S. Mouton, "Comprehension of Own and Outgroup Positions under Intergroup Competition," *Journal of Conflict Resolution, 5* (1961), pp. 304–310; R. R. Blake and J. S. Mouton, "Loyalty of Representatives to Ingroup Positions during Intergroup Competition," *Sociometry, 24* (1961), pp. 177–183; R. G. Corwin, "Patterns of Organizational Conflict," *Administrative Science Quarterly, 14* (1969), pp. 504–520; O. J. Harvey, "An Experimental Approach to the Study Status Relations in Informal Groups," *Sociometry, 18* (1953), pp. 357–367.
4. L. D. Brown, *Managing Conflict at Organizational Interfaces* (Reading, MA: Addison-Wesley, 1983); M. Deutsch, *The Resolution of Conflict* (New Haven, CT: Yale University Press, 1973); D. G. Pruitt and J. Z. Rubin, *Social Conflict: Escalation, Stalemate and Settlement* (New York: Random House, 1986);

B. H. Sheppard, "Third Party Conflict Intervention: A Procedural Frame-work," in B. M. Staw and L. L. Cummings (Eds.), *Research in Organizational Behavior,* vol. 6 (Greenwich, CT: JAI Press, 1984), pp. 141–190; J. A. Wall, "Mediation: An Analysis, Review and Proposed Research," *Journal of Conflict Resolution, 25* (1981), pp. 157–180; R. Walton, *Managing Conflict: Interpersonal Dialogue and Third-Party Roles,* 2nd ed. (Reading, MA: Addison-Wesley, 1987).

5. C. E. Osgood, *An Alternative to War or Surrender* (Urbana: University of Illinois Press, 1962).

6. C. R. Rogers, *On Becoming a Person: A Therapist's View of Psychotherapy* (Boston, MA: Houghton Mifflin, 1961).

7. R. J. Lewicki, J. A. Litterer, D. M. Sanders, and J. W. Minton, *Negotiation,* 2nd ed. (Burr Ridge, IL: Irwin, 1994).

8. R. Fisher, "Fractionating Conflict," in R. Fisher (Ed.), *International Conflict and Behavioral Science: The Craigville Papers* (New York: Basic Books, 1964), pp. 91–109.

9. R. Fisher, "Fractionating Conflict"; F. C. Ikle, *How Nations Negotiate* (New York: Harper & Row, 1964).

10. R. Fisher, W. Ury, and B. Patton, *Getting to Yes: Negotiating Agreement without Giving In,* 2nd ed. (New York: Penguin Books, 1991).

11. R. Fisher, *International Conflict for Beginners* (New York: Harper & Row, 1969).

12. Fisher, Ury, and Patton, *Getting to Yes.*

13. J. Gordon, "Beating the Price Grinder at His Game," *Folio,* May 15, 1993, pp. 31–32.

14. G. F. Shea, "Learn How to Treasure Differences," *HR Magazine,* December 1992, pp. 34–37.

15. R. Bramson, *Coping with Difficult People* (New York: Anchor Books, 1981); R. Bramson, *Coping with Difficult Bosses* (New York: Carol Publishing Group, 1992); J. Bernstein and S. Rosen, *Dinosaur Brains: Dealing with All Those Impossible People at Work* (New York: John Wiley & Sons, 1989); M. Solomon, *Working with Difficult People* (Englewood Cliffs, NJ: Prentice Hall, 1990).

16. W. Ury, *Getting Past No: Negotiating with Difficult People* (New York: Bantam Books, 1991).

17. R. Bramson, *Coping with Difficult People* (New York: Anchor Books, 1981).

18. M. Freedman, "Dealing Effectively with Difficult People," *Nursing 93,* September 1993, pp. 97–102.

19. T. Gordon, *Leader Effectiveness Training* (New York: Wyden Books, 1977).

20. Shea, "Learn How to Treasure Differences."

Chapter 11

1. C. Moore, *The Mediation Process: Practical Strategies for Resolving Conflict* (San Francisco, CA: Jossey-Bass, 1986).

Endnotes

2. See F. Elkouri and E. Elkouri, *How Arbitration Works,* 4th ed. (Washington, DC: BNA, 1985); P. Prasow and E. Peters, *Arbitration and Collective Bargaining: Conflict Resolution in Labor Relations,* 2nd ed. (New York: McGraw-Hill, 1983); and R. N. Corley, R. L. Black, and O. L. Reed, *The Legal Environment of Business,* 4th ed. (New York: McGraw-Hill, 1977).

3. C. Feigenbaum, "Final-Offer Arbitration: Better Theory than Practice," *Industrial Relations, 14* (1975), pp. 311–317.

4. D. Golann, "Consumer Financial Services Litigation: Major Judgments and ADR Responses," *The Business Lawyer.* Vol. 48, May 1993, pp. 1141–1149.

5. T. A. Kochan, *Collective Bargaining and Industrial Relations* (Homewood, IL: Irwin, 1980).

6. G. Long and P. Feuille, "Final Offer Arbitration: Sudden Death in Eugene," *Industrial and Labor Relations Review, 27* (1974), pp. 186–203; F. A. Starke and W. W. Notz, "Pre- and Postintervention Effects of Conventional versus Final-Offer Arbitration," *Academy of Management Journal, 24* (1981), pp. 832–850.

7. V. H. Vroom, "A New Look at Managerial Decision Making," *Organizational Dynamics, 1* (Spring 1973), pp. 66–80.

8. J. C. Anderson and T. Kochan, "Impasse Procedures in the Canadian Federal Service," *Industrial and Labor Relations Review, 30* (1977), pp. 283–301.

9. T. A. Kochan and T. Jick, "The Public Sector Mediation Process: A Theory and Empirical Examination," *Journal of Conflict Resolution, 22* (1978), pp. 209–240; T. A. Kochan, *Collective Bargaining and Industrial Relations* (Homewood, IL: Irwin, 1980).

10. P. J. D. Carnevale and D. G. Pruitt, "Negotiation and Mediation," in M. Rosenberg and L. Porter (Eds.), *Annual Review of Psychology,* Vol. 43 (Palo Alto, CA: Annual Reviews, 1992), pp. 531–582; J. A. Wall and A. Lynn, "Mediation: A Current Review," *Journal of Conflict Resolution, 37* (1993), pp. 160–194; R. J. Lewicki, S. Weiss, and D. Lewin, "Models of Conflict, Negotiation and Third Party Intervention: A Review and Synthesis," *Journal of Organizational Behavior, 13* (1992), pp. 209–252.

11. Carnevale and Pruitt, "Negotiation and Mediation."

12. See W. A. Donohue, *Communication, Marital Dispute and Divorce Mediation* (Hillsdale, NJ: Erlbaum, 1991); K. Kressel, N. Jaffe, M. Tuchman, C. Watson, and M. Deutsch, "Mediated Negotiations in Divorce and Labor Disputes: A Comparison," *Conciliation Courts Review, 15* (1977), pp. 9–12; O. J. Coogler, *Structural Mediation in Divorce Settlement: A Handbook for Marital Mediators* (Lexington, MA: Lexington Books, 1978).

13. K. Duffy, J. Grosch, and P. Olczak, *Community Mediation: A Handbook for Practitioners and Researchers* (New York: Guilford, 1991); P. Lovenheim, *Mediate, Don't Litigate: How to Resolve Disputes Quickly, Privately, and Inexpensively without Going to Court* (New York: McGraw-Hill, 1989); L. Singer, *Settling Disputes: Conflict Resolution in Business, Families, and the Legal System* (Boulder, CO: Westview Press, 1990).

14. R. Coulson, *Business Mediation: What You Need to Know* (New York: American Arbitration Association, 1987).

15. W. Drayton, "Getting Smarter about Regulation," *Harvard Business Review, 59* (July–August 1981), pp. 38–52; R. B. Reich, "Regulation by Confrontation or Negotiation," *Harvard Business Review, 59* (May–June 1981), pp. 82–93; L. Susskind and J. Cruikshank, *Breaking the Impasse: Consensual Approaches to Resolving Public Disputes* (New York: Basic Books, 1987).
16. R. Fisher, *International Mediation: A Working Guide* (New York: International Peace Academy, 1978).
17. Carnevale and Pruitt, "Negotiation and Mediation"; K. Kressel and D. Pruitt (Eds.), *Mediation Research* (San Francisco, CA: Jossey-Bass, 1989).
18. T. A. Kochan and T. Jick, "The Public Sector Mediation Process: A Theory and Empirical Examination," *Journal of Conflict Resolution, 22* (1978), pp. 209–240.
19. C. Moore, *The Mediation Process: Practical Strategies for Resolving Conflict* (San Francisco, CA: Jossey-Bass, 1986).
20. Starke and Notz, "Pre- and Postintervention Effects"; D. W. Grigsby, *The Effects of Intermediate Mediation Step on Bargaining Behavior under Various Forms of Compulsory Arbitration,* paper presented to the Annual Meeting of the American Institute for Decision Sciences, Boston, MA, November 1981; D. W. Grigsby and W. J. Bigoness, "Effects of Mediation and Alternative Forms of Arbitration on Bargaining Behavior: A Laboratory Study," *Journal of Applied Psychology, 67* (1982), pp. 549–554.
21. T. B. Carver and A. A. Vondra, "Alternative Dispute Resolution: Why It Doesn't Work and Why It Does," *Harvard Business Review,* May–June 1994, p. 124.
22. M. A. Rahim, J. E. Garrett, and G. F. Buntzman, "Ethics of Managing Interpersonal Conflict in Organizations," *Journal of Business Ethics, 14* (1992), pp. 423–432.
23. Rahim, Garrett, and Buntzman, "Ethics of Managing Interpersonal Conflict."
24. B. H. Sheppard, "Managers as Inquisitors: Some Lessons from the Law," in M. Bazerman and R. J. Lewicki (Eds.), *Negotiating in Organizations* (Beverly Hills, CA: Sage, 1983), pp. 193–213.
25. Rahim, Garrett, and Buntzman, "Ethics of Managing Interpersonal Conflict."
26. G. M. Flores, "Handling Employee Issues through Alternate Dispute Resolution," *The Bankers Magazine,* July/August 1993, pp. 47–50.
27. From American Bar Association material—Section of Dispute Resolution (1800 M Street, Washington, DC).
28. M. S. Lans, "Try an ADR and You'll Save Yourself a Court Date," *Marketing and the Law,* June 21, 1993, p. 14.
29. D. C. Bergmann, "ADR: Resolution or Complication?" *Public Utilities Fortnightly,* January 15, 1993, pp. 20–22.
30. D. B. Hoffman and N. L. Kluver, "How Peer Group Resolution Works at Northern States Power Co.," *Employment Relations Today,* Spring 1992, pp. 25–30.
31. J. Greenwald, "Resolving Disagreements: Alternative Market Finds ADR Works to Its Advantage," *Business Insurance,* June 7, 1993, p. 45.

Chapter 12

1. E. P. Bettinghaus, *Message Preparation: The Nature of Proof* (Indianapolis, IN: Bobbs-Merrill, 1966).

2. S. Jackson and M. Allen, *Meta-Analysis of the Effectiveness of One-Sided and Two-Sided Argumentation,* paper presented at annual meeting of International Communication Association, Montreal, Quebec, 1987.

3. E. P. Bettinghaus, *Message Preparation;* P. G. Zimbardo, E. B. Ebbesen, and C. Maslach, *Influencing Attitudes and Changing Behavior* (Reading, MA: Addison-Wesley, 1977).

4. R. Fisher, "Fractionating Conflict," in R. Fisher (Ed.), *International Conflict and Behavioral Science: The Craigville Papers* (New York: Basic Books, 1964), pp. 91–109; F. C. Ikle, *How Nations Negotiate* (New York: Harper & Row, 1964).

5. P. C. Feingold and M. L. Knapp, "Anti-Drug Abuse Commercials," *Journal of Communication, 27* (1977), pp. 20–28; C. I. Hovland and W. Mandell, "An Experimental Comparison of Conclusion Drawing by the Communicator and by the Audience," *Journal of Abnormal and Social Psychology, 47* (1952), pp. 581–588; W. J. McGuire, "Inducing Resistance to Persuasion: Some Contemporary Approaches," in L. Berkowitz (Ed.), *Advances in Experimental Social Psychology,* Vol. 1 (New York: Academic Press, 1964), pp. 191–229.

6. J. W. Bowers and M. M. Osborn, "Attitudinal Effects of Selected Types of Concluding Metaphors in Persuasive Speeches," *Speech Monographs, 33* (1966), pp. 147–155.

7. G. S. Leventhal, "Fairness in Social Relationships," in J. W. Thibaut, J. T. Spence, and R. C. Carson (Eds.), *Contemporary Topics in Social Psychology* (Morristown, NJ: General Learning Press, 1976).

8. T. C. Brock, "Effects of Prior Dishonesty on Post-Decision Dissonance," *Journal of Abnormal and Social Psychology, 66* (1963), pp. 325–331.

9. J. W. Bowers, "Some Correlates of Language Intensity," *Quarterly Journal of Speech, 50* (1964), pp. 415–420.

10. P. Gibbons, J. J. Bradac, and J. D. Busch, "The Role of Language in Negotiations: Threats and Promises," in L. Putnam and M. Roloff (Eds.), *Communication and Negotiation* (Newbury Park, CA: Sage, 1992), pp. 156–175.

11. E. P. Bettinghaus, *Persuasive Communication,* 2nd ed. (New York: Holt, Rinehart & Winston, 1980).

12. D. J. O'Keefe, *Persuasion: Theory and Research* (Newbury Park, CA: Sage, 1990).

13. B. S. Greenberg and G. R. Miller, "The Effects of Low-Credible Sources on Message Acceptance," *Speech Monographs, 33* (1966), pp. 135–136.

14. R. A. Swenson, D. L. Nash, and D. C. Roos, "Source Credibility and Perceived Expertness of Testimony in a Simulated Child-Custody Case," *Professional Psychology, 15* (1984), pp. 891–898.

15. D. Tannen, *You Just Don't Understand: Women and Men in Conversation* (New York: Ballantine Books, 1990).
16. S. Westendorf, "Getting the Guys on Your Side," *Working Woman,* July 1993, pp. 15–16.
17. G. Nierenberg, *The Complete Negotiator* (New York: Nierenberg and Zeif, 1976).
18. C. R. Rogers, *Active Listening* (Chicago: University of Chicago Press, 1957).
19. A. G. Athos and J. J. Gabarro, *Interpersonal Behavior: Communication and Understanding in Relationships* (Englewood Cliffs, NJ: Prentice Hall, 1978).
20. W. J. McGuire, "Inducing Resistance to Persuasion: Some Contemporary Approaches," L. Berkowitz (Ed.), *Advances in Experimental Social Psychology,* vol. 1 (New York: Academic Press, 1964), pp. 191–229.
21. D. W. Johnson, "Role Reversal: A Summary and Review of the Research," *International Journal of Group Tensions, 1* (1971), pp. 318–334; C. Walcott, P. T. Hopmann, and T. D. King, "The Role of Debate in Negotiation," in D. Druckman (Ed.), *Negotiations: Social Psychological Perspectives* (Beverly Hills, CA: Sage, 1977), pp. 193–211.
22. F. Tutzauer, "The Communication of Offers in Dyadic Bargaining," in L. Putnam and M. Roloff (Eds.), *Communication and Negotiation* (Newbury Park, CA: Sage, 1992), pp. 67–82.
23. L. Putnam and M. Holmer, "Framing, Reframing, and Issue Development," in L. Putnam and M. Roloff (Eds.), *Communication and Negotiation* (Newbury Park, CA: Sage, 1992), pp. 128–155.
24. Gibbons, Bradac, and Busch, "The Role of Language in Negotiations."
25. J. E. Russo and P. J. H. Schoemaker, *Decision Traps: The Ten Barriers to Brilliant Decision-making and How to Overcome Them* (New York: Simon & Schuster, 1989).
26. G. Karrass, *Negotiate to Close: How to Make More Successful Deals* (New York: Simon & Schuster, 1985).

Chapter 13

1. R. Miller and G. Jentz, *Fundamentals of Business Law* (Minneapolis, MN: West, 1993), pp. 112, 163–164.
2. G. Richard Shell, "When Is It Legal to Lie in Negotiations?" *Sloan Management Review,* Spring 1991, pp. 93–101.
3. Miller and Jentz, *Fundamentals.*
4. J. Z. Rubin and B. R. Brown, *The Social Psychology of Bargaining and Negotiation* (New York: Academic Press, 1975), p. 15.
5. J. R. Boatright, *Ethics and the Conduct of Business* (Englewood Cliffs, NJ: Prentice Hall, 1993); T. Donaldson and P. Werhane, *Ethical Issues in Business: A Philosophical Approach,* 4th ed. (Englewood Cliffs, NJ: Prentice Hall,

1993); J. Rachels, *The Elements of Moral Philosophy* (New York: McGraw-Hill, 1986).

6. R. J. Lewicki, "Lying and Deception: A Behavioral Model," in M. H. Bazerman and R. J. Lewicki (Eds.), *Negotiating in Organizations* (Beverly Hills, CA: Sage, 1983), pp. 68–90.

7. R. J. Lewicki and G. Spencer, "Ethical Relativism and Negotiating Tactics: Factors Affecting Their Perceived Ethicality," paper presented at the meeting of the Academy of Management, Miami, FL, August 1991; R. J. Anton, "Drawing the Line: An Exploratory Test of Ethical Behavior in Negotiations," *The International Journal of Conflict Management, 1* (1990), pp. 265–280.

8. M. Missner, *Ethics of the Business System* (Sherman Oaks, CA: Alfred Publishing, 1980).

9. R. Christie and F. L. Geis (Eds.), *Studies in Machiavellianism* (New York: Academic Press, 1970).

10. R. J. Lewicki and G. Spencer, "Ethical Relativism and Negotiating Tactics: Factors Affecting Their Perceived Ethicality," paper presented at the meeting of the Academy of Management, Miami, FL, August 1991.

11. N. Bowie and R. E. Freeman, *Ethics and Agency Theory* (New York: Oxford University Press, 1992).

12. M. A. Rahim, J. E. Garrett, and G. F. Buntzman, "Ethics of Managing Interpersonal Conflict in Organizations," *Journal of Business Ethics, 14* (1992), pp. 423–432.

13. S. Charmichale, "Focus: Countering Employee Crime," *Business Ethics, 1* (1992), pp. 180–184.

14. S. Milgram, *Obedience to Authority: An Experimental View* (New York: Harper & Row, 1974).

15. S. Bok, *Lying: Moral Choice in Public and Private Life* (New York: Pantheon, 1978).

16. Fisher, Ury and Patton, *Getting to Yes.*

17. G. F. Shea, "Learn How to Treasure Differences," *HR Magazine,* December 1992, pp. 34–37.

Chapter 14

1. R. J. Lewicki, J. A. Litterer, D. M. Saunders, and J. W. Minton, *Negotiation: Readings, Exercises, and Cases,* 2nd ed. (Homewood, IL: Irwin, 1993).

2. A. A. Benton and D. Druckman, "Constituent's Bargaining Orientation and Intergroup Negotiations," *Journal of Applied Social Psychology, 4* (1974), pp. 141–150; A. A. Benton, "Accountability and Negotiations between Representatives," *Proceedings, 80th Annual Convention, American Psychological Association* (1972), pp. 227–228; R. J. Klimoski, "The Effects of Intragroup

Forces on Intergroup Conflict Resolution," *Organizational Behavior and Human Performance, 8* (1972), pp. 363–383; R. R. Haccoun and R. J. Klimoski, "Negotiator Status and Source: A Study of Negotiation Behavior," *Organizational Behavior and Human Performance, 14* (1975), pp. 342–359; J. A. Breaugh and R. J. Klimoski, "Choice of Group Spokesman in Bargaining—Member or Outsider," *Organizational Behavior and Human Performance, 19* (1977), pp. 325–336.

3. A. Hiam, *Closing the Quality Gap: Lessons from America's Leading Companies* (Englewood Cliffs, NJ: Prentice-Hall, 1992).

4. "Strategic Alliances: Guidelines for Successful Management," The Conference Board Report Number 1028 (New York: Conference Board, 1993).

5. C. Berrey, A. Klausner, and D. Russ-Eft, *Highly Responsive Teams: The Key to Competitive Advantage* (San Jose, CA: Zenger-Miller, 1993).

6. F. Stone (Ed.), "Executive Management Forum," Supplement to *Management Review,* American Management Association, May 1994, pp. 3–4.

7. A. Bernstein, "Why America Needs Unions But Not the Kind It Has Now," *Business Week,* May 23, 1994, p. 71.

8. Stone, "Executive Management Forum."

9. Bernstein, "Why America Needs Unions."

10. Stone, "Executive Management Forum."

11. H. J. Thamhain, "Managing Technologically Innovative Team Efforts toward New Product Success," *Journal of Product Innovation Management,* Vol. 7, March 1990, pp. 5–18.

12. Berrey, Klausner, and Russ-Eft, "Highly Responsive Teams."

13. L. Landes, "The Myth and Misdirection of Employee Empowerment," *Training,* March 1994, p. 116.

14. J. J. Sherwood and J. C. Glidewell, "Planned Renegotiation: A Norm-Setting OD Intervention," in J. E. Jones and J. W. Pfeiffer (Eds.), *The 1973 Annual Handbook for Group Facilitators* (San Diego, CA: Pfeiffer, 1973).

15. M. Kaeter, "Repotting Mature Work Teams," Supplement to *Training,* April 1994, pp. 4–6.

16. M. Hequet, "Teams at the Top," Supplement to *Training,* April 1994, pp. 7–9.

17. R. Harrison, "Role Negotiation: A Tough-Minded Approach to Team Development," in W. G. Bennis, D. E. Berlew, E. H. Schein, and F. I. Steele (Eds.), *Interpersonal Dynamics,* 3rd ed. (Homewood, IL: Dorsey, 1973).

18. G. Nadler and S. Hibino, *Breakthrough Thinking* (Rocklin, CA: Prima Publishing & Communications, 1990).

19. B. Geber, "Let the Games Begin," Supplement to *Training,* April 1994, pp. 10–15.

20. M. H. Bazerman, E. A. Mannix, and L. L. Thompson, "Groups as Mixed Motive Negotiations," in E. J. Lawler and B. Markovsky (Eds.), *Advances in Group Processes,* Vol. 5 (Greenwich, CT: JAI Press, 1988), pp. 195–216; J. Brett, "Negotiating Group Decisions," *Negotiation Journal, 7* (1991), pp. 291–310; R. M. Kramer, "The More the Merrier? Social Psychological Aspects of Multiparty Negotiations in Organizations," in M. Bazerman, R. Lewicki, and B. H. Sheppard,

Research on Negotiation in Organizations, Vol. 3 (Greenwich, CT: JAI Press, 1991), pp. 307–332.

21. Bazerman, Mannix, and Thompson, "Groups as Mixed Motive Negotiations."
22. J. Brett, "Negotiating Group Decisions," *Negotiation Journal,* 7 (1991), pp. 291–310.
23. S. E. Taylor and J. D. Brown, "Illusion and Well-Being: A Social-Psychological Perspective on Mental Health," *Psychological Bulletin, 103* (1988), pp. 193–210; T. Tyler and R. Hastie, "The Social Consequences of Cognitive Illusions," in M. Bazerman, R. Lewicki, and B. H. Sheppard (Eds.), *Research on Negotiation in Organizations,* Vol. 3 (Greenwich, CT: JAI Press, 1991), pp. 69–98.
24. R. J. Lewicki, J. A. Litterer, D. M. Sanders, and J. W. Minton, *Negotiation,* 2nd ed. (Homewood, IL: Irwin, 1994); M. Bazerman, R. Lewicki, and B. H. Sheppard, *Research on Negotiation in Organizations,* Vol. 3 (Greenwich, CT: JAI Press, 1991); Nadler and Hibino, *Breakthrough Thinking.*
25. G. Nadler and S. Hibino, *Breakthrough Thinking* (Rocklin, CA: Prima Publishing & Communications, 1990).
26. J. W. Salacuse, "Your Draft or Mine?" *Negotiation Journal,* Vol. 5, No. 4, pp. 337–341.

Chapter 15

1. See R. J. Lewicki, J. Litterer, J. Minton, and D. Saunders, *Negotiation,* 2nd ed. (Homewood, IL: Irwin, 1994).
2. For a more complete—but complex—presentation of these ideas about trust, see R. J. Lewicki and B. B. Bunker, "Trust in Relationships: A Model of Development and Decline," in B. B. Bunker and J. Z. Rubin, *Conflict, Cooperation and Justice* (San Francisco: Jossey-Bass, 1995).

Index

Index

Index

Index